A Collection of
Recipes from the
Fire Departments
& Area Restaurants
of Manatee and
Sarasota Counties
in the State
of Florida.

FIREHOUSE FAVORITES

Firehouse Favorites Dedication

This book is dedicated to the America's bravest – the 1,082,500 firefighters who put their lives on the line to protect life and property. Their selfless sacrifices make all of our lives safer, healthier and happier.

ACKNOWLEDGEMENTS

Firehouse Favorites Inc. wish to thank whole-heartedly the following people who have given their valuable time, recipes and/or expertise to help complete this cookbook.

The local Fire Chiefs of Manatee and Sarasota Counties

The local Firefighters and Paramedics of Manatee and Sarasota Counties

To the Haluska and Kennell families for their sacrifices and support

Participating Businesses and Restaurants

Marketing by Design — Bennie Barton, Carolyn MacMillan and crew

Palm Printing — Randy Hedrick

Chef Rick Munroe — Munroe's Restaurant

Chef Jeff Trefry, Titus Letschert, & Michael Garey — Café L' Europe

Chef Keith Daum & William Herlihy — Café on the Bay

Brian Kehoe — Webmaster

James Carter, Jr. Attorney at Law

John Raffaldi — 1928 Sanford Firetruck Restoration

Barbara Reed — BC Reed Signs

NFPA — Providing facts, statistics and safety tips

Photography — Keith Haluska & Merv Kennell

Fallen Firefighters Photographs — Leigh Flynn & Jim Leo

Editors — Keith & Linda Haluska, Merv Kennell, Shane Kiser, and Chef Rick Munroe

A Very Special Thanks...

To my wife, Linda,

Thanks for your unconditional love & understanding during this project and always. Thanks for believing in me, supporting me, encouraging me and always seeing the best of everything. Thanks for putting up with those many days and nights away from home and dinners without me while I was photographing and eating gourmet food! I love you! Thanks for all your hard work you put into this cookbook while taking great care of our newborn, Nicole and 2-year-old, Marianna. You're one in a million!

Your loving husband,

For Retail Outlets, Ordering Information, Or Advertising Opportunities In Upcoming Editions Check Out Our Web Site At...

www.firehousefavorites.com

FIREHOUSE FAVORITES

Published by Firehouse Favorites, Inc.

6150 State Road 70 East • Bradenton, Florida 34203

Copyright © 2000 Firehouse Favorites, Inc. • All Rights Reserved.

First Printing – November 2000

No part of this book, including interior design, cover design, and recipes may be reproduced or transmitted in any form, by any means (electronic, photocopying, recording, or otherwise) without the prior written permission of the publisher.

Among the sources of material used in the preparation of this book were several pamphlets and brochures produced by the National Fire Protection Asssociation. Courtesy, NFPA, One Batterymarch Park, Quincy, MA 02269

Library of Congress Control Number: 00-136041

ISBN: 0-9705389-0-1

Printed in the United States of America.

Restaurants

Businesses

Thanks To All Of Our Sponsors
• • •

We Couldn't Have Done It Without You!

3

Firehouses are the working homes of the American firefighter. These firehouses are recognized for their warm welcome, camaraderie and pleasant aromas coming from the kitchens. Firefighters' hearty appetites and love for cooking and eating are well known by all. Another characteristic firefighters have in common is a genuine kindheartedness towards people. This unique *Firehouse Favorites Cookbook* has united local fire departments with restaurants and businesses to share their favorite recipes and help aid the neighboring children affected by burn trauma.

Every page will bring you closer to the lives of the firefighters and the sponsors. They will share personal moments and feelings along with the best of recipes. Some of the recipes revealed are not only favorites but also family or restaurant secrets. All pages photographically illustrate each recipe authentically. Your mouth will water just looking at them!

This cookbook has been made possible due to the generous support of the restaurant and business advertisers, as well as our local brothers and sisters in the fire service. The sponsors have shown a sincere concern for the children affected by fire and a great appreciation for the fire service profession. We hope you will patronize these establishments and let them know how very grateful we are for their involvement.

A portion of the proceeds from all book sales will go toward establishing the Manatee-Sarasota Burn Foundation for Children. Thank you for supporting our project. Through your participation, you too have joined in the efforts of our community to make a difference.

Keith Haluska
Firefighter/Paramedic
President
Firehouse Favorites, Inc.

Firehouse Favorites, Inc.
6150 State Road 70 East
Bradenton, Florida 34203

The Haluska Family...
Nicole, Linda, Keith & Marianna

Firehouse Mealtime Memories

It's hard to believe that more than 20 years have passed since I sat down to my first Firehouse Meals. A lot of memories were built sitting around those firehouse tables. From the early years in stations all by myself, to working the Big House with a table full of 6 to 8 crew members sharing stories and food, mealtime was a highlight. I remember my first Fire Chief, Chief Nutter, coming in at about 6 a.m. one morning, after a rough night, and banging on the bunkroom door and hollering "get up, steak and eggs in the conference room!" That meal, like many since, was a time to relax and reflect on the events of the day, good or tragic.

Although I've always been interested in eating, I can't recall exactly when I became interested in cooking. I believe those shifts alone or with a partner who couldn't cook may have been an early motivation. It was never mandatory that we eat together, but I found importance in sharing meals as a crew. As a young Lieutenant, I made it a practice to promote crew meals wherever I was assigned, even if that meant taking on the task of cooking. A lot of ruffled edges seemed to smooth-over during those meals, and my crews seemed to get along better as a result.

I'm reminded that the table talk wasn't always the most appetizing. Firefighters and paramedics seem to enjoy recalling some of the worst things they've seen or smelled during dinner, especially if there were rookies present. One learns early that it's best not to complain about the stories, the cook's choice of menu, or just plain ask too many questions. Twenty-four hours is a long time without a meal. Word travels quickly around the firehouse, and one's ability to cook or not is fair game. Oddly enough, I've never heard of station that didn't have at least one designated cook. Firefighters are a cross section of society with a broad spectrum of tastes, culinary, and ethnic backgrounds that come together to form what we call Firehouse Cuisine.

To put it simply...
  "just plain good eatin."

Merv Kennell
Fire Lieutenant/Paramedic
Vice President
Firehouse Favorites, Inc.

The Kennell Family...
Travis, Linde, Jennie & Merv

A Tribute To Our Fallen Firefighters

"Greater Love has no one than this, that one lay down his life for his friends."
John 15:13

Not Pictured: S.C.F.D. Captain William "Hank" Stowel / 1913-1974

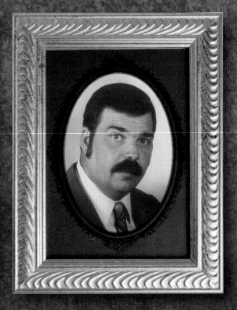

Sara/Brad C.F.R – Captain
"Frank" Colton Wallenstein
1/29/47 – 6/22/90

S.C.F.D. – Lieutenant
Morril "Lonnie" E. Malone
3/13/50 – 8/6/92

S.C.F.D – Lieutenant
Charles "Chuck" R. LaCross
9/20/49 – 8/31/95

A Fireman's Prayer

When I am called to duty God,
wherever the flames may rage, give me strength
to save some life whatever be its age.

Help me embrace a little child before it is too late,
or save an older person from the horror of that fate.

Enable me to be alert and hear the weakest shout,
and quickly and efficiently to put the fire out.

I want to fill my calling and to give the best in me,
to guard my every neighbor and protect his property.

And if according to my fate I am to lose my life,
please bless with your protecting hand
my children and my wife.

S.C.F.D. – Captain
John "Bill" W. Shearer
7/4/51– 6/24/99

S.C.F.D. – Captain
Bruce Campell
8/4/54 – 7/28/99

S.C.F.D. – Firefighter/Paramedic
Michael Yahraus
5/2/68 – 9/12/00

The following pages were painstakingly compiled to take you on a colorful, palate teasing journey through some of the most scrumptious and beautifully displayed foods you've ever laid your eyes on. Prepared by local fire-fighters and chefs, our unique recipe blend of local firehouse and restaurant favorites is sure to be a hit in every cookbook collection and kitchen. Now sit back and relax in your favorite reading chair and sip some Colombian dark roast, while you soak in the delightful pages ahead.

A Collection of
Breakfast Recipes
from the
Fire Departments
& Area Restaurants
of Manatee and
Sarasota Counties
in the State
of Florida.

Breakfast Recipes

FELD ENTERTAINMENT
PRESENTS

RINGLING BROS. AND BARNUM & BAILEY

THE GREATEST SHOW ON EARTH

Where Smiles Never End

*Working together
to help put smiles
back where they belong.*

SUPPORTING OUR LOCAL FIREFIGHTERS

Apple & Cinnamon Coffee Cake
Munroe's Restaurant

Ingredients:

1 cup self rising flour
1 cup whole wheat flour
1/2 tsp baking powder
1/2 tsp salt
1 tbl baking soda
4 tbl margarine
4 tbl light brown sugar

1 tsp ground cinnamon
1 granny smith apple, peeled, cored
  & grated
4 tbl skim milk for recipe
2 tbl skim milk for glazing
1 tbl light brown sugar for glazing

Directions:

1 – Sift flours, baking powder, salt and baking soda into a large mixing bowl. Knead in margarine until the mixture resembles bread crumbs.

2 – Stir in brown sugar and cinnamon, gradually add apple and mix well. Add skim milk to form a soft dough.

3 – Turn the dough onto a floured surface, knead lightly to form a round disc shape.

4 – Place the dough onto a lightly floured cookie sheet, brush the top with skim milk and sprinkle with brown sugar. Score the cake into 8 wedges.

5 – Bake at 400 for 25 minutes or until risen and golden brown.

6 – Serve warm or cold.

Richard Munroe
Chef/Proprietor
Munroe's Restaurant

Brian Gorski
Fire Chief
Sarasota County
Fire Department

Chief Gorski was born in Downers Grove, Illinois, and moved to the Siesta Key area as a nine year old. At age 21 he joined South Trail Fire Department as a volunteer and earned his Paramedic certification prior to being hired in 1977. His love for EMS has brought recognition to Sarasota ever since the early days when he led South Trail Clin-Con teams to 1st place titles in '80, '82, and '84. He was voted firefighter of the year six times on the way to the position he now holds as Fire Chief of the Sarasota County Emergency Services. His work earned Sarasota the prestigious honor of the State EMS Provider of the Year award in 1997.

He and Tracy have a daughter Kaitlin (9) and a son Cameron (5). They love boating, diving and the beaches.

Fire Chief's Breakfast Casserole
Brian Gorski — Fire Chief, Sarasota County Fire Department

Ingredients:

6 eggs beaten together with fork
6 slices bread cubed
1 cup grated cheddar cheese
2 cups milk

1 teaspoon salt
1 teaspoon dry mustard
1 pound brown and serve link sausage

Directions:

1 – Beat eggs together with fork.

2 – Cube bread slices.

3 – Brown sausage, cut up in small pieces.

4 – Mix together all ingredients.

5 – Refrigerate overnight.

6 – Bake in 9x13 pan at 350 degrees for 45 minutes.

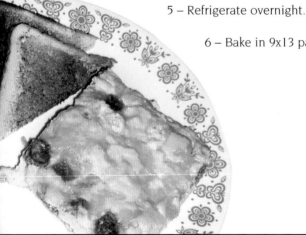

Moist Banana-Nut Bread

Dr. Kantor's Wife: Rona Kantor

Ingredients:

1/2 cup – cooking oil	1/2 teaspoon – baking powder
1 cup – sugar	1/2 teaspoon – salt
2 – eggs, beaten	3 tablespoons – milk
3 – ripe bananas, mashed	1/2 teaspoon – vanilla extract
2 cups – all-purpose flour	1/2 cup – chopped nuts (optional)
1 teaspoon – baking soda	1/3 to 1/2 cup – chocolate chips (optional)

Directions:

1 – Mix oil and sugar together.

2 – Add eggs and banana pulp and beat well.

3 – Add sifted dry ingredients, milk and vanilla.

4 – Mix well and stir in nuts.

5 – Pour into greased and floured loaf pan (9 x 5 x 3).

6 – Bake at 350 degrees for 1 hour.

7 – Cool well and store overnight before cutting.

Makes 1 Loaf.

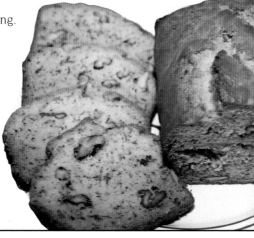

Robert L. Kantor M.D., F.A.C.S.
Kantor Eye Institute & Laser Center

Dr. Kantor has been practicing ophthalmology in Sarasota since 1972 and is the most experienced refractive surgeon in Sarasota and Manatee Counties. He has performed all forms of refractive surgery since 1984 including RK, AK, ALK PRK, and LASIK (Laser Vision Correction) on people from all over the world

Kantor Eye Institute & Laser Center is the largest eye and vision care practice in the area specializing in laser vision correction, cataract surgery, glaucoma, retina diseases, eye muscle surgery, oculoplastics, orbital surgery, neuro-ophthalmology, pediatric ophthalmology and routine eye care. You can visit us virtually for the latest eye care information at www.kantoreye.com

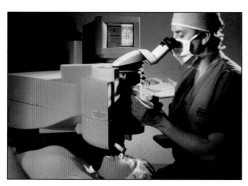
1

**Harold Joslin
Captain, SCFD**

Harold was born in Sarasota in 1957. His father worked for the Florida Park Service and at age 11 his family took up residence in Myakka State Park. His German born mother raised Harold and his sister on a hearty German diet. His plans to become a game warden were set aside when some friends introduced him to the South Trail Fire Department where he immediately became a volunteer. One week later he was hired and has been there 25 years to date.

Harold went on to become a Firefighter, Paramedic, Lieutenant, Training Officer, and in 1999 was appointed Rural Operations Captain.

Harold and Carolyn have been married 18 years and enjoy hunting, fishing, boating, and rural life next to Myakka State Park.

About the recipe...
"The "Camp Scramble" was the result of using a little of everything we had in huntin' camp to make breakfast. It was such a hit, that it I started cooking it for my crew on weekends."

Camp Scramble

Harold Joslin — Captain

Ingredients:

18 eggs
1/4 cup milk
1 package sausage
3/4 cup cubed ham
10-12 strips bacon
butter
3/4 cup chopped green pepper
  (if you desire yellow & red too for color)

1 cup chopped onion
1 small package fresh sliced mushrooms
dash of hot sauce (add to egg mixture)
1 package shredded taco or plain
  cheddar cheese
seasonings - garlic pepper, salt, and
  Italian seasoning
condiments - ketchup and sour cream

Directions:

1 – Beat eggs with 1/4 cup milk (garlic pepper, Italian seasoning, & hot sauce to taste) set aside.

2 – Cook 1 package sausage and crumble. Cook bacon and crumble. Set aside.

3 – In a large skillet, Sauté in butter the green pepper and onion, add mushrooms towards end.

4 – Add to skillet the cubed ham, crumbled sausage and bacon. Add egg mixture and scramble.

5 – When the eggs are done, turn off heat, add cheese and cover to allow cheese to melt.

6 – Serve with potatoes, biscuits and guava jelly. (Potatoes – scrub clean 10 white potatoes, and do not peel. Cook potatoes and drain. Place in large skillet with butter and chopped onions. Add salt, pepper, Lawry's & Everglades seasonings to taste. Sauté til tender and brown.)

Serves 4-6 Hearty Appetite People.

Mom's Ole' Fashioned Raised Donuts

K & K Lawn Service

Ingredients:

3 cups warm water
1/2 cup Crisco
1/2 cup sugar
1 package (2-1/2 teaspoons) dry yeast
2 tablespoons salt
Approximately 8 cups flour

CREAM CHEESE FILLING:
8 ounces cream cheese
1 stick margarine
2 tablespoons vanilla
5 cups powdered sugar

Directions:

1 – Mix yeast with a teaspoon of sugar in a cup.
2 – Add 1 cup warm water to dissolve.
3 – Melt Crisco in a large kettle and then add remaining sugar and salt and stir.
4 – Sift 3 cups flour into mixture.
5 – Add yeast water mixture and mix.
6 – Alternately, add remaining flour and 2 cups water and beat until smooth.
7 – Cover and drape with a warm towel. Let rise for about 1 hour.
8 – Stir down and empty dough on to a floured board. Knead until "elastic."
9 – Use just enough flour to keep hands from getting sticky.
10 – Roll dough to about 1/2" thick. Cut donuts out with a floured juice glass.
11 – Let donuts rise on floured cookie sheet until they are about double in size (approximately 1 hour).
12 – Pour approximately 2" of canola oil into a deep fat fryer or electric skillet and heat to 400 degrees.
13 – Drop each donut gently into the hot oil and fry till golden brown on both sides.
14 – Drain on brown paper and cool.
15 – Roll in powdered sugar or split with serrated knife and fill with cream cheese filling or favorite jellies.

CREAM CHEESE FILLING:
1 – Mix 8 ounces cream cheese, 1 stick margarine and 2 tablespoons vanilla.
2 – Slowly add 5 cups powdered sugar and whip with electric mixer.

Makes Approximately 40 Donuts.

Mark "Papa K" Kennell Sr.
Owner

Mark and his family came to Sarasota in 1961 for a month to escape the bitter cold of upstate New York. He fell in love with the mild climate and tropical beauty and decided to move to Sarasota several months later. They settled into their first Florida home in the Mennonite community known as Pinecraft. In their early Florida days, Mark and his wife Violet raised five children in that 2 bedroom home. After spending 25 years in residential construction, he gave up his contractor's license to establish K & K Lawn Service, which he owns and operates today. His hobbies include hunting, fishing, and eating the catch of the day. He is cordially known as "Porky" to his closest friends and hunting buddies. One look at Violet's ole' fashioned raised donuts and you'll know why!

15

Larry Reed
Battalion Chief
City of Bradenton Fire/Rescue
Florida State Certified
Fire Inspector

A 20-year veteran with the Bradenton Fire Department, Battalion Chief Larry Reed was born in Hanover, PA. on August 24, 1955. When his mother married his step-father, an Army serviceman, he moved to El Paso Texas, Anchorage Alaska, then back to El Paso where Larry grad-uated from high school. In 1980, Larry moved to Bradenton and began his career with the fire service as a dispatcher. He was then transferred to the suppression side of the service and became an engineer in 1986. Working his way up the ranks, he became a Lieutenant in 1991, a Captain in 1995, and ulti-mately a Battalion Chief in 1998. Larry has been mar-ried to wife, Jane, for 4 years and has a stepson, Nick. On Larry's days off he enjoys spending time with Jane, playing golf and dining out at different restaurants.

Baked Victorian French Toast
Larry Reed — Battalion Chief Fire/Rescue & Florida State Certified Fire Inspector

Ingredients:

1 cup packed brown sugar
1/3 cup butter or margarine
3 tablespoons light corn syrup
6-8 slices French bread or
   4-5 slices Texas toast

5 eggs
1 1/2 cups milk
1 or 2 teaspoons cinnamon,
fruit (optional)
powdered sugar (optional)

Directions:

1 – In small saucepan, cook and stir butter, brown sugar and corn syrup until butter melts.
2 – Pour brown sugar mixture into 12 x 7 1/2 x 2 baking dish.
3 – Arrange bread slices in single layer on top of brown sugar mixture (cut to fill in top).
4 – Set baking dish aside.

5 – In medium bowl beat eggs, milk and cinnamon until combined.
6 – Pour egg mixture over bread with baking dish.
7 – Cover and refrigerate 2 – 24 hours. (Longer the better)
8 – Remove cover from baking dish.
9 – Bake at 350 degrees in the oven for 30-35 minutes or until center appears set and top lightly brown.
10 – Let French toast stand for 10 minutes before serving.
11 – When serving, flip French toast over from pan.
12 – Top with fruit or powdered sugar. (Optional)

Makes 6 Servings.

Grits & Cheese Casserole

Big Olaf Creamery – Charity Lambright

Ingredients:

4 cups water (boiling)
1 cup hominy grits
1/3 cup margarine
2 cups shredded cheddar cheese
1 teaspoon Worcestershire sauce

6 drops hot pepper sauce
1 teaspoon salt
3 eggs beaten
sprinkle of paprika

Directions:

1 – Bring water to boil.

2 – Add hominy grits, cover and cook over low heat for 5 minutes, stirring occasionally.

3 – Remove from heat.

4 – Add remaining ingredients (except paprika), mix and pour into a 2 quart casserole dish.

5 – Sprinkle with paprika.

6 – Bake at 275 degrees for 1 hour.

Makes 8 Servings.

Wayne Lambright
Big Olaf Creamery

Wayne grew up in Shipshewana, Indiana, the son of an Amish farmer. He moved to Sarasota in 1986 and using the work ethic instilled in him in his Christian home as a child, he became a residential home builder. Always seeking a challenge, he and his beautiful wife, Charity, entered into a small business venture in 1993, purchasing the Sarasota based "Big Olaf" locations.

When asked what makes Big Olaf special, Wayne smiles and says, "at Big Olaf, we hand make our Premium Ice Cream from scratch, using no preservatives and incorporating whole and natural ingredients. This guarantees a rich and creamy product. We feel it is the finest available."

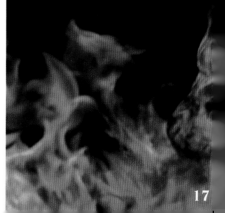

17

Daniel E. Fleischer
Firefighter/EMT

Daniel E. Fleischer is a Firefighter/EMT with the Sarasota County Fire Department. After volunteering for 2 1/2 years, he has just finished his first year as a career Firefighter/EMT. Scuba diving, rollerblading, working out, horseback riding, and "beachin' it" are among his favorite things to do. When asked about his career, he replies, "Everyday I wake up and take a deep breath, reflecting on where I was in the past, how I got to where I am today, and then I look forward to the future. At only 20 years old, I'm proud of who I am and what I do. I thank everyone who helped me get here!"

Training with LPG gas "Night Drill."

Mom's Banana Nut Bread

Daniel Fleischer — Firefighter/EMT

Ingredients:

1/2 cup butter
1 cup sugar
3 eggs
6 mashed over-ripe bananas
3 cups flour

1 tablespoon baking powder
1 teaspoon salt
1/4 teaspoon baking soda
3/4 cup chopped nuts

Directions:

1 – Blend butter and sugar, beat in eggs, stir in mashed bananas.

2 – Blend in flour, baking powder, baking soda and salt.

3 – Stir in nuts.

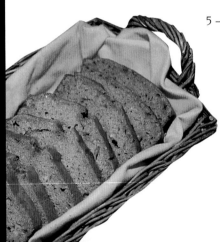

4 – Pour into a greased loaf pan.

5 – Bake for 45 minutes at 300 degrees.

6 – Increase temperature to 350 degrees for 10 minutes more or until toothpick comes out clean.

7 – Sprinkle with powdered sugar.

Dutch Haus Coffee Cake

Dutch Haus Family Restaurant

Ingredients:

BATTER:
1/2 cup butter (1 stick)
1-1/2 cup sugar
2 eggs
2 cups flour
1 teaspoon vanilla
1 teaspoon baking powder
1/2 teaspoon baking soda
1 cup sour cream (regular)

FILLING:
4 tablespoons sugar
1 teaspoon cinnamon
1/2 cup nuts (pecans) chopped

GLAZING:
1/2 cup butter (1 stick)
1/2 cup carnation milk
1/3 cup brown sugar
1/3 cup white sugar

Directions:

1 – To make batter, cream together butter and sugar. Add eggs, mix well.

2 – Add flour, baking powder, baking soda, and vanilla. Mix well.

3 – Add sour cream and set aside.

4 – Mix Filling ingredients; sugar, cinnamon and nuts.

5 – Grease 9x13 cake pan.

6 – Put 1/3 batter mix into cake pan. Sprinkle filling mix over batter.

7 – Put remainder of batter over filling.

8 – Bake at 350 degrees for 45 minutes.

9 – While baking cake, mix glaze ingredients and cook for 5 minutes until syrupy.

10 – Spoon over cake as soon as you remove from oven.

Makes 8 – 12 Servings.

Wagler Children, Michelle, Michael, and Melissa
Dutch Haus
Family Restaurant

All three of the Wagler children have been part of making Dutch Haus a success. Their daughter Michelle did the bookwork until her energies were needed at home raising her own family of four children. All of the delicious desserts at Dutch Haus Restaurant are homemade by Michael and Melissa. They work hard to make sure there are plenty of fresh pies, cakes, cobblers, muffins and cookies ready to serve each morning. The wonderful homemade desserts compliment their Amish Style menu. It is not uncommon to see lines out the door as patrons wait their turn to taste their favorites time and again.

The Wagler's say, "When you visit us at Dutch Haus Restaurant, bring a hearty appetite and we'll see to it you won't go away hungry."

Sausage Biscuits & Gravy

Cliff Prince — Firefighter/Paramedic

Ingredients:

1 pkg. of Jimmy Dean's sage or maple or regular sausage
1 pkg. of Jimmy Dean's hot sausage
1 cup milk

1/8 cup flour
Salt to taste
Pepper to taste

Directions:

1 – Brown sausage in large skillet or pot.

2 – After browned, break up sausage into small pieces.

3 – Add approx. 1 cup of milk and bring up heat to a boil.

4 – Mix 1/8 cup of flour in cold milk and stir into mixture.

5 – Add salt and pepper to taste.

6 – Bake biscuits and enjoy.

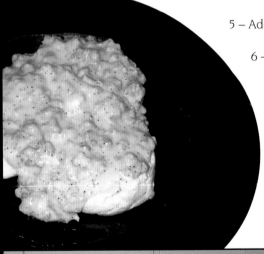

Cliff Prince
Firefighter/Paramedic
SCFD

Native Floridian Cliff Prince moved to this area from his hometown of Jacksonville. Cliff's dream of becoming a firefighter started in 1976 when he tested for Orlando Fire Dept. With limited openings, he found himself selling building supplies for his next 15 years.

During that time, Cliff had a unique opportunity of being hired as personal chef and chauffeur to Ringo Starr who was vacationing in France. He enjoyed the experience and has pictures to prove it.

In 1989, Cliff put himself through Fire and EMT school. He worked for San Carlos Park Fire Department six years before being hired by SCFD in 1997 as a Firefighter/Paramedic.

Water skiing, boating, and caring for his cat "Tess," keep him busy most of his free time.

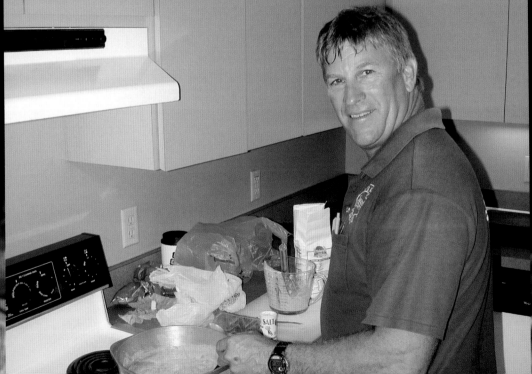

Quiche

Scott Meabon – Firefighter

Ingredients:

Ready made piecrust
1 pound bacon
1 12 ounce package spinach

1 cup grated mozzarella cheese
4 eggs

Directions:

1 – Cook bacon until crisp.

2 – Cook spinach.

3 – Mix eggs together.

4 – Place layer of crushed up bacon on bottom piecrust.

5 – Layer cooked spinach next.

6 – Layer cheese next.

7 – Repeat layers in same order.

8 – Pour in egg mixture making sure it drains down to bottom layer.

9 – Cook at 350 degrees until a knife inserted in the middle comes out clean.

10 – Let stand 5 minutes and slice into 4 equal pieces. Salt and pepper to taste.

Scott Meabon
Firefighter
North River Fire District

Scott was born and raised in Jamestown, New York. Ever since childhood, Scott thought he would be a police officer when he grew up. As fate would have it, he grew weary of long winters and shoveling snow and planned a wholesale change of scenery which landed him in Ellenton, Florida. Some of his friends introduced him to the Fire Department, and he soon became a volunteer. In 1987 he was hired by Ellenton Fire Department as a firefighter, and it has become his life. Ellenton merged with Palmetto to become North River Fire District. He received the "Most Improved Firefighter Award" in 1989.

Scott has two sons, Michael (11) and Justin (13). His hobbies are photography, cooking, and shooting pool.

21

Billy Kimberlin
Firefighter/EMT

Billy is a Firefighter/EMT with the Englewood Fire Department and has been in the Fire Service for ten years. He is Fire Officer 1 certified, and his Firehouse nickname is "Dangerous." Perhaps it's his basketball technique that threatens his Firehouse peers who gave him the rather dubious name. His favorite past time is spending time with his wife, Lori, and sons Devin and Daniel. Billy says, "He got the recipe from his Battalion Chief, (Jim Stuckey) and then modified the ingredients. This Southern Style Biscuits and Gravy recipe is a Firehouse winner every time."

Southern Style Biscuits & Gravy

Billy Kimberlin — Firefighter/EMT

Ingredients:

1 pound Jimmy Dean regular sausage	1 tablespoon pepper (add to taste)
1/2 gallon vitamin D milk	1 tablespoon minced garlic
1/2 cup flour	1 can buttermilk biscuits

Directions:

1 – Brown sausage and add pepper and garlic.

2 – Keep grease in pan.

3 – After browning sausage, sprinkle flour over sausage, covering it.

4 – Brown flour and sausage for 3-5 minutes.

5 – Drop heat to simmer and add milk until it covers the sausage.

6 – Slowly raise heat and keep slowly adding milk until desired thickness.

Makes 4 Servings.

Pumpkin Bread

Robert P. Kilcullen — Lieutenant

Ingredients:

1 2/3 cup all purpose flour
1 1/2 cup sugar
3/4 teaspoon salt
1 teaspoon baking powder
1/2 teaspoon baking soda
1 teaspoon cinnamon

1/4 teaspoon cloves
1/4 teaspoon all spice
1 cup can of pumpkin
1/3 cup shortening or oil
1/3 cup water
2 eggs

Directions:

1 – Combine all ingredients in a large bowl.

2 – Stir mixture until smooth.

3 – Place mixture in a loaf or bread pan sprayed with cooking spray.

4 – Bake for 1 hour at 350 degrees.

5 – Let bread cool slightly before removing from the pan.

6 – Slice, coat with butter, and eat! (Mixture can also be used for muffins, shorten the cooking time.)

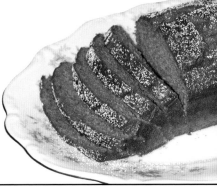

Robert "Bob" Kilcullen
Lieutenant, SCFD

Bob was born and raised in Buffalo, New York . In 1978, he moved to Florida to be with family. He and his Dad signed on as volunteers at South Trail Fire Department at the same time. Bob was hired six months later and has been with the department for 22 years at present. In addition to being a Lieutenant at Station #36-C, Bob also provides a critical element to the health and safety of each firefighter. On his off duty days, Bob services and maintains all self contained breathing apparatus for the firefighters.

Bob and Sharon have enjoyed 21 years of marriage and are proud of their 17-year old daughter, Jessica, who competes as a dancer. Bob enjoys cycling competition with his Lite Speed bicycle.

About the recipe...
"This a family favorite. I bake this bread for my station crew every Christmas. It's best served hot with lots of butter."

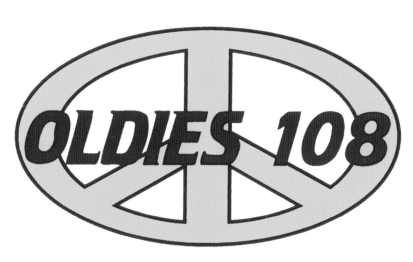
23

SARASOTA MEMORIAL HEALTH CARE SYSTEM

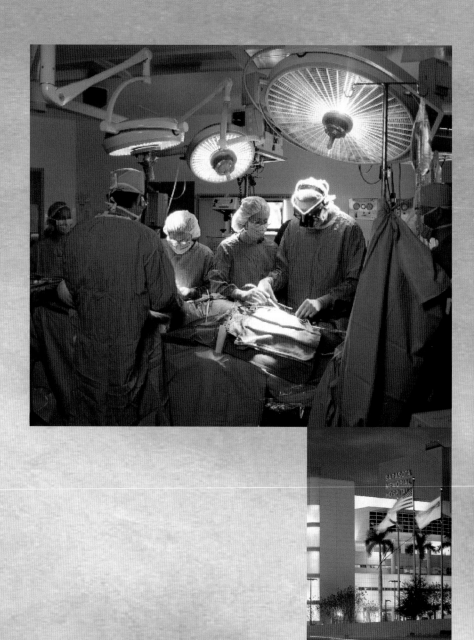

... *is one of only 2.5 percent of all public hospitals to receive accreditation with commendation from the Joint Commission on the Accreditation of Healthcare Organizations.*

... *has the second largest cardiac program in Florida and is among the top 25 in the United States for the number of open-heart surgeries performed annually.*

... *is a leader in robotic and laser surgery. Sarasota Memorial was among the first hospitals in the nation to use a minimally invasive robotic device to perform heart surgery.*

... *One of the first non-academic hospitals in the nation to develop a clinical research service, Sarasota Memorial has conducted almost 200 clinical trials during the past 10 years.*

... *was among the first hospitals in the world to convert its imaging services to an electronic digital format.*

We're creating the future of health care.

SARASOTA
MEMORIAL
HEALTH CARE SYSTEM

Call 917-7777 for more information.

A Collection of
Luncheon Recipes
from the
Fire Departments
& Area Restaurants
of Manatee and
Sarasota Counties
in the State
of Florida.

Luncheon Recipes

Keith Haluska
Firefighter/Paramedic

Keith lived in Rahway, New Jersey, home of the first Fire Department in that state during his early childhood years. In 1980, his family moved to Florida. Keith began a career in sales and marketing for Quaker State Oil and later worked in the insurance and financial field. Interest in the Fire Service stemmed from his appointment to the Bradenton Firefighters Pension Board in which he gained a greater appreciation for firefighters and their profession. In 1995, Keith began volunteering at Braden River Fire Department as a Firefighter and completed his EMT schooling. He then became a paramedic while working for Manatee County EMS. In 1998, he was hired with Sarasota County Fire Department as a Firefighter/Paramedic.

About the recipe...
This is a quick and easy tasty hamburger that firefighters on the run will enjoy.

Aunt Cookie's & Uncle Paul's Hamburger Royal

Keith Haluska — Firefighter/Paramedic

Ingredients:

1 pound hamburger meat	1 teaspoon Worcestershire sauce
1 egg	1/2 small onion chopped finely
1/2 teaspoon salt	1 tablespoon ketchup
1/8 teaspoon black pepper	dash of chili powder

Directions:

1 – Mix all ingredients together well.

2 – Form into hamburger patties.

3 – Grill hamburgers on BBQ.

4 – Enjoy!

Sloppy Joe

Bealls Inc.

Ingredients:

1 pound – ground beef
2 tablespoon – chopped onion
1 clove – chopped clove garlic
2/3 cup – ketchup
1/2 cup – chopped celery (may substitute
   chopped green pepper)

1 tablespoon – sugar
1 tablespoon – vinegar
1 tablespoon – prepared yellow mustard
1/4 teaspoon – salt

Directions:

1 – Brown meat, onions and garlic as for spaghetti sauce.

2 – Add remaining ingredients and simmer for approximately 10 minutes.

3 – Serve on heated or toasted buns.

Makes 4 Servings.

Beall's Inc.

R.M. Beall, founder of Beall's, Inc., moved to Bradenton in 1915 to open the first "Dollar Limit Store" on Main Street. His son, Egbert Beall, was born that year in Bradenton. After college, Egbert married and joined the family business.

His three children all attended Ballard Elementary and found the Sloppy Joes there to be beyond compare. Their mother, Toppa Beall, inquired at the school for the recipe and got a recipe for 250 people; a few more than normally came to dinner. She cut the recipe to feed four and it has been a family favorite since the 1950's.

Merv Kennell
Fire Lieutenant/Paramedic
SCFD

Merv Kennell is vice president of Firehouse Favorites. During the 24 years he has served with Sarasota County Fire Department he has worked in nearly every station and in every capacity at some point in time. Merv is currently a Fire Lieutenant/Paramedic assigned to Station #7 on B-shift, and still loves the job.

Merv and his wife Jennie, enjoy being active with their kids and family through home, school, and church. With a heart for mission work and kids, Merv has recently completed his third mission trip to Haiti to build a church supported orphanage.

Merv is excited by the opportunity to be a part of Firehouse Favorites, which through it's creation of the Sarasota Manatee Children's Burn Foundation, will help unfortunate children and their families when burn trauma disaster strikes.

About the recipe…
"I was first introduced to Russian Chicken while working an overtime shift on another crew. This is my version, partially from memory, and personal taste. It's colorful and the mouth watering aroma keeps the crew nosing around till dinner time."

Hireback Russian Chicken
Merv Kennell — Fire Lieutenant/Paramedic

Ingredients:

3 lbs. boneless chicken breasts
1/2 lb. bacon
1 large Vidalia onion
1 large green pepper
1 large red pepper
1 large yellow pepper

1/2 to 1 tsp. garlic salt (to taste)
pinch ground black pepper
16oz. bottle Russian dressing
    (or western dressing)
1 family sized bag egg noodles (or rice)

Directions:

1 – Cook bacon in microwave until done, but not crispy. Save bacon grease. Set aside bacon.
2 – While bacon is cooking, slice up peppers and onions.
3 – Heat bacon grease in a pan on medium high heat and then brown chicken breasts.
4 – Season with garlic salt and pepper to taste, cover and simmer on medium heat until 1/2 cooked, (approx. 5 minutes) and drain.

5 – Add sliced onions, peppers, and pre-cooked bacon and cover with 3/4 of the dressing.
6 – Cover and simmer, occasionally stirring veggies and turning chicken to avoid burning . Do not over cook.
7 – Boil noodles or rice so that when they are done, the chicken and veggies will be also.

Serving Suggestions:
Serve "Russian Chicken" mixture hot over noodles, with a tossed salad and French bread. Use left over dressing for those who want additional dressing flavor.

Makes 4–6 Servings.

Chopped Chef Salad

Café on the Bay

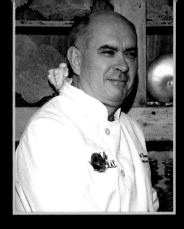

Ingredients:

Salad greens
4 ounces tomato diced
4 ounces diced cooked chicken or turkey
4 hard boiled eggs diced
2 avocados diced

4 ounces black olives diced
4 ounces crisp bacon diced
4 ounces Cheddar cheese diced
4 ounces Swiss cheese diced

Directions:

1 – Put salad greens in bowls.

2 – Top salad greens with 1/4 of each of the above in pie shape wedges.

3 – Serve with your choice of salad dressing.

Makes 4 Salads.

Keith Daum
Executive Chef
Café on the Bay

Keith Daum started in the restaurant business at age 28 to help out a friend during the holiday season. To his surprise, he loved the business so much he enrolled in the C.I.A. and it became his lifelong career. Keith went on to open two 4 star hotels and three other fine dining restaurants in the Rochester, New York area. He became a certified Executive Chef and won two silver medals at the A.C.F. food shows. In September of 1999 he vacationed to Sarasota to visit an old friend, Bill Herlihy. Keith was offered a job as an Executive Chef at Café on the Bay. Not sure about living in Florida, Keith went back home to New York. The rain and snow quickly made up his mind and he is presently with Café on the Bay.

941-383-0440

2630 Harbourside Dr.
Longboat Key, FL 34228

Breakfast Saturday
8:30 AM To 10:30 AM

Sunday Breakfast Brunch
9:00 AM To 1:00 PM

Sunday Lunch
1:00 PM To 3:30 PM

Lunch 6 Days
11:00 AM To 3:00 PM

Dinner 7 Days
4:30 PM To 10:00 PM

Extraordinary cuisine served in a truly exquisite waterfront setting.
Come by land or sea.
Casual attire is welcomed.

29

Robert A. Carlton
Firefighter/EMT

Thirty-two year veteran, Robert A. Carlton, is currently a Firefighter/EMT with Sarasota County Fire Department. Auctions and traveling keep him busy when he is not on duty. Robert's family includes one son, Bobby, one daughter, Denise, and two grandsons, Nathan and Patrick. He also has two lovebirds, two bettas and a Boston terrier named Baby. Robert enjoys his job, family, home, shopping and life in general!

This recipe came from "Ma's kitchen" in Crossville, Tennessee.

Five Cup Salad
Robert Carlton — Firefighter/EMT

Ingredients:

1 cup sour cream
1 cup shredded coconut
1 cup pineapple tidbits

1 cup mandarin oranges
1 cup mini-marshmallows

Directions:

1 – Mix all ingredients well and chill.

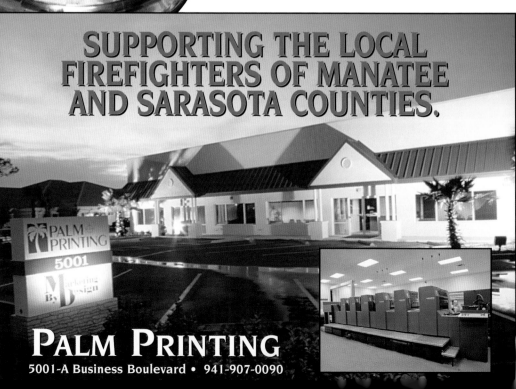

Grouper Reuben

Mar Vista Dockside Restaurant & Pub

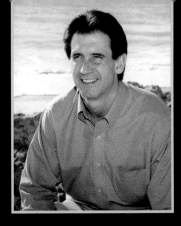

Ingredients:

6 ounce filet of grouper – may substitute another firm fish if unavailable, Mahi works well

1 ounce butter or margarine

1/2-1 ounce drained sauerkraut

1/2 ounce Thousand Island dressing

1 teaspoon horseradish (optional)

2 slices of Swiss cheese

2 slices traditional rye bread or a good Cuban bread

Directions:

1 – Chargrill or sauté fish until tender.

2 – In a medium sauté pan, melt 1 ounce of butter or margarine.

3 – Add sliced bread and grill golden brown, with Swiss cheese to melt.

4 – Add sauerkraut to the cheese, as it will bond. Lightly spread dressing over the kraut.

5 – Top with the fish of your choice and build your sandwich.

6 – Cut in halves or quarters.

7 – Garnish with fresh fruit of your choice and serve.

Steve Ananicz
Chief Operating Officer
Chiles Restaurant Group

Steve Ananicz was born and raised in West Hempstead, New York. Upon receiving a Bachelor's Degree from the University of Central Florida, Steve began his restaurant career in 1975 as Regional Trainer for Steak & Ale and quickly advanced as General Manager at stores in Atlanta, GA and Orlando, FL. He joined the Chiles Group in 1986 as General Manager of the Sandbar Restaurant. In 1999 Steve became Chief Operating Officer overseeing the operations of all three Restaurants. Steve, his wife Marianne and their two sons live in Bradenton, where they enjoy the beautiful Gulf Coast. He stays very active in the community by coaching Little League and soccer teams for his sons as well as raising money for many local and national charities.

Todd Mead
Firefighter/EMT

After completing Fire and EMT school, Todd worked as volunteer firefighter with Nokomis Fire Department for one year. He was hired by Charlotte County Fire & EMS as a Firefighter/EMT shortly thereafter and has been with them 4 years at present. He is currently taking his last class in the Fire Officer 1 series with a goal to become a Fire Lieutenant. Todd enjoys spending time with his wife, Delores, and their three children, Paige, Lindsay and Andrew. Todd and Delores are both alumni of Sarasota Christian School and all three children currently attend school there as well.

About the recipe...
Todd says, "The Rueben Sandwich recipe is a favorite of the crews and was passed down to me by a fellow firefighter, and modified to taste."

Reuben Sandwich
Todd Mead — Firefighter/EMT

Ingredients:

1/2 pound of corned beef per person (2 sandwiches per person),
3 slices of Swiss cheese per sandwich
16 ounce bottle of thousand island dressing for every 6 sandwiches

16 ounce bag of sauerkraut for every 6 sandwiches
rye bread
butter

Directions:

1 – Place the sauerkraut in a saucepan and heat on medium.

2 – Heat a grill to 375 degrees or a frying pan to medium to medium-high heat.

3 – Butter the slices of bread on one side.

4 – Place 1 1/2 slices of cheese on a slice of bread.

5 – Place about 5 slices of corned beef on the cheese.

6 – Drain and place some sauerkraut on the corned beef.

7 – Place about 2 tablespoons of thousand island dressing on the sauerkraut.

8 – Place 1 1/2 slices of cheese on the dressing.

9 – Place the other slice of bread on the sandwich and grill.

10 – Serve with a slice of dill pickle and chips.

Tips – So everyone can eat together, heat oven to 250 degrees and turn off. Place sandwiches as they are finished being grilled in oven on a cookie sheet. (Do not leave in oven too long it will dry out bread, making it crispy.) Purchase extra thousand island for dipping.

Bird of Paradise

Café on the Bay

Ingredients:

1 whole golden pineapple cut in 1/4
toasted sliced almonds
1 1/2 pounds cooked turkey or chicken diced
1/4 cup celery diced

2 tablespoons red onion diced
1 cup mayonnaise
1/4 cup sour cream
4 tablespoons honey

Directions:

1 – Mix all above ingredients to make salad, except pineapple.

2 – Cut the core from each 1/4 pineapple. Score pineapple.

3 – Place pineapple on plate and top with salad.

4 – Garnish with almonds.

Makes 4 Servings.

Bill Herlihy
General Manager
Café on the Bay

Twenty-two years ago, Bill Herlihy began working in the restaurant business in the Finger Lake Region in Western New York. He moved to Rochester, New York in 1984, where he first met Café on the Bay's current Executive Chef, Keith Daum. In 1988, Bill decided to relocate to sunny Florida and 2 years later he met Michael Garey and Titus Letschert. Shortly thereafter, he started as a dining room captain at Café L' Europe. After 6 years of learning from "the best" Bill became General Manager of Café on the Bay. Keith Daum and Bill were reunited after 12 years. Bill has a nine-year old daughter, Delanie, and is very active in local charities. He has been the Co-Chairperson of the St. Jude's Gourmet Luncheon on Longboat Key for the last five years.

941-383-0440

**2630 Harbourside Dr.
Longboat Key, FL 34228**

Breakfast Saturday
8:30 AM To 10:30 AM

Sunday Breakfast Brunch
9:00 AM To 1:00 PM

Sunday Lunch
1:00 PM To 3:30 PM

Lunch 6 Days
11:00 AM To 3:00 PM

Dinner 7 Days
4:30 PM To 10:00 PM

**Extraordinary cuisine served in a
truly exquisite waterfront setting.
Come by land or sea.
Casual attire is welcomed.**

Jim Papa
Firefighter/EMT

Jim Papa is a Firefighter/ EMT and has been with the City of Bradenton Fire Department for the past three years.

An avid Tampa Bay Buccaneer football fan, Jim goes to as many games as possible and does not miss out on the tailgate parties either! He also enjoys fishing and playing basketball. Michelle, his wife, is what Jim says he loves the most in life. This hot dog recipe is great for a firefighter who might get called out any minute or a mom who needs a quick and easy meal for the kids to enjoy.

Rescue drill with LPG

Poops Superdog
Jim Papa — Firefighter/EMT

Ingredients:

hot dogs
bread
mayonnaise
ketchup

mustard
onion
jalapeno pepper
tomatoes

Directions:

1 – Cook hot dogs the way you like them! (grilled, boiled, etc.)

2 – Chop onions, tomatoes, and jalapeno pepper.

3 – Put mayonnaise on bread, so the dog will stick to the bread. (very important)

4 – Put ketchup & mustard on the dog, so the toppings will stick to the dog. (very important)

5 – Place topping on dog.

6 – Enjoy!

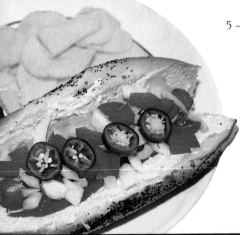

34

Island Seafood Salad

Phillippi Creek Restaurant

Ingredients:

SALAD:
1/2 cup Dijon Vinaigrette dressing
3 (each) large shrimp
4 (each) large sea scallops
3 (each) 1-2 ounce lobster tail
1 head romaine lettuce chopped coarse
1/4 cup carrots finely chopped
1/4 cup chopped tomatoes

1/4 cup red cabbage finely chopped
1/4 cup green peas
small green pepper
small onion
1 hard boiled egg

DIJON VINAIGRETTE DRESSING
8 ounces Dijon mustard
2 tablespoons yellow mustard

4 tablespoons oregano
4 tablespoons granulated garlic
2 tablespoons paprika
1 tablespoon black pepper
1/2 tablespoon salt
2/3 cup sugar
1/3 cup lemon juice
1/3 cup soy sauce
1 quart salad oil
1 cup red wine vinegar

Directions:

SALAD:
1 – Grill shrimp, lobster tails, and scallops.
2 – Mix 1/2 cup of Dijon vinigarette and chopped romaine lettuce.
3 – Spread romaine lettuce evenly on plate.
4 – Garnish corner of plate with carrots, red cabbage, tomato, and green peas.
5 – Slice egg in half, garnish on plate.
6 – Mix 2 tablespoons vinaigrette dressing and seafood.
7 – Garnish plate with seafood and slice of onion and green pepper.

DIJON VINAIGRETTE DRESSING:
1 – In a medium size mixing bowl, mix all above ingredients well.
Servings yield 1 quart.

Ricky Orduno
Chef/Kitchen Manager
Phillippi Creek

Roy LaLone
Owner
Phillippi Creek

Experience casual waterfront dining at "the place to go" for seafood. Located in a tropical setting, this family restaurant features a multiple choice of fresh local seafood daily. Outdoor and indoor waterfront dining. Open 11 a.m. daily, serving lunch and dinner on the waterfront.

PHILLIPPI CREEK
VILLAGE
OYSTER BAR

941-925-4444

**5353 South Tamiami Trail
Sarasota**

**Sunday – Thursday
11 AM To 10:30 PM**

**Friday – Saturday
11 AM To 11 PM**

**Water Front Dining
In The Old Florida
Tradition**

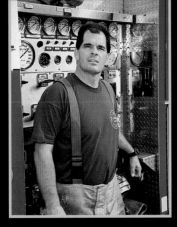

Michael "Mike" Martino

Firefighter/Paramedic
SCFD

Mike was born and raised on Long Island, New York. In 1980 he married his high school sweetheart, Linda. Mike worked for the railroad and in construction until 1988 when he and Linda decided to escape the cold, frigid north and make Sarasota, Florida, their new home.

In search of a new career path, Mike was introduced to the fire department by a friend who was a firefighter. Mike was hired in 1989, by Sarasota Fire Department as a firefighter. In 1994 he became a paramedic at Station #1, the busiest firehouse in the department. Since 1997 he has represented the SCFD firefighters in collective bargaining.

Mike and Linda enjoy music, golfing, running, bicycling, and swimming, with their eight-year old son Michael.

36

Bacon Cheese Loaf

Mike Martino — Firefighter/Paramedic

Ingredients:

1 loaf of french bread	4 tsp.of Dijon mustard
1/2 cup of diced green shallots	2/3 cup of butter
1/4 lb. of baby swiss cheese thinly sliced	1/2 tsp. black pepper
8-12 strips of bacon	

Directions:

1 – Slice bread in 1 inch slices attached at bottom.

2 – In bowl combine butter, shallots, pepper, and mustard. Mix together by hand.

3 – Spread mixture on bread.

4 – Place cheese between slices of bread.

5 _ Drape bacon over each slice.

6 – Place loaf on baking sheet and bake at 400 degrees for 20-25 minutes or until bacon is crisp.

7 – Remove from oven and serve.

Stuffed Piquillo Peppers

Café L' Europe

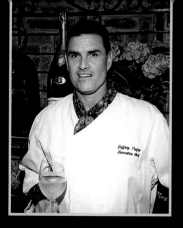

Ingredients:

8 Piquillo peppers
8 ounces jumbo lump crabmeat
1 tablespoon mayonnaise
2 teaspoons seasoned breadcrumbs
1 tablespoon chopped fresh basil

salt and pepper
1 handful mixed greens
1 tablespoon Balsamic vinegar
1/4 cup extra virgin olive oil

Directions:

1 – Remove piquillos from can and rinse carefully.

2 – Remove shell and cartilage from crabmeat.

3 – Mix with mayonnaise, basil and breadcrumbs.

4 – Season with salt and pepper.

5 – Stuff peppers with crab mixture, place on plate. Cover with plastic wrap.

6 – Warm in microwave oven for 30 seconds at a time until hot all the way through.

7 – Mix greens with Balsamic vinegar and olive oil.

8 – Place on plate and arrange piquillos around.

Makes 4 Servings.

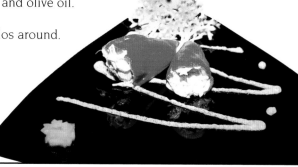

Jeff Trefry
Executive Chef
Café L' Europe

Upon graduation from the prestigious Culinary Institute of America, Jeff moved west to Santa Barbara, California and worked as a pastry chef for the El Encanto Hotel. To broaden his knowledge of the culinary arts and hone his skills, Jeff moved east and spent three years at Café L' Europe in the early 1980's. Jeff's career path led him to the Five-Star Five-Diamond Ritz Carlton Resort in Naples and he was promoted to Executive Sous Chef. In 1989, promotion placed Jeff as Executive Chef in charge of culinary operations at the Ritz Carlton in Kansas City, Mo. He then worked in Bermuda and Hilton Head Island, S.C. but is now back with Café L' Europe as Executive Chef. Jeff executes New European Cuisine with his own imagination and personal style. He is married to Janet and has three children – Megan, Jack and Mike.

Byron Teates
Shift Commander,
Fire Officer 1 Instructor,
Haz-Mat Team Inspector
and EMT

A 25 year veteran, Byron Teates has spent the last 15 years with Braden River Fire Department. He is a Shift Commander there and has also acquired Fire Officer 1, Instructor, Haz-Mat Team, Inspector and EMT over the years. Byron is an avid out-doorsman enjoying the peace-ful woods and water along with hunting, fishing, and gardening. He and his wife, Cathy, also love to spend time with their three grandchil-dren, soon to be four.

About the recipes....
This is one of Byron's grandmothers favorites.

Tuna Chip Casserole

Byron Teates — Shift Commander, Fire Officer 1 Instructor,
Haz-Mat Team Inspector and EMT

Ingredients:

2 – 6 ounce cans tuna
2 – 10 ounce cans cream of mushroom
  soup

1/2 cup milk
10 ounce bag potato chips
salt and pepper to taste

Directions:

1 – In a casserole dish, mix all ingredients except chips.

2 – Crush chips into small pieces in bag.

3 – Mix 1/2 of chips into casserole with other ingredients.

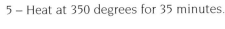

4 – Sprinkle remaining 1/2 of chips on top of casserole.

5 – Heat at 350 degrees for 35 minutes.

Makes 6 Servings.

Tortilla Wrap

Café on the Bay

Ingredients:

4 – 12" Tortilla shells
8 ounces deli Turkey sliced or
   any deli meat

1 ounce Alfalfa sprouts or shredded lettuce
1 small red onion sliced thin
5 ounce herbed cheese soft

Directions:

1 – Whip herbed cheese.

2 – Spread on tortilla shell.

3 – Spread out all other ingredients leaving 3" with just cheese.

4 – Roll shell with just the cheese at bottom.

5 – Cut in half and it should be a pinwheel.

Bill Herlihy

General Manager
Café on the Bay

Twenty-two years ago, Bill Herlihy began working in the restaurant business in the Finger Lake Region in Western New York. He moved to Rochester, New York in 1984, where he first met Café on the Bay's current Executive Chef, Keith Daum. In 1988, Bill decided to relocate to sunny Florida and 2 years later he met Michael Garey and Titus Letschert. Shortly thereafter, he started as a dining room captain at Café L' Europe. After 6 years of learning from "the best" Bill became General Manager of Café on the Bay. Keith Daum and Bill were reunited after 12 years. Bill has a nine-year old daughter, Delanie, and is very active in local charities. He has been the Co-Chairperson of the St. Jude's Gourmet Luncheon on Longboat Key for the last five years.

941-383-0440

2630 Harbourside Dr.
Longboat Key, FL 34228

Breakfast Saturday
8:30 AM To 10:30 AM

Sunday Breakfast Brunch
9:00 AM To 1:00 PM

Sunday Lunch
1:00 PM To 3:30 PM

Lunch 6 Days
11:00 AM To 3:00 PM

Dinner 7 Days
4:30 PM To 10:00 PM

**Extraordinary cuisine served in a
truly exquisite waterfront setting.
Come by land or sea.
Casual attire is welcomed.**

Irl H. Orr
Firemedic
SCFD

Irl grew up in Indianapolis, Indiana, the son of an Irishman. In his wilder days he traveled the U.S. as a drummer for a group known as "The Chessman" who had several recordings with Columbia Records. After the band, he decided to drum up a little business of his own hanging wallpaper, which he did for 18 years. In 1980 he moved to Sarasota and was hired by SCFD in '82.

He and his wife, Gini, have 10 children and 22 grandchildren. He enjoys his hobbies of deep sea fishing and diving on his days off with his own fishing charter business "Tarpon Tyme" out of Englewood.

Irl is affectionately called "Grandpa" by his young firefighter peers and grandchildren. He will retire later this year.

About the recipe...
"This is a very light dessert with a fruity, mouth pleasing taste."

Spaghetti Pie
Irl H. Orr — Firemedic

Ingredients:

1 pound ground beef
1 green pepper
1 onion
32 ounce jar spaghetti sauce
12 ounce package cheddar cheese

12 ounce package mozzarella cheese
12 ounce package spaghetti noodles
  cooked and drained
Parmesan cheese

Directions:

1 – In a large skillet, sauté pepper, onion and ground beef.

2 – Add spaghetti sauce and mix well.

3 – In 13x9 pan, put small amount of sauce to coat bottom.

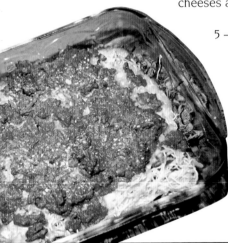

4 – Place half of spaghetti noodles on sauce, top with half of cheeses and cover with half of sauce.

5 – Repeat layers.

6 – Sprinkle with Parmesan cheese.

7 – Bake uncovered at 350 degrees for 30-40 minutes.

*Optional – add mushrooms and/or olives

Makes 12 Servings.

Shrimp and Avocado Salad

Café on the Bay

Ingredients:

4 ripe avocados split
salad greens
1 pound shrimp cooked
1/2 cup mayonnaise

1/4 cup ketchup
1 ounce cognac
1 ounce chopped chives
dill to taste

Directions:

1 – Mix mayonnaise, ketchup, cognac, chives, and dill.

2 – Place greens on plate.

3 – Place avocado (2 halves) on top of greens.

4 – Fill avocado with cooked shrimp.

5 – Spoon dressing over shrimp.

6 – Serve chilled.

Makes 4 Servings.

Café on the Bay

Nestled in the Longboat Key Moorings, along beautiful Sarasota Bay, sits Longboat Key's Hidden Gem...Café on the Bay. Elegant yet casual, her charm beckons seafarers and landlubbers alike for breakfast, lunch or dinner. You will delight in an offering of extraordinary cuisine. Enjoy the indoor dining room or the covered outdoor terrace, both featuring spectacular marina and bay views. Or you may simply wish to enjoy your favorite cocktail or one of our own exotic creations at our Marker 15 Lounge. This is one "Port of Call" you will wish to visit over and over again! Inquire about our sunset special and the pre-fixed dinner offering. Breakfast Saturday 8:30 AM – 10:30 AM Sunday Breakfast Brunch 9:00 AM – 1:00 PM Sunday Lunch 1:00 PM – 3:30 PM Lunch 11:00 AM – 3:00 PM Dinner 4:30 PM – 10:00 PM In the Longboat Key Moorings Marina behind Publix – right out of guard gate, second left.

941-383-0440

**2630 Harbourside Dr.
Longboat Key, FL 34228**

Breakfast Saturday
8:30 AM To 10:30 AM

Sunday Breakfast Brunch
9:00 AM To 1:00 PM

Sunday Lunch
1:00 PM To 3:30 PM

Lunch 6 Days
11:00 AM To 3:00 PM

Dinner 7 Days
4:30 PM To 10:00 PM

Extraordinary cuisine served in a
truly exquisite waterfront setting.
Come by land or sea.
Casual attire is welcomed.

Merv Kennell
Fire Lieutenant/Paramedic
SCFD

My love of the fire service began at 15 years old when I would go to the fire station to visit my brother Mark, a Paramedic/Firefighter. I volunteered until 3/30/78 when I was hired. I loved the challenges the fire/rescue service offered me and in 1979 (while attending Sarasota Fire Academy), I became the first 18 year old State Certified Paramedic in Florida. Twenty-two years later the challenges remain and the experiences of my past are priceless. I thank God daily for his many blessings. The most special of which are my wife Jennie, daughter Linde' and son Travis. This one's for my crew..."Isn't it a Great Day to be Alive!"

About the recipe...
Long before I had ever heard of a calzone, my sister Marcia made this delicious recipe from the Mennonite Community in Lowville, New York. I make it for the crew to eat while watching the Buc's.

Old Fashioned Sausage Bread

Merv Kennell — Fire Lieutenant/Paramedic

Ingredients:

2 pounds mild ground sausage
2 loaves frozen bread dough
(homemade if you're brave)
2 medium Spanish onions
(Vidalia if possible)
2 green peppers

1 small can mushrooms slices(optional)
2 cups shredded mozzarella cheese
1/4 tsp. each seasonings: salt, pepper,
garlic powder
16 oz jar spaghetti sauce
(your favorite brand)

Directions:

1 – Thaw frozen bread dough and let raise.
2 – Fry sausage on medium heat with seasonings until approx. 1/2 cooked.
3 – Add onions, peppers, and mushrooms, and finish cooking sausage.
4 – Drain vegetable/meat mixture.
5 – Sprinkle dough with flour and roll flat. Place on a greased cookie sheet.
6 – Place half of vegetable/meat mixture on each rolled loaf and sprinkle 1 cup of cheese over each.
7 – Pinch dough together and lightly butter the top.
8 – Place in the oven @ 400 degrees for approx. 15 minutes or until golden brown. *You should swap racks in the oven 1/2 way through cooking so both loaves cook evenly. Tip:Ventilated cookie sheets help avoid over cooking bottom of loaf.
9 – Warm spaghetti sauce on stove while loaves are cooking.
10 – Remove from oven and slice into 2" strips, placing two on each plate as one serving. You may pour sauce on each plate or serve in small bowl for dipping.

Makes 8 Servings (or 4 fireman).

Grilled Vegetable Sandwich

Café on the Bay

Ingredients:

4 Portobello mushroom large
1 Yellow pepper
1 Red pepper
1 Green pepper
1 Eggplant
1 Zucchini

1 Yellow squash
4 Flat bread or pita bread
Olive oil
Salt and pepper to taste
1 small round Brie cheese

Directions:

1 – Cut pepper in fourths.

2 – Cut eggplant and squash in 1/4 inch slices.

3 – Marinate vegetable in olive oil and salt and pepper.

4 – Grill or bake in oven until soft.

5 – Layer vegetable on bread and top with Brie.

SINCE 1832 . . .

AMERICAN LaFrance

THE INCOMPARABLE HERITAGE
OF AMERICAN LAFRANCE.

WWW.AMERICANLAFRANCE.COM

AMERICAN LaFrance

A Collection of
Hors d'oeuvre
Recipes from the
Fire Departments
& Area Restaurants
of Manatee and
Sarasota Counties
in the State
of Florida.

Hors d'oeuvre Recipes

Terrence "Terry" Kehoe
Battalion Chief
SCFD

Terry was born in 1958 in Chicago, Illinois, one of six sons (all who became Firefighters). Steeped in tradition, he recalls getting his first Chicago Fire Department uniform at age nine. He would wear it when he rode with his Deputy Chief father, and once as a teenager, he sucked smoke along side his brothers assigned to Engine or Ladder companies.

Terry was 16 when his family moved to Florida. He was hired by South Trail Fire District as a Firefighter/ Paramedic in 1978. He later became a Lieutenant, Battalion Captain, and is presently a Battalion Chief with SCFD.

Terry and his wife of 21 years, Trish, have a 14-year old daughter, Tracy. His hobbies include fishing, photography, and being a "die-hard Chicago Cubs Fan!"

Chicago Style Pizza Dip

Terrence Kehoe — Battalion Chief

Ingredients:

8 ounce package cream cheese
1 teaspoon dried Italian seasoning
1 cup shredded mozzarella cheese
3/4 cup shredded Parmesan cheese
12 ounce can tomato sauce
8 ounce can tomato sauce
2 teaspoons chopped green pepper

2 teaspoons chopped green onions
salt and pepper to taste
garlic powder to taste
OPTIONAL TOPPINGS:
2 teaspoons chopped pepperoni
2 teaspoons cooked sausage
2 teaspoons chopped mushrooms

Directions:

1 – Preheat oven to 350 degrees.

2 – Combine creams cheese and Italian seasoning and mix in small bowl. Spread in bottom of 9"-10" pie plate.

3 – Mix mozzarella cheese and Parmesan cheese together. Sprinkle mixture over cream cheese.

4 – Mix tomato sauce and paste together. Add salt, pepper and garlic to taste.

5 – Spread over cheese layer.

6 – Top with green pepper, onion, and any additional toppings.

7 – Spread remaining cheese over toppings.

8 – Bake 15-18 minutes or until cheese is melted.

9 – Serve with crackers.

Conch Fritters

Mar Vista Dockside Restaurant & Pub

Ingredients:

8 ounce conch meat
2 ounces bread crumbs
1/4 teaspoon salt
2 eggs
1/2 ounce jalapenos
2 ounces green peppers

3 ribs scallions
dash Tabasco
dash cayenne pepper
1/4 teaspoon Worcestershire sauce
Japanese bread crumbs or regular bread
   crumbs as needed

Directions:

1 – Ground conch meat.

2 – Finely dice vegetables, add all remaining ingredients with enough breadcrumbs to bind mixture.

3 – Mix and form into 1 one-ounce balls and roll in Japanese breadcrumbs.

4 – Deep fry in 350-degree oil until golden brown.

5 – Average cooking time is 2 to 3 minutes.

6 – The fritters should be golden brown when done.

7 – Garnish with lemon wedge and cocktail sauce.

Yields: 12 *one-ounce portions*.

Barbara Hough

**General Manager of
Mar Vista Dockside
Restaurant & Pub**

Barbara Hough, born and educated in Syracuse, New York moved to Anna Maria Island after college in 1976. She began working at the Sandbar Restaurant in 1986 as a Server. She quickly moved up to Head Wait and shortly thereafter became an Assistant Manager. She was then promoted to General Manager of Mar Vista Pub in late 1995 and has made the restaurant her second home enjoying the Old Florida Charm which Mar Vista does so well. Barbara has two unforgettable children, a very bright son of 15 and a beautiful daughter, age 13. She is a big sports fan and jumps at the chance of catching any football game. We advise you to never stand in the way of her Buffalo Bills.

941-383-2391

**760 Broadway
Longboat Key**

**Lunch 11:30 AM To 5 PM Daily
Dinner 5 PM To 10 PM Sun-Thurs
Dinner 5 PM To 10:30 PM Fri & Sat**

A Taste of Old Florida

Indoor & Outdoor Dining on the Water!

Victoria Gross
Firefighter/Paramedic
SCFD

Victoria was born in San Antonio, Texas, in 1969. With a father in the Air Force, she lived in Germany and Fayetteville, N.C., before striking out on her own in 1990. No stranger to moving, she easily adapted to life in Tampa, Fla. She was working as a bank secretary when her best friend suggested she try firefighting as a career. She attended the Florida State Fire College in Ocala to attain her certification. In 1993 she was hired by Hillsborough County as a Firefighter/EMT. She became a paramedic in 1995 and is most excited to have joined S.C.F.D. in January 1999.

Victoria has been married four years to Jeff, a Sarasota Sheriff's Detective. They enjoy raising "Bandit," their search and rescue dog.

About the recipe...
Great for those last minute parties or unexpected guests. It's simple to make, and tastes great!

Victoria's - Last Minute Dip
Victoria Gross — Firefighter/Paramedic

Ingredients:

16 oz. refried beans	1/2 to 1 pkg. taco seasoning
16 oz. sour cream	2 tbs. mayonnaise
12 oz. guacamole dip	2 cups shredded cheddar cheese

Directions:

1 – Procure a 9x13 pan or 2 round pie plates.

2 – Spread beans on bottom of pans.

3 – Next spread guacamole dip on top of bean layer.

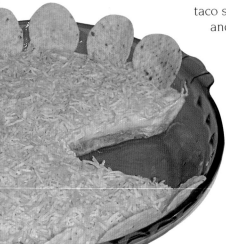

4 – In a separate bowl, mix mayonnaise, sour cream, and taco seasoning (start with 1/2 pkg. of taco seasoning and add more "to taste").

5 – Then layer the sour cream mix on top of guacamole.

6 – Sprinkle heavy with cheese.

7 – If you have time, refrigerate for 30 minutes.

8 – Serve this appetizer with Tostito's or your favorite crackers.

Stone Crab, Corn & Potato Fritters

The Colony Restaurants

Ingredients:

3/4 pound stone crab, weight after shell removed
1 tablespoon olive oil
1/2 cup onion, fine diced
1 tablespoon garlic, minced
2/3 cup sweet corn kernels, blanched and chilled
4 tablespoon chives, minced

2/3 cup russet potatoes, peeled and small diced, blanched in boiling salted water and chilled
2 whole medium eggs
2/3 cup milk
1/4 cup buttermilk
1 1/3 cup all purpose flour

1 1/2 teaspoon baking soda
1 1/2 teaspoon baking powder
Ground black pepper to taste
Ground white pepper to taste
Kosher salt to taste

Dining Room
The Colony Restaurants

The Colony Restaurants have enjoyed a quarter century of international recognition receiving numerous awards such as the prestigious DiRoNA Award and The Wine Spectator's Award of Excellence since 1982, as well as being a member of Nation's Restaurant News Fine Dining Hall of Fame. In addition, The Colony receives national and international praise for its annual Stone Crab, Seafood & Wine Festival – which for the past ten years has brought together premier culinary and wine-making professionals to celebrate the opening of the Florida Stone Crab season.

Directions:

1 – Over low heat sauté the onion and garlic in olive oil.

2 – In a small mixing bowl combine eggs, milk and buttermilk.

3 – In a large bowl, sift flour, baking soda and powder, black and white pepper and kosher salt. Then pour the wet ingredients into the dry ingredients and mix well.

4 – Add the well-cooled corn and potatoes, garlic, onions and chives.

5 – Squeeze the crabmeat to remove any excess moisture. Shred the crabmeat into medium to large pieces using fingers. Add it to the rest of the ingredients and mix well.

6 – Using a 1-ounce ladle, drop batter into a lightly oiled, HOT cast iron skillet and fry until golden brown on both sides.

Makes 6 Servings.

Daniel E. Fleischer
Firefighter/EMT

Daniel E. Fleischer is a Firefighter/EMT with the Sarasota County Fire Department. After volunteering for 2 1/2 years, he has just finished his first year as a career Firefighter/EMT. Scuba diving, rollerblading, working out, horseback riding, and "beachin' it" are among his favorite things to do. When asked about his career, he replies, "Everyday I wake up and take a deep breath, reflecting on where I was in the past, how I got to where I am today, and then I look forward to the future. At only 20 years old, I'm proud of who I am and what I do. I thank everyone who helped me get here!"

The heat is on!

Roswitha's Seven Layer Dip
Daniel Fleischer — Firefighter/EMT

Ingredients:

2 cups refried beans
2 cups sour cream
2 cups mayonnaise
2 cups chopped tomatoes

2 cups guacamole
taco seasoning to taste
2 cups shredded cheese (any type)

Directions:

1 – In a 10" pie dish, layer ingredients starting with refried beans.

2 – Blend 1 cup of sour cream and 1 cup mayonnaise and layer on top of beans.

3 – Sprinkle taco seasoning on top for next layer.

4 – Add guacamole for next layer.

5 – Blend remaining sour cream (1 cup) and mayonnaise (1 cup) and layer on top.

6 – Layer tomatoes on top and sprinkle with cheese for final layer.

7 – Serve with tortilla chips.

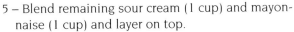

Easy Tomato Salsa

Munroe's Restaurant

Ingredients:

4 Lg ripe tomatoes, chopped
3 Jalapenos, seeded & chopped
8 green onions, chopped

2 cloves, garlic
8 sprigs, cilantro
1 tbsp salt

Directions:

1 – Lace all ingedients in food processor, blend unti a coarse texture is achieved.

2 – Store in refrigerator for one hour before serving.

NFPA Factoids And Kitchen Fire Safety Tips

Question:
How many fires did public Fire Departments respond to in 1999?

Answer:
1,823,000.

"Heat Oil Slowly"
Heat oil slowly over a moderate heat, and don't leave it for a second.

Information Courtesy of NFPA

Top Photo:
Keith Haluska at Munroe's during a photo shoot for the news media.

Bottom Photo:
1928 Sanford Firehouse Favorites Promo Vehicle

51

Richard Munroe

Chef/Proprietor
Munroe's Restaurant

Locals and seasonal visitors alike enjoy the bistro setting of Munroe's Restaurant. Proven to be Sarasota's favorite restaurant with casual elegance, friendly service, and creative, American foods.

Whether you start off your meal with one of our famous appetizers or finish with one of our colorful desserts, you won't go away disappointed.

For the late night guest, we offer live entertainment upstairs, with a late night menu and premium bar.

Chilled Mussels with Caviar Vinaigrette

Munroe's Restaurant

Ingredients:

4 mussels
1 ounce caviar
1 ounce balsamic vinegar
1 ounce olive oil

1/2 teaspoon minced red bell pepper
1/2 teaspoon minced green bell pepper
1/2 teaspoon minced chive
1 anchovy fillet

Directions:

1 – Poach mussels until they open then chill immediately.

2 – Place the anchovy in a mixing bowl and mash with a wooden spoon, add balsamic vinegar – mix well, then add olive oil while stirring.

3 – Place mussels on a plate; sprinkle the minced peppers and chive over each mussel. Drizzle vinaigrette over the mussels and plate. Dollop each mussel with caviar.

52

Buffalo Oysters

King Creole

Ingredients:

12 fresh oysters in a shell
8 celery sticks
4 ounces blue cheese dressing
1 stick melted butter
2 ounces Louisiana hot sauce
1 ounce Cajun power garlic sauce

pinch black pepper
pinch white pepper
pinch granulated onion
1 cup sifted seasoned flour
2 cups oil for frying

Directions:

SAUCE:

1 – Combine melted butter, hot sauce, garlic sauce, black pepper, white pepper and onion in a jar with lid.

2 – Shake until all ingredients are combined.

OYSTERS:

2 – Shuck oysters and save 1/2 the shells.

3 – Dredge oysters in flour.

4 – Heat oil to 375 degrees in a large skillet.

5 – Add oysters in a single layer and cook until golden about 2 minutes.

6 – Arrange oyster shells on a platter and fill shells with the sauce.

7 – Place one oyster in each shell and serve with blue cheese and celery sticks.

Richard Drumgools
Executive Chef
King Creole

King Creole, Sarasota' newest addition to downtown nightlife, faithfully captures the charm and pulse of New Orleans, by recreating the look and feel of an authentic French Quarter venue. Serving up traditional Creole and Cajun fare, as well as a lively lineup of quality entertainment every night, King Creole guarantees to take you on a sensory visit to the Crescent City amid the aromas of zesty Jambalayas, Crawfish Etouffee, warm Beignets & Coffee, and the sounds of hot Jazz and cool Blues. Executive Chef, Richard Drumgools' latest challenge has proven his mettle in mastering all types of cuisines. Richard is a member of the American Culinary Federation, and has worked in many fine restaurants and clubs from Cape Cod to Florida. King Creole is open six days, featuring lunch, dinner, and a late night menu.

941-365-7474

1991 Main Street • Sarasota

**Monday – Thursday
11:30 AM To Midnight
Friday • 11:30 AM To 1:00 AM
Saturday • 5 PM To 1 AM**

Authentic Cajun & Creole Cuisine

- **Nightly Live Entertainment**
- **Late Night Menu**
- **Catering**
- **Private Parties**

Keith Daum
Executive Chef
Café on the Bay

Keith Daum started in the restaurant business at age 28 to help out a friend during the holiday season. To his surprise, he loved the business so much he enrolled in the C.I.A. and it became his lifelong career. Keith went on to open two 4 star hotels and three other fine dining restaurants in the Rochester, New York area. He became a certified Executive Chef and won two silver medals at the A.C.F. food shows. In September of 1999 he vacationed to Sarasota to visit an old friend, Bill Herlihy. Keith was offered a job as an Executive Chef at Café on the Bay. Not sure about living in Florida, Keith went back home to New York. The rain and snow quickly made up his mind and he is presently with Café on the Bay.

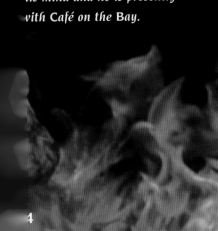

Clams Casino
Café on the Bay

Ingredients:

24 large clams
1/2 cup diced red pepper
1/4 cup diced green pepper
1 tablespoon chopped parsley
1/2 pound butter

1/4 cup bread crumbs
1 lemon juice
Tabasco to taste
3 strips of bacon to garnish

Directions:

1 – Heat butter.

2 – Lightly cook pepper in butter.

3 – Add all other ingredients.

4 – Shuck clams and top with mixture.

5 – Cut chunks of bacon to top clam.

6 – Bake at 350 degrees in oven until bacon in browned.

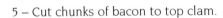

Lump Crab Canapés

Munroe's Restaurant

Ingredients:

2 ounces jumbo lump crab picked
3 croutons
1 lemon juice of
1/2 teaspoon minced fresh garlic

1 lime zest of
1/2 ounce caviar
1/2 ounce red onion julienne
1 pinch minced chive

Directions:

1 – Place crab lumps, lemon juice, lime zest and red onion in a mixing bowl – toss gently, keeping the crab lumps in tact.

2 – Spoon crab mix over the croutons.

3 – Garnish with caviar and flavored oils.

Brian Kehoe
**EMS Quality
Assurance Captain
SCFD**

In 1962, the Kehoe family of firefighters was blessed with the arrival of Brian. His father was a chief in the Chicago Fire Department, which undoubtedly shaped the lives of Brian, his five brothers and two sisters. Upon his retirement, Brian's father moved their family to Punta Gorda, Florida, where Brian grew up.

There was never any doubt in Brian's mind about what career path he'd follow. In 1981, Brian joined the South Trail Fire Department (currently Sarasota County) as a firefighter. His love for EMS led him to paramedic school and eventually to the position he holds today as a Quality Assurance EMS Captain.

Brian's wife, Erin, was a volunteer firefighter with Fruitville Fire Department before they met. Their four-year old daughter, Shannon, is the light of their lives.

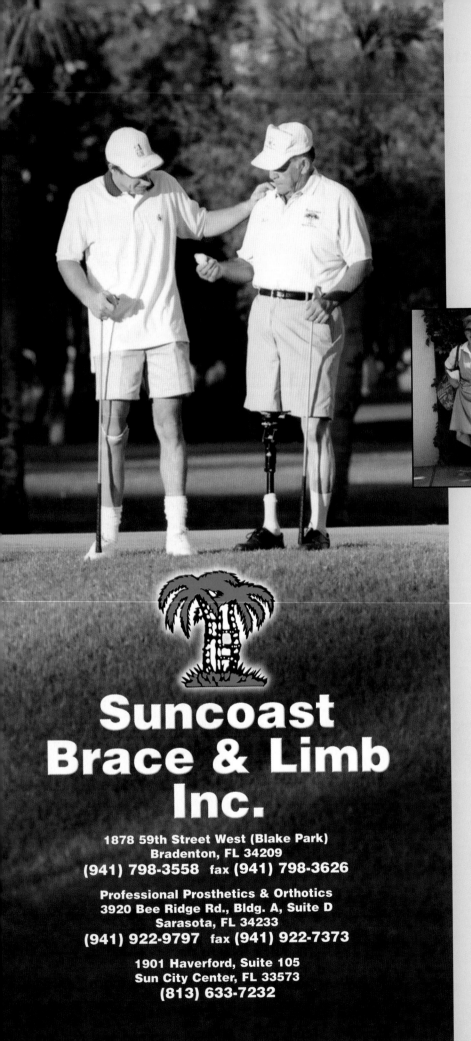

A Collection of
Appetizer Recipes
from the
Fire Departments
& Area Restaurants
of Manatee and
Sarasota Counties
in the State
of Florida.

Appetizer Recipes

Ed Chiles

Owner
Chiles Restaurant Group

Ed Chiles graduated from the University of Florida in 1978 with a degree in Political Science. He worked at Joe's Stone Crab, the venerable Miami Institution for a year and then joined a partnership to purchase and operate the Sandbar Restaurant in 1979. This partnership included Lawton Chiles, Ed's father and past Governor of Florida along with Wilbur Boyd, and Dennis Fecteau. In 1990 Chiles purchased the Mar Vista Dockside Restaurant and Pub and again in 1993 purchased the former Harbor House now known as the Beach House Restaurant. Ed and his wife Anne take great pride in their development of the three restaurants. Their daughters Ashley and Christin have also began to get their feet wet in the business by filling in as hostesses and bussers whenever needed.

Clam Chowder

Mar Vista Dockside Restaurant & Pub

Ingredients:

1/2 pound lightly salted butter
2 cups flour
4 celery ribs – diced
2 medium onions – diced
5 medium potatoes – peeled, diced, and blanched
1 quart heavy cream

1/2 quart half & half
2 bay leaves
3 teaspoons white pepper
3 cans chopped clams, drained & reserve juices
2 cans clam juice

Directions:

1 – In a two gallon pot, slowly melt butter. When completely melted, add chopped onions and celery. Cook until almost clear.

2 – Add flour and blend thoroughly.

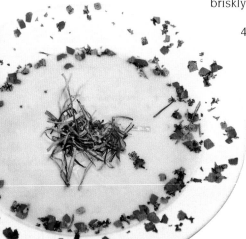

3 – Add the juice from the chopped clams and clam juice. Turn up heat to medium high and bring to a slow boil. Whisk briskly, being careful not to burn the bottom.

4 – When the liquid has thickened, add the heavy cream, half & half, blanched potatoes, and white pepper.

5 – Turn heat down to lower temperature for approximately 10 minutes.

6 – Serve hot with Saltine crackers or oyster crackers.

7 – This should yield 2 gallons.

Easy Fig "Shortcake"

Munroe's Restaurant

Ingredients:

1 tube plain biscuit dough
6 dried figs
2 oz boursin cheese
2 Tbl honey

1 Tbl sugar
1 Tbl flour
2 oz fruit puree (papaya, mango, etc.)

Directions:

1 – Open biscuit dough and add 1 minced fig, 1 tbl honey, 1 tbl flour and 1 tbl sugar - mix to incorporate evenly.

2 – Divide into silver dollar size scones and place on a greased sheet pan - bake until crisp.

3 – Slice remaining figs and mix with 1 tbl honey.

4 – To plate the dish spread 1 side of each scone with softened boursin cheese and fan on the plate as shown.

5 – Spoon the figs over the top and garnish with fruit puree and pecans.

Top Photo:
Rick Munroe's daughter, Ashley

Bottom Photo:
Rick Munroe in his kitchen having fun with us, while helping us cook our meals for the cookbook.

59

Dana Anderson
Firefighter/Paramedic

Dana started his career as a volunteer firefighter 8 years ago and was hired 4 years later as a Firefighter/EMT. Dana put himself through Paramedic school while working full time at the second busiest station in his department, Sarasota County Fire Department Station #11-A. His hobbies include water sports, traveling, race cars, and antique automotive restoration. After he and his father restored a 1925 Dodge Touring Car, they began their current project of restoring the second motorized pumper the Sarasota Fire Department owned. This 1926 Seagrave Suburbanite was found, literally in pieces, in a local junk yard. Upon completion, he and his father hope to enter it in the coast-to-coast Great American Race...any interested sponsors out there?

Station 11 Ham & Bean Soup

Dana Anderson – Firefighter/Paramedic

Ingredients:

1 large left over ham bone with meat
  (if not available, substitute 3-4 cups
  chopped ham)
2 large bags of 15 bean, dry mixed beans

1 large white onion
1 pound spicy ham sausage
3-4 bay leaves
3-4 teaspoons black pepper

Directions:

1 – It is best to start this soup early in the morning. The longer it cooks the better.

2 – In a large pot soak the beans in cool water for at least 3 hours.

3 – Remove beans and rinse.

4 – Put beans, chopped onion, sausage, bay leaves, pepper and ham bone in large stew pot. Top with water almost to the top of pot. (If a ham bone is not available you may substitute 3-4 cups of chopped ham.)

5 – Simmer ingredients at a low-medium heat for 3 to 4 hours.

6 – Serve with salad and cornbread.

7 – Costs less than $20.00!

Makes 8 Servings

Scallop Martini

Michael's Seafood Grille

Ingredients:

24 medium scallops
2 oranges
2 grapefruits
1/2 golden pineapple
1/2 teaspoon chiles
2 limes

1 teaspoon cilantro chopped
1/4 teaspoon sugar
salt & pepper
1 tomato (fresh or smoked)
sliced plantain for garnish

Directions:

1 – Grill or sear the scallops.

2 – Peel and segment the orange and grapefruits into a bowl. Squeeze the juice from the core into the bowl. Peel the pineapple, dice and add to the fruits and juice.

3 – Add the chiles and cilantro. Squeeze the juice from the limes. Let sit for at least one hour.

4 – To serve: Spoon some of the fruit salsa into a martini glass. Place scallops on top of fruit. Garnish and serve.

Makes 6 Servings.

Martha Wright
Chief Financial Officer
Chiles Restaurant Group

Martha Wright, Chief Financial Officer came to Bradenton, in 1979 from the small town of Avon Park, Florida. After working several years in the banking industry and in private accounting, she joined the Sandbar Restaurant in 1982. She earned her Bachelor's Degree in Accounting from the University of South Florida in 1987 and feels that by getting her degree while working in the restaurant was a great advantage, there is nothing like hands on experience. Martha enjoys remaining active in the community as well, where she was the first woman elected to the Crewe in the Hernando DeSoto Historical Society in 1993 and also served as President in 1998. When the time comes to get away, you can find her with Taylor on their boat cruising the inter coastal.

Conch Chowder

Sandbar Restaurant

Ingredients:

1 pound conch meat	9.5 ounces tomato juice	dash Tabasco sauce
2 ribs celery	9.5 ounces V-8 juice	dash cayenne pepper
3 1/2 ounces Spanish onions	20 ounces whole tomatoes	1/2 teaspoon granulated garlic
6 ounces green peppers	.5 ounces Sherry	
3 ounces carrots	2 bay leaves	
4 large potatoes	1/2 teaspoon basil	
	1/2 teaspoon oregano	

Directions:

1 – Sauté all veggies until aldente.

2 – Add one gallon of water and all ingredients except the potatoes.

3 – Cook potatoes in a separate pot until slightly tender.

4 – Bring soup to a boil and skim fat from the top.

5 – Add cooked potatoes and serve.

Yields: 1 gallon

Mushroom A La Daum

Café on the Bay

Ingredients:

1 pound mushrooms (any fresh mushroom)
olive oil
phyllo pastry
salt and pepper to taste

SAUCE:
2 cups cream
3 tablespoons French mustard
1 tablespoon chopped fresh herbs of choice

Directions:

1 – Chop mushrooms and cook in sauté pan. Season.

2 – Let cool and drain.

3 – Layer phyllo in four layers, painting each layer with olive oil.
(You must work fast with this pastry.)

4 – Place mushroom in middle of pastry.

5 – Fold up to make a pouch.

6 – Bake in 350-degree oven on oiled pan until golden brown.

7 – Make sauce: reduce cream to 1/2.
Add mustard and herbs.

8 – Serve on plate, placing mushroom pouch on sauce.

Makes 4 Servings.

Café on the Bay

Nestled in the Longboat Key Moorings, along beautiful Sarasota Bay, sits Longboat Key's Hidden Gem...Café on the Bay. Elegant yet casual, her charm beckons seafarers and landlubbers alike for breakfast, lunch or dinner. You will delight in an offering of extraordinary cuisine. Enjoy the indoor dining room or the covered outdoor terrace, both featuring spectacular marina and bay views. Or you may simply wish to enjoy your favorite cocktail or one of our own exotic creations at our Marker 15 Lounge. This is one "Port of Call" you will wish to visit over and over again! Inquire about our sunset special and the pre-fixed dinner offering. Breakfast Saturday 8:30 AM – 10:30 AM Sunday Breakfast Brunch 9:00 AM – 1:00 PM Sunday Lunch 1:00 PM – 3:30 PM Lunch 11:00 AM – 3:00 PM Dinner 4:30 PM – 10:00 PM In the Longboat Key Moorings Marina behind Publix – right out of guard gate, second left.

Dennis Esposito
Firefighter/Paramedic

I became a fire fighter in 1987 after some good advice from my grandfather. He was a retired NYC fire fighter and said, "Stop bartending and get a real job." After I started working in the fire service I realized that I would like to do more. I became an EMT and went on to Paramedic School. I even finished an associate degree in emergency medicine and became fire officer one certified.

I feel that I'm a very lucky guy. I get paid for doing a job I love to do. Even after 14 years of service I still can't believe it when I climb into a fire truck or rescue. The crews you work with are like family. Every call is different and challenging. The fire service is an extremely rewarding job.

Firehouse cooking can also be challenge. Food that is prepared needs to have the ability to be able to sit, if the station gets a call, and still taste good when the crew returns. My ceviche dish can be left, in the fridge, and taste the same hours later. I hope you have fun making and eating it.

Sarasota Summer Ceviche
Dennis Esposito — Firefighter/Paramedic

Ingredients:

1 pound firm mild fish (orange roughy)	2 tablespoons olive oil
1/2 cup Vidalia onion	1 teaspoon oregano
2 cups ripe tomatoes, diced	2 cups ripe avocados
3 tablespoons fresh parsley, chopped	salt & pepper to taste

Directions:

1 – Cut fish into small cubes and place in a bowl.

2 – Cover with lemon juice and let stand in refrigerator covered for at least 6 hours.

3 – Add the remaining ingredients EXCEPT avocado and refrigerate 3 more hours.

4 – When ready to serve, stir in avocado.

5 – Serve with your favorite tortilla chips.

Makes 6 Servings.

Shrimp Alex

Café on the Bay

Ingredients:

12 large shrimp
12 slices of bacon
1-pound feta cheese
1 bag spinach

1 juice lemon
8-ounce sherry
3 ounce butter

Directions:

1 – Butterfly shrimp and clean.

2 – Cut feta in block to fit shrimp.

3 – Place feta on shrimp.

4 – Wrap bacon around shrimp and feta.

5 – Bake in oven at 350 degrees until bacon is brown.

6 – Heat up sherry and lemon juice. Fold in butter.

7 – Steam spinach.

8 – Place shrimp over spinach and spoon on sauce.

Makes 4 Portions.

Keith Daum
Executive Chef
Café on the Bay

Keith Daum started in the restaurant business at age 28 to help out a friend during the holiday season. To his surprise, he loved the business so much he enrolled in the C.I.A. and it became his lifelong career. Keith went on to open two 4 star hotels and three other fine dining restaurants in the Rochester, New York area. He became a certified Executive Chef and won two silver medals at the A.C.F. food shows. In September of 1999 he vacationed to Sarasota to visit an old friend, Bill Herlihy. Keith was offered a job as an Executive Chef at Café on the Bay. Not sure about living in Florida, Keith went back home to New York. The rain and snow quickly made up his mind and now he is presently with Café on the Bay.

941-383-0440

2630 Harbourside Dr.
Longboat Key, FL 34228

Breakfast Saturday
8:30 AM To 10:30 AM

Sunday Breakfast Brunch
9:00 AM To 1:00 PM

Sunday Lunch
1:00 PM To 3:30 PM

Lunch 6 Days
11:00 AM To 3:00 PM

Dinner 7 Days
4:30 PM To 10:00 PM

Extraordinary cuisine served in a truly exquisite waterfront setting.
Come by land or sea.
Casual attire is welcomed.

Richard, Adela and Casey Gonzmart
Owners
Columbia Restaurant

Our family has been creating some of Florida's favorite Spanish cuisine for nearly 100 years. We feature the freshest seafood and steaks as well as our won tradition family recipes. Through the years we have received some of the highest awards in the restaurant industry, but our highest praise comes from our loyal customers who dine with us again and again.

Join us daily for lunch or dinner, and take in the beautiful sites of St. Armands Circle while enjoying the delicious dishes our chef prepares especially for you.

The Gonzmart family looks forward to welcoming you to the Columbia Restaurant!

Black Bean Soup – Frijoles Negros

Columbia Restaurant

Ingredients:

1 pound black beans, dried
2 quarts water
2 medium onions, chopped fine
1 bay leaf
2 green peppers, cut in strips
1/2 cup olive oil
1 teaspoon oregano

4 cloves garlic, minced
1/4 teaspoon ground cumin
1 tablespoon salt
1/2 teaspoon black pepper
White rice, cooked
Chopped onions for garnish

Directions:

1 – Before washing beans, spread on flat surface and pick out broken beans and foreign particles.

2 – Wash bean thoroughly and soak overnight in 2 quarts of water.

3 – Next day, pour beans and water into a 4-quart soup kettle and bring to a boil. Cover and cook over medium heat.

4 – Meanwhile, in a skillet, sauté onions and green peppers in olive oil until light and golden.

5 – Add crushed oregano, bay leaf, cumin and garlic.

6 – Add mixture and beans, stirring well.

7 – Add salt and pepper and cook slowly over low heat. Cover until beans are tender (at least 1 hour).

8 – Serve over white rice and top with chopped onions.

Makes 4 Servings.

Mom's Scrumptious Nut Roll

Chelena & Associates

Ingredients:

BREAD:
6 cups sifted flour
1 teaspoon salt
1/2 pound butter or
    margarine
3 tablespoons sugar

3 eggs
1 cup sour cream
2 packages (1/4 g.)
    dry yeast
1/2 cup warm milk
*2 eggs whites (optional)

FILLING:
1 1/2 cup sugar
1 pound ground walnuts
1/4 teaspoon cinnamon
1/4 teaspoon lemon juice

Directions:

1 – Dissolve yeast in milk.

2 – Combine flour, butter, salt, sugar, eggs and sour cream.

3 – Add yeast and milk mixture.

4 – Blend well.

5 – Divide dough in to four parts and roll out each part thin as for jellyroll.

6 – Mix filling ingredients together in a bowl.

7 – Spread nut mixture on dough evenly. Roll lengthways and place in greased pan. Allow to rise for 1 hour or until doubled in bulk.

8 – *(Optional) Put 2 egg whites in a bowl. Brush egg whites evenly on rolls. (This will make roll appear shiny when done.)

9 – Bake at 350 degrees for 35-40 minutes.

Makes 4 Nut Rolls.

Ted and Bunny Chelena

Chelena & Associates

Ted and Bunny Chelena are insurance agents specializing in long term care since 1988. Most Americans would suffer financial devastation if they required an extended nursing home stay or other long term care services. As a way to protect against the high cost of personally financing this kind of care, many seniors have turned to long term care insurance. On a personal side, Ted and Bunny have two sons, two daughters and ten grandchildren. They enjoy the theater, dancing, taking nature walks and watching sunsets at the beach.

*About the recipe...
This nut roll-kolachki is our family favorite that was brought to this country from Eastern Europe in the early 1900's. It can be enjoyed at any time, but it is most popular at Christmas and Easter.*

Big Daddy's Baked Potato Soup
Jerry Jensen — Firemedic

Ingredients:

4 large potatoes
2/3 cup butter
2/3 cup flour
1 1/2 quarts whole milk
4 chopped green onions

1 cup sour cream
2 cups bacon (cooked crisp, crumbled)
5 ounces grated cheddar cheese

Directions:

1 – Heat oven to 350 degrees, bake potatoes until tender.

2 – Melt butter in a medium saucepan. Slowly blend in the flour with a wire whisk until thoroughly blended. Gradually add milk to the butter-flour mixture, whisking constantly.

3 – Cut potatoes in half, scoop out insides and set aside.

4 – Chop half the peels and discard the remainder.

5 – When milk is very hot, whisk in potatoes.

6 – Add green onions and potato peels.

7 – Whisk well; add sour cream and crumbled bacon. Heat thoroughly.

8 – Add cheese a little at a time until melted in.

9 – Serve with sourdough bread and a salad.

10 – Happy Eating!

Jerry Jensen
Firemedic
SCFD Sta.#8-C

Jerry ("Big Daddy J") Jensen moved to southwest Florida from Wisconsin to become a firefighter after working 15 years with General Motors. Starting later in life in his career gave him a unique perspective, since there weren't too many 35 year-old "rookies."

He loves to work out and competes individually and as member of the over 40 relay team in the Firefighter Combat Challenge. He is proud to have competed in the "World Combat Challenge Finals." At 6'4" and 275 pounds, there aren't many doors that can hold back the "J - Tool." His grown children, Emilie, Jeremy and Alice, often wonder when their father will grow out of this stage.

Jerry loves his free time and enjoys spending time hiking and traveling with his wife, Tina.

Mushroom Strudel

Café L' Europe

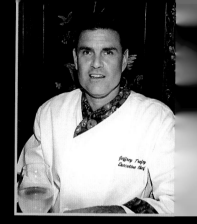

Ingredients:

3 sheets filo pastry
2 ounces melted butter
2 tablespoons olive oil
1 shallot chopped fine
1/2 pound white mushrooms
1/2 pound shiitake mushrooms

1/2 pounds Portobello mushrooms
1 cup chicken stock
1 cup port wine
1/2 cup dry bread crumbs
1 teaspoon thyme
salt and pepper

Directions:

1 – Slice all mushrooms very fine.
2 – Heat olive oil in a large pot.
3 – Sauté shallot until lightly browned.
4 – Add mushrooms and sauté for 5 minutes.
5 – Add chicken stock, port wine and thyme. Cook down until almost all of the liquid has evaporated.
6 – Season with salt and pepper and stir in breadcrumbs. The mixture must be firm and dry. Allow to cool.
7 – Take one sheet of filo and carefully brush with butter. Place another sheet on top and brush with butter. Put another sheet on top and brush with butter.
8 – Working with the filo with the narrow end towards you, place 1/2 of the mushroom mix evenly on the end. Tightly roll the filo 1/2 way up to form a tight roulade. Cut and seal the edge with butter. Brush the outside with butter and set aside.
9 – Follow these directions with the remaining mix.
10 – Cut each roulade into 2 pieces.
11 – Bake at 350 degrees until golden brown, about 10 minutes.

Makes 4 Servings.

Jeff Trefr_

Executive Che_
Café L' Europe

Upon graduation from the prestigious Culinary Institute of America, Jeff moved west to Santa Barbara, Californic and worked as a pastry che_ for the El Encanto Hotel. To broaden his knowledge of the culinary arts and hone his skills, Jeff moved east and spent three years at Café L Europe in the early 1980's Jeff's career path led him to the Five-Star Five-Diamond Ritz Carlton Resort in Naples and he was promoted to Executive Sous Chef. Ir 1989, promotion placed Jef_ as Executive Chef in charge o_ culinary operations at th_ Ritz Carlton in Kansas City Mo. He then worked ir Bermuda and Hilton Head Island, S.C. but is now back with Café L' Europe as Executive Chef. Jeff executes New European Cuisine witl_ his own imagination and personal style. He is married to Janet and has three children — Megan, Jack and Mike

941-388-4415

431 St. Armands Circle

Lunch 11 AM – 3:30 PM Mon-Sat
Lunch 12 PM – 3 PM Sunday
Dinner 5 PM – 10 PM Nightly

New European Cuisine and Classic Continental Cuisine

• • •

World Class Wine List
Gracious Refined Service

CAFÉ L'EUROPE

6

Lee Guidry
Chef
Osteria Northern
Italian Restaurant

Lee was born in Charleston, South Carolina. He grew up in New Orleans and started cooking in Ft. Walton Beach. He attended the University of South Alabama and graduated from Delgado Culinary Program in New Orleans, Louisiana. Lee is a chef that truly enjoys his work and is continually creating exciting and innovative dishes to serve at Osteria Northern Italian Restaurant in Sarasota, Florida.

Zuppa Di Pesce

Osteria Northern Italian Restaurant

Ingredients:

4 1/2 - 5 pounds assorted fish and seafood
1 cup olive oil
3 tablespoons chopped green onion or scallion
3 tablespoons chopped fresh garlic
3 tablespoons chopped fresh parsley

4 cups fresh chopped tomato
3 bay leaves
1/4 teaspoon red pepper
1/2 quart clam juice
1 cup Pinot Grigio or other white wine
sliced Italian bread

Directions:

Any type of fish and seafood can be used, we suggest mussels, clams, octopus, squid, scallops, lobster, shrimp, filet of fish: swordfish, sole, and snapper.

1 – Thoroughly clean the fish, discarding heads and tails. Clean and chop cuttlefish and/or squid. Wash and scrub the mussels and clams, and soak them in a bowl of cold salted water for one hour to allow the sand to fall to the bottom of the bowl.
2 – Pour the olive oil into a large pan over high heat; add the onion, garlic and parsley. Saute for five minutes; add seafood, which requires the longest cooking time; the octopus, squid, clams and mussels.

3 – Cover with clam juice and wine, add the red pepper, bay leaves and tomato.
4 – Bring to a boil, and then reduce heat.
5 – Simmer for approximately 20 minutes, then add the lobster tail, and filets of fish and continue cooking for 10 minutes.
6 – Add the scallops and shrimp and cook for another 5 minutes, or until the meat is cooked and tender but not breaking up.
7 – Rub the Italian bread with garlic and toast.
8 – Put fish and seafood in a large bowl surrounded by Italian bread, ladle broth over top and serve immediately.
Makes 6 Servings.

Papaya Soup

Munroe's Restaurant

Ingredients:

1 ripe papaya, peeled and seeded
3 oz simple syrup
1 tbl honey

1/2 tsp vanilla extract
1 oz raspberry syrup for garnish

Directions:

1 – Place papaya, syrup, honey and vanilla in a blender to puree.

2 – Strain thru a fine mesh strainer into a chilled bowl.

3 – Garnish with raspberry syrup and fresh berries as shown.

Richard Munroe
Chef/Proprietor
Munroe's Restaurant

Locals and seasonal visitors alike enjoy the bistro setting of Munroe's Restaurant. Proven to be Sarasota's favorite restaurant with casual elegance, friendly service, and creative, American foods.

Whether you start off your meal with one of our famous appetizers or finish with one of our colorful desserts, you won't go away disappointed.

For the late night guest, we offer live entertainment upstairs, with a late night menu and premium bar.

Munroe's

U̲rban B̲istro - V̲intage T̲avern

941-316-0609

**1296 First Street
Sarasota
Lunch Monday – Friday
Dinner Monday – Saturday
5:30 PM To 10:00 PM
Closed Sundays**

Sarasota's Favorite Restaurant

- American cuisine
- Bistro setting
- Live entertainment upstairs
- Desserts • Appetizers
- Late Night Menu
- Premium Bar
- Catering Available

Gary "Indian" Ewing
Lieutenant
Sarasota Bradenton Airport
C.F.R.

Gary grew up in the middle of the Osage Indian Reservation in Hominy, Oklahoma. With a great respect for the Osage Tribe, he's proud to bear the nickname "Indian."

During the six years Gary served in the Navy, he used his training as an expert salvage diver and demolition expert in Vietnam. After serving his tour of duty, he was hired by Sarasota Bradenton Airport as a crash fire rescue firefighter. He was the second Firefighter hired for the original crew of seven. He's spent 25 years in the CFR business, and this 57 year old officer is still in great physical condition.

Gary is single and has a 26-year old daughter "Brandy." He enjoys gun smithing, hunting, fishing, and boating in his free time.

About the recipe... "I've been making my Chowder ala Indian recipe at the Firehouse for 20 years or more. The guys love it with a touch of tobasco sauce to heat it up a little."

Sarasota Bradenton International Airport Crash Rescue Truck 3.

"Chowder ala Indian"
Gary Ewing — Lieutenant, Sarasota Bradenton Airport C.F.R.

Ingredients:

1 gal. milk (2 %)
8 oz. sliced mushrooms
4 lg. onions (white or Vidalia)
1 bunch celery
4 – 5 potatoes (diced)
1 stick butter (not margarine)
2 – 14 oz. cans whole kernel corn
4 large cloves garlic cloves

2 – 12 oz. cans Miller lite beer
To taste Everglades seasoning
To taste Lowery seasoning salt
choice of any one or more in combination:
  5 – 8 fillets fish
  3 – 4 lbs. shrimp
  2 lbs (shucked) clams
  3 cartons (shucked) oysters

Directions:

1 – Place butter, onions, celery, mushrooms, garlic and beer in bottom of a large pot.

2 – Place seafood over ingredients and simmer until fillets can be shredded with a fork or (5 - 8 minutes).

3 – Then pour in milk and (undrained) corn.

4 – Add seasoning salt to taste.

Tips: The recipe can be done in any quantity. The key is to cover the ingredients with 2 – 3 inches of milk before cooking.

Makes 6 Firemen Servings.

Leek & Lobster Stuffed Artichoke with Basil Oil and Balsamic Vinaigrette

Ophelia's

Ingredients:

ARTICHOKES:
3 large whole artichokes
2 leeks cut in half and
fine sliced
1 pound fresh lobster meat
coarse diced
1/2 pound butter
2 cloves
garlic fine sliced
1/2 cup white wine

1/2 teaspoon thyme
1/2 cup chopped parsley
1 cup dry bread crumbs
1/2 cup asiago cheese
grated
salt & pepper.

BALSAMIC VINAIGRETTE:
3 shallots
1 teaspoon sugar

1 clove garlic
1 teaspoon dry mustard
1/2 cup balsamic vinegar
1 cup extra virgin olive oil
salt & pepper

BASAL OIL:
approximately 30 basil
leaves
1 cup extra virgin olive oil.

Directions:

ARTICHOKES:
1 – Trim the thorny tops by cutting approximately 1/2 to 1 inch off top and trim outer leaves off stem leaving 2 inches of peeled stem and steam until tender.
2 – Cut length wise in half and scoop out fribrous choke with spoon.
3 – Saute leeks and garlic in 1/2 pound of butter, add lobster meat, wine and herbs.
4 – When leeks are soft mix in breadcrumbs and cheese and allow to cool.
5 – Stuff the cavities of the artichoke halves and bake for 15 minutes at 375 degrees or until golden brown.

BALSAMIC VINAIGRETTE:
Mix all together.

BASAL OIL:
Mix leaves and oil in blender.

Jane Ferro
Ophelia's

Jane Ferro, a native of Massachusetts, began her career at Anthony's Pier 4 in Boston. Moving to Cape Cod, she and her husband renovated and opened the Playhouse Restaurant in 1976, in Dennis, at America's oldest Summer Theater, the Cape Playhouse. In 1988 they renovated and opened Ophelia's on the Bay. Jane fell in love with Sarasota and in 1990 sold the Playhouse Restaurant and moved to Siesta Key. Jane enjoys working the front of the house with the wait staff and meeting the guests. Jane also does the wedding part of the business, which is her favorite. Jane and Stan have two children, Tim and Kristina, who also work at the restaurant and will soon be off to college.

Michael Garey
General Manager
Café L' Europe

Michael Garey was born and raised in Buffalo, New York. He moved to Sarasota, Florida as a teenager and began in the restaurant business as a busboy in 1977. In 1979 he started as a busboy at the Café L' Europe. Moving up the ladder, he became a dining room captain in 1981 and assistant manager in 1982. In 1984, he left Café L' Europe to help open and manage Mr. Wong's Chinese restaurant. Michael came back to Café L' Europe in 1986 as General Manager, the title that he holds today. Mr. Garey is currently President of the St. Armands Merchants Assoc. and conceived and organized two events for the Florida Wine Festival, the Wine Marker's Dinner, and Sip and Shop. He is married to his wife, Catherine and has three daughters, Alexandra, Jenna and Amelia.

Seviche of Sea Scallops

Café L' Europe

Ingredients:

16 jumbo sea scallops
3 ounces orange juice
3 ounces lemon juice
3 ounces lime juice
4 tablespoons red onion finely chopped
1 tablespoon chopped chives
1/2 chopped jalapeno

1 teaspoon chopped garlic
1 tablespoon chopped cilantro
2 ounces olive oil
salt and pepper
16 grilled asparagus spears
8 ounces yellow gazpacho
(see recipe from gazpacho trio)

Directions:

1 – Mix together juices with onion, chives, jalapeno, garlic, cilantro, olive oil, salt and pepper.

2 – Marinate raw scallops in this mixture overnight.

3 – To present place scallops with asparagus and sauce with yellow gazpacho.

Makes 4 Servings.

Strawberry Sashimi

Munroe's Restaurant

Ingredients:

1 oz saki

1/4 tsp minced ginger

1/4 tsp sugar

6 large strawberries

Directions:

1 – Slice strawberries thin and fan on a plate as shown.

2 – Mix the saki with the ginger and sugar, let stand for 5 minutes then drizzle over berries.

3 – Garnish with fresh berries.

Linda Haluska with her two daughters Marianna and Nicole cooking cookies.

James "Herm" Herrmann

Firemedic
Sarasota Bradenton
Airport C.F.R.

Herm was born in Boise, Idaho, in 1960, the oldest of seven children. In 1981 he came to Sarasota, fell in love with the fishing, and never left.

As a former Air Force Fire Protection Specialist, it was only natural for him to become a volunteer firefighter upon exiting the service. He spent seven years volunteering between Anna Maria and Parrish Fire Departments before being hired by Sarasota Bradenton Airport Crash Fire Rescue as an airport firemedic.

Herm and Lori have been married 14 years and have two children, Jameson (9) and Lily (3). He enjoys hunting, salt water fishing, and coaching soccer for the North River Sharks.

Sarasota Bradenton International Airport Crash Rescue Truck 3.

Stuffed Pepperoncini

James Herrman — Firemedic

Ingredients:

16 pepperoncini (large)
8 oz. fetta cheese (drained)
1 lb. smoked bacon
16 oz. Italian bread crumbs

4 eggs
1 cup flour
24 oz (or less) oil (for frying)
8 oz. bottle ranch dressing

Directions:

1 – Drain and dry pepperoncini, make small cuts in peppers.

2 – Cook bacon until done, and chop into small bits.

3 – Make egg wash with a little water.

4 – Stuff peppers with bacon and cheese.

5 – Roll peppers in flour, then egg wash, then bread crumbs.

6 – Then drop into hot oil (375 deg.) for 1 1/2 minutes or golden brown.

7 – Serve with "ranch dressing" for dipping.

Servings: 16 pieces = 4 people / 4 per serving

76

Black Bean Soup

Durango Oak Fire Steakhouse

Ingredients:

2 pounds bacon (raw)
3 - #10 cans black beans
4 cups diced red onions
2 1/2 ounces minced garlic
2 1/2 cups diced green peppers
1 1/2 tablespoons oregano

2 1/2 cups salad oil
1 cups white vinegar
2 cups water
1/2 cup each of toppings – cheese,
  red onions, chives

Directions:

1 – Cook bacon on sheet tray in 350 degree oven until well done. Chop into small pieces, drain and set aside.

2 – Open black beans and place in kettle.

3 – Combine all other ingredients (except bacon) in a blender and blend until well chopped. Place mixture and chopped bacon in steam kettle with beans. Turn the kettle on high.

4 – Bring the soup to a boil (should be a milky consistency).

5 – Remove from the steam kettle and place in an ice bath to chill rapidly.

6 – It can be served later by preheating in the microwave to 165 degrees.

7 – Top each bowl of beans with a tablespoon of each of the following: shredded cheese, chives and red onions. Serve with 2 packages of saltines.

Fred B. Bullard Jr.
Chairman and Chief Executive Officer
Durango

Fred B. Bullard Jr. co-founded the Company in 1991 and has served as a director since the Company's inception. In addition, Mr. Bullard has served as Chairman and Chief Executive Officer since June 1995. In this capacity, he has been responsible for the Company's overall leadership, direction and strategic thinking. Additionally, Mr. Bullard has applied his vast real estate experience to secure attractive lease agreements for the 26 restaurants.

Mr. Bullard has also served as Chairman and Chief Executive Officer of the Bullard Group, a privately held investment group since 1975. Mr. Bullard has been in the real estate development and construction business since 1968, building shopping centers, office buildings and planned community housing developments throughout Florida.

Mr. Bullard graduated from the University of Florida with a Bachelor of Arts in Business Administration. Mr. Bullard currently serves on the University of Florida Foundation Board, the Council of 100 Board of Directors, and the Shands Hospital Board of Directors in Gainesville, Florida.

941-378-0595
5451 Fruitville Road
Sarasota

941-761-9516
5502 Cortez Road West
Bradenton

941-496-8383
4369 South Tamiami Trail
Venice

Voted #1 Steak House
Across Florida By
Florida Today
Venice Gondolier
and *Naples News Press*

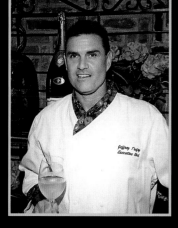

Jeff Trefry
Executive Chef
Café L' Europe

Upon graduation from the prestigious Culinary Institute of America, Jeff moved west to Santa Barbara, California and worked as a pastry chef for the El Encanto Hotel. To broaden his knowledge of the culinary arts and hone his skills, Jeff moved east and spent three years at Café L' Europe in the early 1980's. Jeff's career path led him to the Five-Star Five-Diamond Ritz Carlton Resort in Naples and he was promoted to Executive Sous Chef. In 1989, promotion placed Jeff as Executive Chef in charge of culinary operations at the Ritz Carlton in Kansas City, Mo. He then worked in Bermuda and Hilton Head Island, S.C. but is now back with Café L' Europe as Executive Chef. Jeff executes New European Cuisine with his own imagination and personal style. He is married to Janet and has three children – Megan, Jack and Mike.

Lobster Bisque
Café L' Europe

Ingredients:

5 pounds lobster in shells (preferably live Maine)
1 onion
2 red delicious apples
4 celery stalks
2 carrots
1 tablespoon olive oil
2 ounces Brandy
1/4 cup tomato paste
1 teaspoon paprika
1 tablespoon thyme
5 bay leaves
2 quarts clam juice
1/2 quart cream
1/4 cup cornstarch mixed with 1/2 cup water
salt and pepper

Directions:

1 – Chop lobster in shell into large chunks.

2 – Chop onion, apples, celery and carrots into a large dice.

3 – In a large 2 gallon pot, sear off Lobster in olive oil until Lobster is red in color.

4 – Add diced vegetables and apples and sauté for 5 minutes.

5 – Deglaze with Brandy and flame.

6 – Stir in tomato paste, paprika, thyme, and bay leaves.

7 – Add clam juice and simmer for 45 minutes.

8 – Strain and reserve Lobster.

9 – Bring Lobster stock back to a simmer and thicken with cornstarch slurry.

10 – Add cream and sherry.

11 – Cook for an additional 5 minutes.

12 – Add salt and pepper to taste.

13 – Remove Lobster from shell and chop. Add chopped lobster to soup as garnish.

Makes 10 Servings.

Vichyssoise – Cold Potato Soup

Sarasota University Club

Ingredients:

1 white onion large peeled and
  roughly sliced
2 stalks leeks rinsed and roughly sliced
3 pounds Yukon gold potatoes peeled
  and quartered
2 quarts water

8 cubes chicken bouillon
1/4 teaspoon thyme dry
4 bay leaves
1/2 quart heavy cream
salt and pepper to taste
sour cream and chives to garnish

Directions:

1 – Sauté onions and leeks on medium heat until soft.

2 – Add herbs, potatoes, water and bouillon.

3 – Simmer on medium heat until potatoes are cooked and fall apart with a fork.

4 – Puree in food processor or blender and pass through strainer or china cap, push through as much as possible and discard all that won't.

5 – Refrigerate for at least four hours or overnight.

6 – Before serving, add one half quart of heavy cream and mix well. Add salt and pepper taste.

7 – Serve in a chilled bowl, topped with a dollop of sour cream and chopped chives.

Makes 6 – 8 ounce bowls.

John R. Halling
Executive Chef
Sarasota University Club

Recently taking charge of the Sarasota University Club kitchen, Chef John brings a combination of classic French, International cuisine and traditional Florida cooking styles. Formerly of Francoise et Henri, Cape Codder Hotel in Cape Cod, and Bayou Bills, Treasure Island Florida. These and other Chef positions have allowed Chef John a wide range of experience to please many different palates. The recipes that Chef John presents are some of his personal favorites. Chef John finds them easy to prepare and very flavorful. The Sarasota University Club hopes you enjoy these recipes and they provide many enjoyable dining experiences.

79

Michael L. Fitzgerald
Firefighter

Michael L. Fitzgerald has been in the fire service for 13 years and is a 1st Class Firefighter with the Cedar Hammock Fire Department. In 1998, Michael was the CHFD Firefighter of the Year nominee. He also owns a successful irrigation company. Spending time with his wife of six years, Robin and two children, Savannah and Christian, is what he loves most in life. Seeing the joy in the eyes of his children when he arrives home after every shift is what life is about! When asked about the recipe, Michael replies, "The wings are an authentic recipe from Buffalo, NY, and the chicken salad is the best he's ever had! Really!"

Firehouse Chicken Wings
Michael L. Fitzgerald — Firefighter

Ingredients:

2 pounds chicken wings
2 - 16 ounce bottles of
  Louisiana hot sauce

1 stick butter or margarine
1/2 cup vinegar

Directions:

1 – Deep fry or bake wings until well done.

2 – Place in a bowl or a basket lined with a paper towel to absorb the excess grease.

3 – Melt butter in a medium sized pot.

4 – Add hot sauce and vinegar. (Make sure you don't cook the hot sauce. It'll kill the heat.)

5 – Stir until well mixed.

6 – Place wings, a few at a time, into sauce and coat liberally.

7 – Remove and place in a large bowl or serving dish.

8 – Repeat until all are done.

9 - Pour remaining sauce over wings.

*These will be pretty hot, so adjust the amount of hot sauce to your liking.

Makes 3–4 Servings.

Butternut Squash Soup
with Walnuts and Curry

Cuoco Matto Restaurant

Ingredients:

3 cups butternut squash
   puree
1/2 teaspoon ground cloves
1/2 teaspoon ground cinnamon
1/2 teaspoon freshly grated nutmeg
2 tablespoons unsalted butter
1 teaspoon curry powder
salt & pepper
4 cups whole milk
2 tablespoons cornstarch
1 cup heavy cream
1/2 cup chopped walnuts

NOTE:
You can use frozen butternut squash puree if you're pressed for time, just make sure it contains nothing but squash and salt, or the flavor of the soup will be altered. Frank Bologna uses fresh squash and bakes it until tender, then scoops out the flesh and mashes it with a potato ricer while it is still hot. If you plan to use fresh squash, you'll need about 3 pounds of fresh squash to obtain 3 cups of pureed squash.

Directions:

1 – In a food processor, combine the squash, cloves, cinnamon, nutmeg, butter, curry, salt, pepper, and 1 cup of the milk until smooth.

2 – Transfer to a large pot; simmer, adding all but 2 tablespoons of the milk by the 1/4 cup until thick.

3 – Heat until boiling.

4 – Dissolve the cornstarch in the remaining milk; whisk into the boiling soup; add the cream and bring to a boil. Cook until thick, whisking constantly, and serve hot, garnished with walnuts.

Makes 8 Servings.

Frank Bologna
Executive Chef & Co-Owner
Cuoco Matto Restaurant

In Italian "cuoco" means cook or chef and "matto" means crazy. Frank Bologna is the Executive Chef and co-owner of this "Crazy Chef Italian Restaurant." Guests can dine or enjoy a drink at the bar, amongst the warm and entertaining ambiance of an open kitchen with an authentic wood-burning oven. The splendid tastes of Rosticceria Cucina Toscana (rustic Tuscan cuisine) are featured along with a distinct wine list at reasonable prices. Warm delicious Foccacia bread with a tangy balsamic vinegar and oil dipping sauce, is served promptly with every meal. Everyone will enjoy the personable, attentive service, superb food, and cozy atmosphere found at Cuoco Matto.

Gary Wooten
General Manager
Sandbar Restaurant.

Gary Wooten was born in Columbus, Ohio and graduated from Otterbein College in 1977. He went on to graduate school at Emporia State University in Emporia, Kansas studying Student Personnel. He began his employment with the Miami Valley Hospital as Residence Director in Dayton, Ohio in 1978. Later, Gary relocated to Anna Maria Island and joined the Chiles Restaurant Group holding multiple positions and yet ten years later still enjoying all that the industry has to offer as General Manager to the Sandbar Restaurant. Gary has several hobbies, his favorite being fundraising and charity work. Gary is very active in community organizations such as Partners in Education in which we were voted the number one business for our participation in Manatee County.

Oysters Rockefeller

Sandbar Restaurant

Ingredients:

1 ounce bacon
1 ounce Spanish onion
1/2 ounce white wine
1/2 ounce chicken bouillon
4 ounces 1/2 & 1/2
4 ounces heavy cream

6 ounces frozen spinach or 12 ounces fresh spinach
4 ounces roux (roux = 1 to 1 butter and flour)
parmesan cheese

Directions:

1 – Sauté onions and bacon until onions are tender.

2 – Add white wine and reduce. Add heavy cream, half and half, and chicken base. Bring to a slow simmer and then add roux until thickened. If using frozen spinach, squeeze out excess water before adding.

3 – Simmer 5 minutes and cool.

4 – To prepare, shuck oysters and rinse any grit from them.

5 – Place rock sauce on the oyster covering to the edge of the shell.

6 – Top with grated parmesan cheese (enough to cover sauce).

7 – Bake in a 450 degree oven until slightly browned.

8 – Garnish with 1 lemon and parsley.

Yields: 4 portions

82

Swordfish Carpaccio

Osteria Northern Italian Restaurant

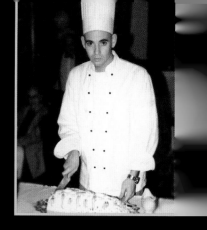

Ingredients:

1 swordfish filet
2 lemons
1 lime
salt & pepper to season

drizzle extra virgin olive oil
fresh radicchio
fennel leaves
toasted Italian bread

Directions:

1 – Remove skin from one swordfish filet, marinate in the juice of two fresh lemons and one fresh lime for approximately 20-30 minutes.

2 – Dry the fish and slice into thin pieces.

3 – Sprinkle with salt and pepper.

4 – Drizzle with extra virgin olive oil.

5 – Serve on a bed of fresh radicchio and top with fennel leaves and toast.

Lee Guidry

Chef
Osteria Northern
Italian Restaurant

Lee was born in Charleston South Carolina. He grew up in New Orleans and started cooking in Ft. Walton Beach He attended the University of South Alabama and graduated from Delgado Culinary Program in New Orleans Louisiana. Lee is a chef that truly enjoys his work and is continually creating exciting and innovative dishes to serve at Osteria Northern Italian Restaurant in Sarasota, Florida

941-388-3671

29 1/2 N. Blvd. of the Presidents
Sarasota
Serving Dinner 7 Days A Week
4:30 PM To 10:30 PM Daily

Served the very best in authentic Northern Italian cuisine for over 15 years.

Vegetable Soup

Jerry Palmer — Hazardous Waste Specialist

Ingredients:

2-3 eye of round steaks (or other lean beef)
5 large potatoes
32 ounce can V-8 juice
32 ounce can water
1 bag frozen mixed vegetables
1 medium size onion (1/2 cup diced)

1 small head cabbage
1 can beef consommé
1 beef bouillon cube
1/4 stick margarine
salt & pepper to taste

Directions:

1 – Trim any excess fat from the steaks and cut into 3/4 inch cubes.

2 – Using a stockpot, on medium heat brown meat in the margarine.

3 – While meat is browning, dice onion and add to pot. Add bouillon cube.

4 – While meat and onions continue to cook, peel potatoes and cut into good-sized pieces.

5 – Add potatoes, consommé, mixed vegetables, V-8 juice and water.

6 – Increase heat setting to high to bring to a boil.

7 – While heating, dice cabbage into 1/2 to 3/4 inch pieces and add to pot.

8 – After it comes to a boil, reduce heat and simmer until the cabbage and potatoes are cooked.

9 – Start to finish, on the table in less than 1 hour.

Makes 6-8 Servings.

Jerry Palmer
Hazardous Waste Specialist

Jerry grew up in Wayne County, Ohio. The fifth child in a family of 10 kids, his family was self sufficient. Being farmers, they raised their own meat and vegetables and made their own hand churned butter from fresh cream.

Jerry and his wife, Maryanne, have been married nearly 20 years. They share three grown children: Kimberly Denver, Co.), Michael Coshocton, Ohio), and Matthew (Toledo, Ohio).

After 25 years with Bell and Howell, he left a position of operations manager with responsibilities that included their hazardous waste disposal program. Jerry joined SCFD Hazardous Waste Division) in 1998, applying his experience to work as an inspector in the Small Quantity Generators Program and responding to occasional hazardous materials spills in the county.

About the recipe...
"This recipe for Vegetable Soup is a quick, delicious creation of mine. I've been making it for nearly 30 years and have never found a person who didn't think it was great!"

Quit hogging the Nozzle!

4

Tuna & Lobster Martini
with Absolut Pepar Aioli

Ophelia's

Mitch Rosenbaum

Ophelia's

Ingredients:

8 ounces thick cube of Yellowfin Tuna
12 ounces fresh lobster meat
   (tails & claw mixture)
4 egg yolks
4 cloves garlic
1/2 cup white wine vinegar
1/2 teaspoon cayenne
1 teaspoon salt

1/2 cup cubed French bread without crust
pinch crushed chili
1 ounce Absolut Pepar
1 cup extra virgin olive oil
2 tablespoons cracked black peppercorns
baby greens and fresh chives to garnish
1/2 teaspoon of paprika

Directions:

1 – Encrust Tuna Steaks with peppercorn and kosher or sea salts and quick sear on all sides at about 30 seconds per side, cool in freezer immediately.

2 – In a food processor combine yolks, garlic, vinegar, cayenne, salt, bread, chili, paprika, and vodka, gradually incorporating oil until emulsified.

3 – Chill and combine with large pieces of lobster.

4 – Slice tuna into thin uniform pieces of rare tuna.

5 – To assemble place two slices of tuna on side of martini glass, place small bed of baby greens in glass, four pieces of dressed lobster meat over top, garnish with fresh chive and lime slices.

Chef Mitch Rosenbaum comes to Ophelia's from the top Manhattan's corporate executive dining rooms to the Four Star Restaurants of Boston and Cape Cod. Living in the lower East side of New York City, Mitch was creatively influenced by China Town and Little Italy. He traveled through France, Spain Portugal and Morocco to expand his culinary talents. Upon returning to the United States, Mitch was known throughout the restaurant elite as Chef, and became Chef-Owner of the critically acclaimed Cielo Café, a 20 seat restaurant with European style dining in Wellfleet, Massachusetts Eventually he opened a larger establishment, Mitchell's Bistro, in Eastham Massachusetts known for its eclectic mix of New American, Indian Latin American and Portuguese preparations. With so many transplanted New Englanders at Ophelia's on the Bay, Mitch has quickly become a welcome and valuable part of the family

Ophelia's
on the bay

941-349-2212

9105 Midnight Pass Road
Siesta Key
Open 7 Days A Week
5 AM To 10 PM

All Decked Out For
A Private Party

8

Café L' Europe

Now celebrating its twenty seventh anniversary, Café L' Europe continues to be one of Sarasota's most beautiful and popular restaurants. A multitude of awards have been received over the years from such publications as The Wine Spectator, Sante' Award of Excellence and Florida Trend as well as the prestigious DIRONA award; bearing witness to the high quality of food. Pleasing aromas and beautiful presentations preview the finest of Continental Cuisine and New European Cuisine from elaborate appetizers to elegant entrees and truly decadent desserts. Completing the scene is a superb selection of wines from the finest vineyards of Europe and California. The final ingredient essential to fine dining is the high level of professional service. The warm welcome on arrival hints at the care taken by every person at Café L' Europe to ensure your dining pleasure.

Gazpacho Trio

Café L' Europe

Ingredients:

TRADITIONAL GAZPACHO:
1 cucumber peeled, seeded, and diced
1 red pepper diced
2 tomatoes diced
1 clove garlic chopped
1/4 red onion chopped
2 ounces red wine vinegar
1 tablespoon chopped fresh basil
1 dash Tabasco
2 cups tomato juice
2 cups V-8 juice

2 ounces extra virgin olive oil
salt and pepper

YELLOW GAZPACHO:
1 tablespoon garlic
1/2 yellow pepper
2 ripe yellow tomatoes
2 slices dry French bread
1/4 cup olive oil
1 tablespoon red wine vinegar
salt and pepper

WHITE GAZPACHO:
1/2 green pepper
1 cucumber peeled and seeded
2 slices white bread crust removed
1/4 cup toasted almonds
1 tablespoon garlic
2 tablespoons chopped fresh basil
2 tablespoons white wine vinegar
1/4 cup olive oil, salt and pepper

Directions:

TRADITIONAL GAZPACHO:
Combine all ingredients and chill well.

YELLOW GAZPACHO:
Combine all ingredients in a blender until smooth. Chill well.

WHITE GAZPACHO:
Process all ingredients in blender until smooth. Chill well.

Makes 4 Servings.

Lobster Frit

Café on the Bay

Ingredients:

2 cups vegetable or salad oil
4 lobster tails
1/2 cup flour
4 eggs
1 tablespoon chopped parsley

SAUCE:
4 ounces sherry
8 ounces butter
1 ounce lemon juice
3 ounces Asiago cheese

Bill Herlihy
General Manager
Café on the Bay

Directions:

1 – Pull lobster tail from shell. Cut down center and flatten out.

2 – Heat oil in sauté pan.

3 – Whip eggs and add parsley in a bowl.

4 – Roll lobster meat in flour and egg mixture.

5 – Cook in hot oil. (Do NOT let oil get too hot.)

6 – Make sauce: Reduce sherry and lemon juice to 1/3. Fold in butter just before serving.

7 – Add Asiago to finish.

Makes 4 Servings.

Twenty-two years ago, Bill Herlihy began working in the restaurant business in the Finger Lake Region in Western New York. He moved to Rochester, New York in 1984, where he first met Café on the Bay's current Executive Chef, Keith Daum. In 1988, Bill decided to relocate to sunny Florida and 2 years later he met Michael Garey and Titus Letschert. Shortly thereafter, he started as a dining room captain at Café L' Europe. After 6 years of learning from "the best" Bill became General Manager of Café on the Bay. Keith Daum and Bill were reunited after 12 years. Bill has a nine-year old daughter, Delanie, and is very active in local charities. He has been the Co-Chairperson of the St. Jude's Gourmet Luncheon on Longboat Key for the last five years.

941-383-0440

2630 Harbourside Dr.
Longboat Key, FL 34228

Breakfast Saturday
8:30 AM To 10:30 AM

Sunday Breakfast Brunch
9:00 AM To 1:00 PM

Sunday Lunch
1:00 PM To 3:30 PM

Lunch 6 Days
11:00 AM To 3:00 PM

Dinner 7 Days
4:30 PM To 10:00 PM

Extraordinary cuisine served in a truly exquisite waterfront setting. Come by land or sea. Casual attire is welcomed.

A Collection of
Salad Recipes
from the
Fire Departments
& Area Restaurants
of Manatee and
Sarasota Counties
in the State
of Florida.

Salad Recipes

Richard, Adela and Casey Gonzmart

*Owners
Columbia Restaurant*

Our family has been creating some of Florida's favorite Spanish cuisine for nearly 100 years. We feature the freshest seafood and steaks as well as our won tradition family recipes. Through the years we have received some of the highest awards in the restaurant industry, but our highest praise comes from our loyal customers who dine with us again and again.

Join us daily for lunch or dinner, and take in the beautiful sites of St. Armands Circle while enjoying the delicious dishes our chef prepares especially for you.

The Gonzmart family looks forward to welcoming you to the Columbia Restaurant!

1905 Salad – Ensalada 1905

Columbia Restaurant

Ingredients:

SALAD:
1/2 head iceberg lettuce
2 ripe tomatoes, cut in eighths
2 stalks celery, sliced
1/2 cup Swiss cheese, cut in julienne strips
1/2 cup ham, cut in julienne strips
   (or turkey or shrimp)
1/4 cup green Spanish olives, pitted
2 teaspoons grated Romano cheese

DRESSING:
1/8 cup white wine vinegar
1/2 cup extra-virgin Spanish olive oil
4 cloves garlic, mined
1 teaspoon Worcestershire Sauce
Salt and pepper to taste
1 teaspoon oregano
2 teaspoons lemon juice

Directions:

1 – Toss together all salad ingredients except Romano cheese.

2 – Mix garlic, oregano, and Worcestershire sauce in a bowl.

3 – Beat until smooth with a wire whisk.

4 – Add olive oil, gradually beating to form an emulsion.

5 – Stir in vinegar and lemon juice and season with salt and pepper.

6 – Add dressing to salad and toss well. Add Romano cheese and toss one more time.

Makes 4 Servings.

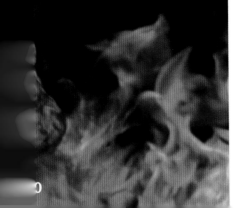

Mary Mixon's Ambrosia

From the Kitchen of Mixon Fruit Farms Inc.

This recipe is a simple, delicious, fresh citrus fruit salad, so easy to make anyone can do it.

Ingredients:

Mixon Oranges (navels are excellent) sectioned or cut into chunks; quantity varies according to amount of people to be served; oranges are the main ingredient

Pineapple (canned, unsweetened, drained; cut in small chunks, just enough to flavor)
Coconut (shredded, small amount)
Red Maraschino Cherries (cut in halves)

Directions:

1 – Combine oranges, pineapple and cherries. (It should be juicy.)

2 – Chill.

3 – About one hour before serving, mix in coconut.

4 – For a festive look, sprinkle more coconut on top and add a few cherries for decoration.

5 – Best when served fresh.

6 – This is my "By Guess and By Golly" recipe. Use amounts of all ingredients to suit your personal taste — heavy on the oranges. You can't go wrong.

7 – Enjoy!

Mary

Mixon Fruit Farms Inc.

A trip to Florida is not complete without a stop at Mixon's 350-acre grove. Bring your camera and plan to stay awhile.

Stroll the grove, tour our plant, picnic in the grove with our deli sandwiches and baked goods. Taste our famous Orange Swirl Ice Cream and Homemade Fudge both made with fresh orange juice. Sample Florida's best citrus and juice. Shop in our gift shop offering a lovely selection of Florida jellies, marmalades and candies, gourmet food items, novelties and Florida souvenirs.

Grove fresh fruit baskets, mesh bags, airline packs, and gift fruit shipping is available. Mixon's is known worldwide for Southern hospitality. Plan a visit soon.

Tom Klauber
**Food & Beverage Director
The Colony Restaurants**

The Colony's Director of Food & Beverage Operations Tom Klauber is also Chef/Proprietor of Longboat Key's popular Pattigeorge's restaurant. Tom began his culinary career by working at his family's resort, later attending the University of Houston's Hotel & Management School, and earning a degree from the Culinary Institute of America. He then traveled and studied abroad, receiving his diploma from La Varenne's Ecole de Cuisine in Paris, France. He gained experience in fine restaurants in Paris, Florence and Amsterdam before returning to The Colony, where he worked as executive chef and food and beverage director from 1982 to 1992. Prior to opening PGs in 1998, Tom was chef/owner at Gieusseppi Wong in Aspen.

Tom Klauber has received numerous accolades, including being recognized in "Chefs in America" as one of the outstanding chefs in the United States, and receiving the James Beard Foundation "Rising Stars of American Cuisine" Award.

Asian Slaw
The Colony Restaurants

Ingredients:

1 cup red cabbage, shredded
1 cup snow peas, julienne
1/4 cup daikon radish, peeled and julienne
1/4 cup bean sprouts
1/2 cup carrot, julienne
1/4 cup red bell pepper, julienne
1/4 cup yellow bell pepper, julienne

1 tablespoon black sesame seeds
1 tablespoon sesame oil
1 tablespoon vegetable oil
1/4 cup soy sauce
1 tablespoon ginger, minced
1 teaspoon garlic, minced
2 tablespoon scallions, sliced

Directions:

1 – Combine all ingredients and toss. Hold for service.

the Colony Restaurants

**Monday – Saturday
Lunch: 11:30 AM To 2:30 PM
Dinner: 6:00 PM To 10:00 PM
Sunday Brunch:
10:00 AM To 2:00 PM**

941-383-5558
**1620 Gulf of Mexico Drive
Longboat Key**

• • •

Enjoy an award-winning dining experience complemented by an unparalleled wine list with *spectacular* views of the Gulf of Mexico.

- **Prestigious DiRoNA Award**
- *The Wine Spectator's* **Award of Excellence**
- **Five Star Diamond Award for outstanding hospitality from the American Academy of Hospitality Sciences**
- **Member of** *Nation's Restaurant News* **Fine Dining Hall of Fame**

Sunset Salad

Beach House Restaurant

Ingredients:

1 cup chopped Romaine lettuce, rinsed
1 cup chopped Red leaf lettuce, rinsed
1 carrot, grated
4-5 sliced radishes
1/2 red onion, shaved thin

1 ounce alfalfa sprouts
2 hard boiled eggs, sliced or chopped
2 ounces chopped walnuts
1 tomato, quartered
2 chicken breasts, sautéed or grilled

Bobby Wheeler
Executive Chef
Beach House Restaurant

Bobby Wheeler is a long time resident of Bradenton. He began his culinary career as Apprentice Chef with L'Auberge Du Bon Vivant, which was one of the premier French restaurants on Longboat Key. He first joined the Sandbar Restaurant in 1981 where he was the Kitchen Manager and Chef for four years. He later worked as Executive Chef for Beach Bistro during which time they earned the 1996 Golden Spoon Award. The Chiles Group was fortunate to once again join forces with Bobby in 1998 when he returned as Executive Chef of the Beach House Restaurant. Bobby currently serves as Corporate Chef overseeing all the restaurants. Bobby's knowledge, experience and dedication to quality rank him as one of our areas finest chefs.

Directions:

1 – Toss lettuces, carrots and radishes in a bowl. You may also add shredded red cabbage for color.

2 – Assemble on serving plates and place the tomatoes, alfalfa sprouts and eggs around the edges of the plates. Place the sliced eggs to accompany the colors.

3 – Top the salad with shaved onions and sliced chicken breast.

4 – Garnish with the chopped walnuts and serve with your favorite dressing.

5 – You may also serve this beautiful salad with grilled shrimp or salmon filet.

Makes 2 Generous Portions.

Rick Haller
Firemedic

Rick was born in Chicago, but moved to Sarasota as a child and has been here ever since. Rick worked for Sarasota County doing aquatic plant control for seven years and was a volunteer firefighter most of that time. His dedication landed him a position as Volunteer Lieutenant before leaving the group to take a rookie firefighter position with SCFD two years ago. Somewhere along the way he picked up the nick-name "porkchop" and it stuck to this day.

He loves camping, open pit BBQ, fishing, 4-wheelin' and boating. Don't let his quiet demeanor fool you into thinking he's timid. He successfully crossed 300 miles of ocean with his 23' Mako on a round trip to the Berry Islands in the Bahamas with some firefighters. Now that's adventure!

The crew at Doctors Hospital ER.

Broccoli Salad
Rick Haller — Firemedic

Ingredients:

1 head broccoli
8-10 slices bacon (cooked and crumbled)
1 cup raisins (regular or light)
2-4 tablespoons chopped sweet onion

1/2-1 cup mayonnaise
1-2 tablespoons vinegar
2-4 tablespoons sugar
1 cup shredded cheddar cheese

Directions:

1 – Mix all ingredients.

2 – Chill 4-6 hours.

Makes 8 Servings.

Rick's Cafe Cous Cous

Munroe's Restaurant

Ingredients:

16 oz. Cous cous
1/2 tsp ground cinnamon
1 tsp ground tumeric
1 tsp ground cumin
1 tsp ground coriander
1/4 tsp black pepper
1/2 tsp nutmeg
1/2 tsp red pepper flakes
1 tsp saffron threads

1 tsp salt
1 cup raisins
2 cloves garlic, minced
1 large tomato, diced
1 small red onion, diced
1 lemon, juice of
1 orange, juice of
2 cups chicken stock

Directions:

1 – Rinse cous cous in a fine strainer with cold water.

2 – Place cous cous in a bowl and mix in all remaining ingredients.

3 – Put cous cous in a casserole dish with stock and bake at 400 until liquid is absorbed (about 20 minutes.

4 – Serve with grilled meats, fish or chicken.

Keith Haluska stands by engine 61 Tele-Squirt.

Fanny Yoder
Head Cook
Der Dutchman Restaurant

Fanny Yoder and her husband Emanuel have been cooking and baking "Amish Style" their whole lives. The experience they gained both at home and in their bakery in Ohio, has been a palatable one to Der Dutchman Restaurant patrons.

With our roots from the Amish community in Ohio where we have seven other restaurant locations, we bring a taste of our culinary heritage to the community in Sarasota.

When you've finished feeding that hearty appetite, don't forget to take a stroll through our well known bakery and Carlisle Gifts shop for some take home goodies.

Pasta Salad
Der Dutchman Restaurant

Ingredients:

6 cups of Rotini Noodles
1 teaspoon salt
1 large green pepper
1/2 medium purple onion

1 large tomato
2 cups Italian dressing
1/2 cup sugar

Directions:

1 – Put on kettle to boil.

2 – When starting to boil, put Rotini into water and turn off heat. Let sit in water for 30 minutes.

3 – Rinse with cold water until pasta feels cool.

4 – Chop pepper, onion, and tomato and set aside.

5 – Mix Italian dressing, seasoning, and sugar together.

6 – Toss until mixed.

7 – Serve cold and fresh.

Makes 8-10 Servings.

Mandarin Orange Salad

Rick Pride — Firefighter/Paramedic

Ingredients:

CARAMELIZED ALMONDS:
1/4 cup chopped slivered almonds
2 tablespoons sugar

SALAD:
1 bunch romaine
1 bunch green onions chopped with tops
1 cup chopped celery
1 – 11 ounce can mandarin oranges, drained

DRESSING:
1/4 cup oil
2 tablespoons vinegar
2 tablespoons sugar
1/2 teaspoon salt
dash Tabasco
dash pepper

Directions:

CARAMELIZED ALMONDS:
1 – Heat almonds and sugar over medium heat until sugar melts and almonds turn brown, stirring constantly.

2 – Remove from heat and cool.

SALAD:
1 – Wash and tear romaine into bite size pieces.

2 – Toss romaine with celery, onion and oranges.

DRESSING:
1 – Mix all together.

2 – Just before serving, toss romaine mixture with dressing.

3 – Top with almonds.

Richard "Rick" Pride
Firefighter/Paramedic
SCFD

Boston, Massachusetts, was home to Rick until he was eight years old. His father was a department store manager with an opportunity to relocate to the Sunshine State. In 1978 they picked Sarasota to call home, and that is where Rick did most of his growing up. He recalls a desire to be a fireman as far back as his memory permits. In 1992 (at age 22) his opportunity came when he was offered a firemedic position with Sarasota County Fire Department. Five years later he put himself through paramedic school. He is currently working at Station #11 on B-shift.

Married just four years, Rick and Lisa enjoy fitness, boating, and travel, when Lisa can get away from her work as an interior designer.

About the recipe...
"The Mandarin Orange Salad is a tasty recipe that my wife Lisa found years ago. I tried it out on my crew at Station #11-B it was a definite hit."

Station #11 takes "pride" in their cooking.

9

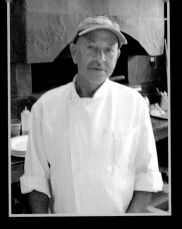

Giovanni (Gigi) Mauri

Executive Chef
Cosimo's Brick Oven
Trattoria & Bar

Born and raised in the Piedmont Region of Italy, Executive Chef Giovanni (Gigi) Mauri has been in the restaurant business for over four decades, with stops in Switzerland, London, and Washington, D.C. before arriving in Southwest Florida in 1990.

At Cosimo's Brick Oven, Chef Gigi and his staff skillfully combine "Old World" Italian Cuisine with New World flavors and techniques to create an unforgettable dining experience.

If you're in the mood for a wood-fired pizza, specialty salad, signature pasta, or the famous calamari, you must try Cosimo's Brick Oven! And don't forget the daily specials or the extensive and afford-able wine list!

Winner, Best New Restaurant, Sarasota Herald Tribune, 1999

"Gargano Salad"

Cosimo's Brick Oven Trattoria & Bar

Ingredients:

4 Sliced Plum Tomatoes
10 - 12 Calamata Olives
1/2 cup Feta Cheese
1 cup Mixed Greens

1 oz. Balsalmic Reduction
1 Tbs Olive Oil
Pinch Dried Oregano
6 Red Onion Slices

Directions:

1 – Arrange tomatoes and olives in a circle aorund edge of plate, with mixed greens in the center.

2 – Top tomatoes with Feta cheese.

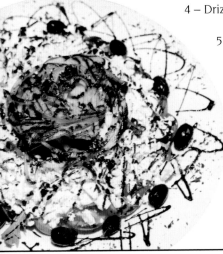

3 – Top with oregano and olive oil.

4 – Drizzle Balsalmic Reduction over Tomatoes and Onion.

5 – Parsley Garnish

Tip: To make your own "Balsalmic Reduction." Boil vinegar in a pan till it is reduced to 10%. Let it cool to thicken.

Makes 1 Serving.

98

Strawberry & Field Green Salad

Michael's Seafood Grille

Ingredients:

SALAD:
1- 6 ounce package field greens (available in most produce sections)
1 tomato diced 1/4"
1/2 pint strawberries hulled & sliced
1 small red onion sliced
1/2 cup crumbled Gorgonzola or Bleu Cheese

BALSAMIC VINAIGRETTE:
1/4 cup Dijon mustard
1/4 cup fresh basil leaves
3 cloves garlic
1 shallot or 1 tablespoon chopped red onion
2 tablespoons powdered sugar
pinch of salt & pepper
1/4 cup balsamic vinegar
1 cup vegetable oil

SPICED WALNUTS:
1/2 cup large spiced walnuts
1/2 cup powdered sugar
pinch cayenne pepper
vegetable oil

Directions:

BALSAMIC VINAIGRETTE DRESSING: 1 – Process all ingredients into a food processor (except balsamic vinegar) until chopped fine. 2 – Add balsamic vinegar. 3 – Drizzle in 1 cup vegetable oil to finish.
Yields 1 pint.

SPICED WALNUTS: 1 – Bring 1 quart of water to boil in medium pot. 2 - Add nuts and boil for 7 minutes. Drain well. 3 – Place hot nuts in a mixing bowl and cover with sugar and pepper. Toss to coat well. 4 – In a small pan add enough oil so that when adding the nuts, they will be completely submerged.
5 – Heat oil to approximately 350 degrees, or just until when 1 nut is added bubbles will form around it.
6 – Add the nuts coated with the sugar and fry for 4 minutes, adjusting the heat to keep the nuts simmering. 7 – Remove with slotted spoon and drain on paper towels.

SALAD: 1 – Toss lettuce with just enough Balsamic dressing to lightly coat leaves.
2 – Portion lettuce onto 4 plates and garnish with tomatoes, strawberries, onion, cheese, and walnuts.

Richard E. Kirby

Chaplain for Braden River Fire and Rescue

Richard E. Kirby is the Chaplain for Braden River Fire and Rescue and has been involved in the fire service for 11 years. Married with grown children, he spends his spare time building model aircrafts. This recipe is one of his special favorites at Christmas because of its festive colors. When asked what's most important in life to Richard, he replies, "Serving God and my fellow man."

Sauerkraut Salad

Richard Kirby

Ingredients:

1 quart sauerkraut
1/2 cup diced green pepper
1/2 cup diced celery
1/2 cup (more or less) diced onion
4 oz. jar diced pimentos

1/2 cup white vinegar
1 1/2 cup sugar
1 cup (or less) oil
3/4 cup water

Directions:

1 – Rinse and drain sauerkraut

2 – Add other ingredients

3 – Mix; Let sit few hours – best overnight

4 – Keeps well in refrigerator a long while

Mediterranean Salad with Fresh Oregano Vinaigrette

The Colony Restaurants

Ingredients:

SALAD:
8 cups mixed spring greens
1 roasted red bell pepper, sliced
8 ounces calamata olives, halved
1/4 cup capers
1 small red onion, coarsely chopped
8 whole peppercini

1 large tomato, coarsely chopped
1 cucumber, peeled and thinly sliced
1/2 cup crumbled feta
Fresh Oregano Vinaigrette (see recipe)

VINAIGRETTE:
1/4 cup red wine vinegar
1 cup extra virgin olive oil
2 tablespoons finely minced fresh oregano
1 aspoon dried thyme or 1 tablespoon fresh
1 clove garlic, finely minced
Salt and freshly ground pepper to taste

Directions:

SALAD:

1 – In large bowl, gently toss all ingredients except feta and peppercini, with dressing.

2 – Divide evenly among 4 plates.

3 – Sprinkle with feta and garnish each with 2 peppercini.

VINAIGRETTE:

1 – Mix all ingredients. Pour over top of salad.

Makes 4 Servings.

Amy Knox
*Chef/Manager of Tastebuds
The Colony Restaurants*

As Chef/Manager of Tastebud's Gourmet Market and Wine Shop at The Colony Beach & Tennis Resort, Amy Knox does what she loves best – creating. From a very young age, Amy spent summers with her grandmother learning aspects of canning and preserving.

At 16, Amy became head cook of a dude ranch in Wyoming, serving three meals a day, seven days a week to as many as 200 guests and staff. In middle school, Amy studied French with the thought of going to France one day and studying with great chefs.

After graduating from the University of Denver, Amy attended the Culinary Institute of America, where she excelled on the Dean's list and as group leader.

Chef Knox moved to Sarasota in 1996 to work as night supervisor for the fine dining line in The Colony Dining Room. There she met Tom Klauber, then Executive Chef at The Colony. Amy aided Tom in the opening of his popular Longboat Key restaurant, Pattigeorge's, in 1998. She served as Sous Chef until May of 2000, when Tom brought her back to The Colony to manage Tastebud's.

Michael L. Fitzgerald
Firefighter

Michael L. Fitzgerald has been in the fire service for 13 years and is a 1st Class Firefighter with the Cedar Hammock Fire Department. In 1998, Michael was the CHFD Firefighter of the Year nominee. He also owns a successful irrigation company. Spending time with his wife of six years, Robin and two children, Savannah and Christian, is what he loves most in life. Seeing the joy in the eyes of his children when he arrives home after every shift is what life is about! When asked about the recipe, Michael replies, "The wings are an authentic recipe from Buffalo, NY, and the chicken salad is the best he's ever had! Really!"

Firehouse Chicken Salad

Michael L. Fitzgerald — Firefighter

Ingredients:

3 cups shredded, cooked chicken
1 cup finely chopped celery
1 cup chopped, seedless red grapes
1 cup chopped pecans

1/2 cup finely chopped onion
3/4 to 1 cup mayonnaise
1/2 cup heavy whipping cream, salt to taste

Directions:

This takes a little bit of time to prepare, but it's well worth the wait.

1 – Use 2-3 large chicken breasts or dark meat will work as well, and boil or bake chicken.

2 – Measure out whipping cream while chicken is cooking. Using a hand mixer or whip, begin whipping cream. (Your hand mixer should be set on whip setting, and cream should thicken after 2 minutes.) When the cream will no longer pour out of the bowl, it should be done. It should be very thick. Set aside.

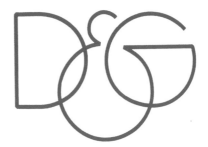

3 – Chop the remaining ingredients.

4 – After the chicken has cooked and been allowed to cool, begin shredding or coarsely chop in food processor.

5 – Combine all ingredients and place in refrigerator for one hour.

6 – Serve on a bed of leaf lettuce or hoagie roll with red leaf lettuce and tomato.

Café Pear Salad

Café on the Bay

Ingredients:

2 pears – peeled
corded and cut in 1/2
3 tablespoons olive oil
2 tablespoons honey

4 bunches arugula or any other green mix
Roquefort cheese
1/4 cup Balsamic vinegar

Directions:

1 – Place oil and honey in sauté pan. (Do not let burn.) Add 1/2 pear to hot mixture. Cook slowly until pear softens.

2 – Pull out pear and chill.

3 – Add Balsamic vinegar to pan mixture. Add more oil if needed. (This is the dressing and serve at room temperature.)

4 – Place green on plate. Slice pear to fan. Place fanned pear on greens.

5 – Garnish with a wedge of Roquefort cheese.

6 – Spoon dressing on salad.

Bill Herlihy
General Manager
Café on the Bay

Twenty-two years ago, Bill Herlihy began working in the restaurant business in the Finger Lake Region in Western New York. He moved to Rochester, New York in 1984, where he first met Café on the Bay's current Executive Chef, Keith Daum. In 1988, Bill decided to relocate to sunny Florida and 2 years later he met Michael Garey and Titus Letschert. Shortly thereafter, he started as a dining room captain at Café L' Europe. After 6 years of learning from "the best" Bill became General Manager of Café on the Bay. Keith Daum and Bill were reunited after 12 years. Bill has a nine-year old daughter, Delanie, and is very active in local charities. He has been the Co-Chairperson of the St. Jude's Gourmet Luncheon on Longboat Key for the last five years.

941-383-0440

**2630 Harbourside Dr.
Longboat Key, FL 34228**

Breakfast Saturday
8:30 AM To 10:30 AM

Sunday Breakfast Brunch
9:00 AM To 1:00 PM

Sunday Lunch
1:00 PM To 3:30 PM

Lunch 6 Days
11:00 AM To 3:00 PM

Dinner 7 Days
4:30 PM To 10:00 PM

**Extraordinary cuisine served in a
truly exquisite waterfront setting.
Come by land or sea.
Casual attire is welcomed.**

Michael Garey
General Manager
Café L' Europe

Michael Garey was born and raised in Buffalo, New York. He moved to Sarasota, Florida as a teenager and began in the restaurant business as a busboy in 1977. In 1979 he started as a busboy at the Café L' Europe. Moving up the ladder, he became a dining room captain in 1981 and assistant manager in 1982. In 1984, he left Café L' Europe to help open and manage Mr. Wong's Chinese restaurant. Michael came back to Café L' Europe in 1986 as General Manager, the title that he holds today. Mr. Garey is currently President of the St. Armands Merchants Assoc. and conceived and organized two events for the Florida Wine Festival, the Wine Marker's Dinner, and Sip and Shop. He is married to his wife, Catherine and has three daughters, Alexandra, Jenna and Amelia.

Stuffed Calamari Salads

Café L' Europe

Ingredients:

8 calamari heads
2 cups mixed greens
1 package enoki mushrooms
Belgium endive leaves
16 small asparagus tips grilled
1 chopped shallot

4 large basil leaves
1 teaspoon garlic
2 ounces white wine vinegar
1 tablespoon grain mustard
1 tablespoon honey
8 ounces olive oil

Directions:

1 – In a blender, prepare dressing. Add shallot, basil, garlic, vinegar, mustard, and honey to the blender jar and blend. Add in olive oil slowly and season with salt and pepper.

2 – On a hot grill; mark off the calamari and asparagus.

3 – Season the inside of the calamari with salt and pepper.

4 – Toss the greens with a little bit of dressing and stuff the calamari.

5 – Finish with asparagus, enoki mushrooms and endive

Makes 4 Servings.

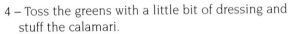

04

Holiday Pasta Salad
Munroe's Restaurant

Ingredients:

6 ounces cooked linguini
4 ounces turkey breast julienne
2 ounces toasted pecans
2 ounces Lingonberry jam

1 scallion sliced
1 ounce red onion julienne
1 teaspoon brown sugar
1 ounce cranberry juice

Directions:

1 – Sauté onions in a pan until tender, add sugar and cranberry juice and cook until caramelized.

2 – Add jam and remove from heat. Toss pasta with sauce and fold in remaining ingredients.

3 – Chill for one hour before serving.

Merv cooking in "Munroe's Kitchen."

People's Community Bank

We salute our firefighters.

A Collection of
Entree Recipes
from the
Fire Departments
& Area Restaurants
of Manatee and
Sarasota Counties
in the State
of Florida.

Entree Recipes

Richard Munroe
Chef/Proprietor
Munroe's Restaurant

Locals and seasonal visitors alike enjoy the bistro setting of Munroe's Restaurant. Proven to be Sarasota's favorite restaurant with casual elegance, friendly service, and creative, American foods.

Whether you start off your meal with one of our famous appetizers or finish with one of our colorful desserts, you won't go away disappointed.

For the late night guest, we offer live entertainment upstairs, with a late night menu and premium bar.

Braised Domestic Lamb Shanks

Munroe's Restaurant

Ingredients:

4 14-18 ounce domestic lamb shanks
1 yellow onion, chopped into large pieces
1 stalk, celery sliced 1" thick
2 medium carrots, sliced & halved
4 fingerling or Yukon potatoes,
   peeled & halved

2 medium parsnips, sliced & halved
2 sprigs, fresh rosemary
4 ounces unsalted butter
4 cloves garlic – crushed
1 tablespoon salt & pepper
1 quart water

Directions:

1 – In a large metal braiser or saucepan on high heat – brown the lamb shanks on all sides, remove from pan & reserve.

2 – Add butter and all vegetables – sautee to bloom the vegetables, add garlic, rosemary and water. Remove from heat.

3 – Place lamb shanks upright in pan (liquid should cover half the shank) – cover with a lid or aluminum foil and braise in an oven at 350 degrees for three to 2 1/2 hours.

4 – Remove from pan when meat is tender and falling off the bone – place shank in a large bowl (pasta bowl) and evenly distribute braising vegetables, potatoes & stock around and over the shank.

5 – Garnish with fresh rosemary sprigs.

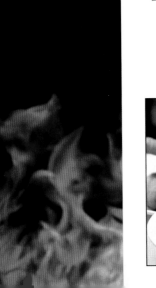

Sublamation Shrimp

Kevin Baker — Firefighter/Paramedic

Ingredients:

8 large tomatoes, peeled and chopped
1 cup onions chopped
1 cup celery, chopped
8-12 large Jalapeno peppers
   (8 hot, 12 for flashover), chopped, seeds
   and stems removed
4 pounds shrimp pealed and deveined
2 tablespoons garlic

1 teaspoon crushed red pepper
1 teaspoon black pepper
2 tablespoons sugar
3/4 tablespoon salt
3 tablespoons oil
3 or 4 cups rice (uncooked)
parmesan cheese

Directions:

1 – Combine all ingredients EXCEPT tomatoes, shrimp, sugar and salt in a pan. Stir-fry on high heat until onions are clear or tender.

2 – Add tomatoes, sugar and salt. Boil until most of the water has evaporated. Be sure to stir occasionally to prevent sticking. Stirring is required more often, and the heat should slowly be reduced as the sauce thickens.

3 – As the sauce starts to thicken, it is a good time to start the rice.

4 – Once the sauce is nearly free from water, add shrimp and reduce to a medium heat. Stir the shrimp in and cover. Cook on medium heat for 10 minutes or until all the shrimp are done and stir occasionally. (Do not overcook).

5 – Add rice to your plate, cover with spicy shrimp, sprinkle with parmesan cheese and enjoy!

This recipe is fun as you can add or subtract ingredients for your personal taste. Try adding any combination of the following: 1/4 cup red bell pepper, 1 cup mushrooms, 3 tablespoons of soy sauce or teriyaki sauce. You may add 2 tablespoons of curry, 1 teaspoon of cinnamon, and 2 more tablespoons of sugar for an Indian flair. Mix and match and enjoy the preparation of the food as much as the meal.

This is to feed 6-8 hungry Firefighters, so adjust accordingly.

Kevin Baker
Firefighter/Paramedic

Kevin Baker is a Firefighter/ Paramedic with Sarasota County Fire Department at Station #11-B. This is his 15th year with the Fire Service. Single with two children, Kevin enjoys fishing, boating, scuba diving, and growing hot peppers. Sunsets on the water are what he loves the most.

Seasoned veteran seasons the supper.

Anna Marie Yoder
Yoder's

Mary Lou Emrich and Anna Marie Yoder, daughters of Levi and Amanda Yoder, manage Yoder's. Mom and Dad Yoder along with their two daughters founded Yoder's restaurant on Main Street Sarasota in 1975. What began as a small 45 seat restaurant soon was enlarged to over 100 seats with lots of people waiting in long lines to eat. In 1983 Yoder's moved their location to Bahia Vista Street where they continue the tradition today with that same "at home" atmosphere, serving the highest quality home cooking made from scratch, with fast, friendly service as Sarasota's original Amish restaurant.

Chicken & Dumplings Customers' Favorite

Yoder's

Ingredients:

1 Large stewing chicken	Poultry seasoning
3 – 4 quarts of water	1/2 cup diced celery
6 cups flour	1/2 cup diced onion
7 eggs beaten	1 cup diced carrots
1 tablespoon baking powder	1 cup frozen peas
2 tablespoons salt (divided)	2 tablespoons cornstarch mixed in
Black Pepper	1/2 cup cold water

Directions:

1 – Place the chicken in a large pot, cover chicken with water and bring to boil, reduce heat to medium high and continue cooking until done. (Approximately 40 minutes or center of breast meat reaches 180 degrees.)

2 – Mix flour, baking powder and 1 tablespoon salt together. Add eggs and mix with pastry mixer to a pie crust consistency. (If needed add small amount of chicken broth).

3 – Remove chicken from broth and let cool.

4 – Add black pepper, poultry seasoning and 1 tablespoon salt to chicken broth to taste. Add celery, onion, carrots and peas to the seasoned broth. Bring to boil and reduce heat to simmer.

5 – Roll out dough on floured surface to about 1" thickness. Cut into 1" squares. Drop squares into simmering vegetable broth when all are cut and continue simmering until tender. (about 10 minutes)

6 – Add corn starch rue to simmering broth and bring to boil and remove from heat.

7 – Pull chicken meat off of bone and add to broth mixture.

Makes 6 – 8 Servings. Enjoy!

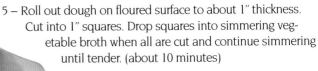

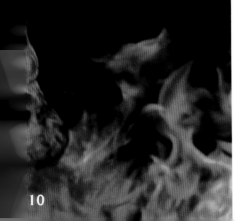

10

Smoked Chicken

Stacey Bailey — Firefighter/EMT

Ingredients:

2 whole chickens
2 whole lemons
2 oranges

2 apples
1 bottle BBQ sauce
1 smoker (any type)

Directions:

1 – Thaw chickens and peel skin with hand (try not to break) and make a cavity.

2 – Slice lemons, oranges, and apples into small pieces or slices.

3 – Place all in between chicken meat and skin and in body cavity.

4 – Close skin with toothpicks so all meat is enclosed by skin.

5 – Smoke at medium or ideal temperature for 2 1/2 – 3 hours.

6 – The last 1/2 hour apply sauce for you taste.

Portions: 1 to 2 per whole chicken.

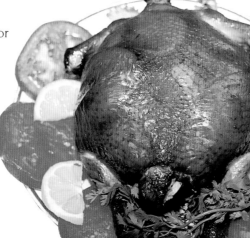

Stacey Bailey
**Firefighter/EMT
Braden River
Fire Department**

Stacey began his firefighting career with the City of Bradenton 7 years ago. Presently he is with the Braden River Fire Department as a Firefighter/ EMT. Over the years, Stacey studied and completed his education for Fire Officer 1 and Hazmat Technician. He is married to wife, Teresa, and enjoys the outdoors by fishing and golfing. Going to church and cooking also tops his list. Stacey, nicknamed "Beetle Bailey," got this favorite firehouse recipe from a fellow Firefighter/EMT, Pat Conrey. When asked what he loves most in life, "Helping others and my wife, Teresa."

Braden River Engine 611 with Stacey Bailey at the wheel.

111

Michael Garey
General Manager
Café L' Europe

Michael Garey was born and raised in Buffalo, New York. He moved to Sarasota, Florida as a teenager and began in the restaurant business as a busboy in 1977. In 1979 he started as a busboy at the Café L' Europe. Moving up the ladder, he became a dining room captain in 1981 and assistant manager in 1982. In 1984, he left Café L' Europe to help open and manage Mr. Wong's Chinese restaurant. Michael came back to Café L' Europe in 1986 as General Manager, the title that he holds today. Mr. Garey is currently President of the St. Armands Merchants Assoc. and conceived and organized two events for the Florida Wine Festival, the Wine Marker's Dinner, and Sip and Shop. He is married to his wife, Catherine and has three daughters, Alexandra, Jenna and Amelia.

Tuna Scallopine with Caper Pesto
Café L' Europe

Ingredients:

3 pounds tuna loin
3 ounces olive oil
salt and cracked black pepper

PESTO:
1 cup fresh basil leaves
3 tablespoons capers
1/4 cup roasted garlic cloves
1/2 cup toasted pine nuts
1/2 cup grated grana padana cheese
1/2 cup extra virgin olive oil

Directions:

1 – In a blender, combine all ingredients for pesto. Blend until smooth.

2 – Cut tuna loin into thin slices.

3 – Season with salt and cracked black pepper.

4 – In a hot skillet, quickly sear tuna on both sides.

5 – Tuna is best when served medium rare.

6 – Remove from pan and serve immediately.

Makes 6 Servings.

Mexican Chicken

Tim Beattie — Firefighter/Paramedic

Ingredients:

1 chicken
16 ounce Doritos
10.5 ounce can cheddar cheese soup

10.5 can cream of chicken soup
1 small can green chilies
8 ounce bag yellow rice

Directions:

1 – Cook and debone chicken.

2 – In 8x12 pan, add cheddar cheese soup and cream of chicken soup with 2 cans of water. Mix with fork.

3 – Add chicken.

4 – Chop green chilies and add to pan.

5 – Crush bag of Doritos. Spread crushed Doritos over top of mixture covering it.

6 – Bake at 350 degrees for 30 minutes on center rack.

7 – Prepare rice.

8 – Serve chicken over rice.

Makes 4-6 Servings.

Tim Beattie
Firefighter/Paramedic
SCFD

Tim Beattie, a Firefighter/Paramedic with Sarasota County Fire Department has been in the Fire Service for 18 years. He is a man of many "hats." Twelve of his 18 years, he has been a Swat Medic; he is also a Bayflite Flightmedic, BTLS instructor and criminal justice instructor. Tim loves his job and would not do anything else.

The most important thing in life to him is his wife and two-year old son. He and his wife love to travel and have been all around the United States, Europe and Caribbean several times. "Ma Beatle" is his nickname for his "Ma Beatle's Firehouse Cooking" the last 16 years at the fire stations. His meals are quite economical, too, never costing more than $7.00 a person for lunch and dinner.

Tim shows his son the "office."

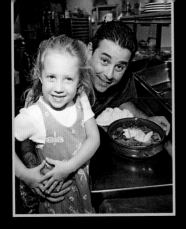

The Munroe family
Susan, Max, Rick, Ashley.

Med Style Poached Snapper
Munroe's Restaurant

Ingredients:

2 – 8oz red snapper fillets, boned
1 medium carrot, chopped
1 medium parsnip, chopped
2 plum tomatoes, sliced thick
2 cloves garlic, peeled & crushed

1 tsp, saffron threads
1/4 cup white wine
2 tsp olive oil
1 medium yellow onion, chopped
1 stalk celery, sliced
1 yukon gold potato, chopped

1/4 cup kalamata olives, chopped
1 tbl capers
1 tbl chopped fresh basil
1 tbl chopped fresh marjoram
2 oz basil pesto
1 tbl s&p

Directions:

1 – Sweat onions in a large sauce pot, add wine and reduce by 1/2.

2 – Add all other vegetables and simmer until potatoes are cooked.

3 – Add capers, olives & garlic simmer for two minutes.

4 – Lay the snapper fillets in the stock and poach until cooked, remove immediately and place in serving bowl.

5 – Add seasonings to the stock, bring to a boil and ladle vegetables and stock over fish.

6 – Stir pesto into finished plate and serve immediately.

Simple Chicken Enchiladas

Keith Haluska's wife – Linda Haluska

Ingredients:

1 1/2 pounds chicken, cooked & diced
16 ounce can refried beans
16 ounce can sour cream
1 package taco seasoning mix
2 cups water

2 – 10 ounce cans enchilada sauce
3 cups shredded cheddar cheese
6 – 8 flour tortillas
Optional – chopped onions & chopped
    green peppers if desired

Directions:

1 – Pre-heat oven to 350 degrees.

2 – Spread 1/4 to 1/2 can of enchilada sauce into a 13x9 baking dish to lightly cover bottom and set aside.

3 – Cook and dice chicken. Place diced chicken in skillet; add taco seasoning mix and 2 cups of water. Bring to a boil, and then simmer chicken in mix for 15 minutes.

4 – Mix refried beans and sour cream in a bowl.

5 – Spread about 2-3 tablespoons of bean mixture on to each tortilla.

6 – Place approximately 3/4 cup of chicken on top of bean mixture and sprinkle with a little cheddar cheese. (May add onions & green peppers on top of chicken if desired).

7 – Roll up tortilla and place a little bit of bean mixture on edge of tortilla seams to close.

8 – Place tortillas in baking dish and pour remaining enchilada sauce over top of tortillas. Generously sprinkle cheddar cheese over sauce.

9 – Cover and bake 30 -35 minutes.

10 – Place a little sour cream and a few diced green onions over top of enchiladas. Recommended side dish is yellow rice.

Makes 4 – 6 Servings.

Keith Haluska
Firefighter/Paramedic
SCFD

In 1980, Keith's family moved to Bradenton, Florida, after living in New Jersey and Michigan. One of his favorite adventurous hobbies in this 'new town' of Bradenton was motorcross racing. He competed in Open A Class motorcross racing throughout Florida and loved life in the "fast lane." However, he slowed down just a little when he met his true love, Linda, and married her in 1988. Keith joined the Fire Service in 1995 and eventually became a firefighter/paramedic. This career changed his life incredibly. "I've been blessed with so many things but most of all my wife and two precious daughters, Marianna and Nicole," Keith says.

About the recipe... This was the first dinner my very brave wife, then girlfriend, made for my entire family! We all loved it and her ever since!

John R. Halling
Executive Chef
Sarasota University Club

Recently taking charge of the Sarasota University Club kitchen, Chef John brings a combination of classic French, International cuisine and traditional Florida cooking styles. Formerly of Francoise et Henri, Cape Codder Hotel in Cape Cod, and Bayou Bills, Treasure Island Florida. These and other Chef positions have allowed Chef John a wide range of experience to please many different palates. The recipes that Chef John presents are some of his personal favorites. Chef John finds them easy to prepare and very flavorful. The Sarasota University Club hopes you enjoy these recipes and they provide many enjoyable dining experiences.

Italian Stuffed Flank Steak
Sarasota University Club

Ingredients:

8 ounces Fresh spinach, trimmed and washed
1/2 cup Italian Style Bread Crumbs
1/2 cup Fresh Grated Parmesan Cheese
1/4 cup Olive Oil
2 cloves Garlic, chopped

3 Red Bell Peppers, roasted, peeled, cored and split in half (you may substitute whole, canned roasted peppers)
4 ounce Proscuitto Ham, thinly sliced
1 Flank Steak, 1 1/2 pounds (Ask your butcher to butterfly)

Directions:

1 – Preheat oven to 350.

2 – In a hot saucepan, add 2 tablespoons of olive oil and chopped garlic. Sauté until brown, add spinach and take off the heat. Stir until spinach wilts.

3 – Transfer spinach, garlic and oil mixture to a bowl. Add cheese, breadcrumbs and remaining olive oil. Mix well.

4 – Lay out steak on work surface, season with salt and pepper. Arrange roasted peppers in one layer on the steak. Top with a layer of Proscuitto and spread spinach mixture on top of both.

5 – Starting with the long side, roll the steak up like a jellyroll. Tie with string at 2 inch intervals. Brush with a little olive oil and season with salt and pepper.

6 – Place steak in a shallow baking pan and bake for 40 minutes for medium-rare. Let stand for 10-15 minutes before slicing and serving.

7 – Slice steak 3/4 inch thick and topped with Calamata olives, scallions and diced tomatoes.

Makes 2-4 Servings.

Linguine With 2 Clam Broth Sauce

Susan Shyne — Firefighter/EMT

Ingredients:

1 pound box linguine noodles
4 cans chopped clams
1 bottle clam juice
1 small can sliced black olives

1 bunch green onions
2 tablespoons fresh chopped garlic
2 tablespoons olive oil
1 package fresh mushrooms, sliced

Directions:

(Approximately 30 minutes prep time... great for on duty crews of firefighters.)

1 – Sauté garlic in olive oil on medium heat for 2 minutes.

2 – Add green onions and mushrooms on medium heat for 5 minutes.

3 – Add canned olives, canned clams with juice, and bottle of clam juice.

4 – Simmer 15 minutes.

5 – You can prepare noodles as directed, while it's simmering. Do NOT overcook.

6 – Just prior to serving, heat clam mixture on high for five minutes.

7 – Pour over noodles and enjoy!

8 – Suggested side servings include garlic bread and tossed salad.

Makes 4 Servings.

Susan "Suzie" Shyne
Firefighter/EMT
SCFD

Susan, or "Susie" to her peers and crew, is working on completing her 11th year as a Firefighter/EMT with Sarasota County Fire Department. She is currently assigned to A shift at Station #4 (known for its night-life and unusual calls). Susie holds a position as one of the department's public Education Instructors

As a single woman, she spends her off-duty hours enjoying her hobbies that include aerobics, running, boating, travel and wining and dining. "Tony and "Charlie" think she's the greatest and could probably benefit from eating her low fat tasty linguine. Her two cats weigh in at 25 pounds each

1

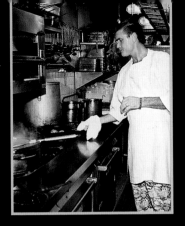

Jeff Trefry
Executive Chef
Café L' Europe

Upon graduation from the prestigious Culinary Institute of America, Jeff moved west to Santa Barbara, California and worked as a pastry chef for the El Encanto Hotel. To broaden his knowledge of the culinary arts and hone his skills, Jeff moved east and spent three years at Café L' Europe in the early 1980's. Jeff's career path led him to the Five-Star Five-Diamond Ritz Carlton Resort in Naples and he was promoted to Executive Sous Chef. In 1989, promotion placed Jeff as Executive Chef in charge of culinary operations at the Ritz Carlton in Kansas City, Mo. He then worked in Bermuda and Hilton Head Island, S.C. but is now back with Café L' Europe as Executive Chef. Jeff executes New European Cuisine with his own imagination and personal style. He is married to Janet and has three children – Megan, Jack and Mike.

Rock Lobster in Banyuls Wine

Café L' Europe

Ingredients:

4-6 ounce rock lobster tails
1 pound ripe tomatoes
1 ounce olive oil
1 carrot
2 shallots
3 cloves garlic

5 ounces prosciutto
salt and cayenne pepper
3 tablespoons calvados
1 cup Banyuls wine
4 ounces crème fraiche

Directions:

1 – With a heavy gauge knife, cut the lobster tail into medallions according to the natural divisions in the tail.

2 – Skin, seed and chop tomato fine.

3 – Peel and chop carrot fine.

4 – Mince shallot and garlic together.

5 – Slice prosciutto in a fine julienne.

6 – In a heavy saucepan, heat olive oil very hot. Drop in lobster medallions and sear until shell is bright red.

7 – Add carrot, tomato, shallot and garlic and cook out for a couple of minutes.

8 – Add prosciutto and deglaze with calvados.

9 – Cook out alcohol. Add banyuls and simmer.

10 – Finish with crème fraiche and season with salt and cayenne pepper.

Makes 4 Servings.

Fake Steak and Potatoes

John Hanlon — Firefighter/EMT

Ingredients:

MARINADE:
2 tablespoons olive oil
1 teaspoon liquid smoke-hickory
1 tablespoon soy sauce
water (small amount to make 1/4 cup
  marinate)
1 teaspoon balsamic vinegar
2 cloves garlic

VEGETABLES:
4 Portobello mushrooms, washed
  and drained
4 baked potatoes

OPTIONAL:
Fresh pineapple slices or thin apple slices

Directions:

1 – Mix all marinade ingredients (should equal 1/4 cup).

2 – Wash and drain mushrooms.

3 – Pour marinade over mushrooms, imbedding garlic pieces into mushroom bottoms.

4 – Marinate for 1/2 hour.

5 – Place mushrooms bottom side up in broiler pan.

6 – Broil approximately 3 minutes; turn and broil tops approximately 2 minutes, until fork tender. Watch constantly so it doesn't burn.

7 – Add fruit slices and broil 1 minute.

8 – Serve with baked potato and salad for a delicious healthy meal.

Makes 4 Servings.

John Hanlon
Firefighter/EMT
SCFD

After a three-year stint in the Army, John started his fire-fighting career in Cedar Rapids, Iowa, at age 21. His brother was a juggler for a circus and taught him the craft. During his 10 years with Cedar Rapids, John would travel Iowa doing juggling gigs as "Gilbert." In 1987 he tested for a position with Sarasota Fire Department and was chosen, so he moved here to continue his career as a firefighter.

His wife, Mary, is a firefighter paramedic on the same shift. His daughter, Heather, is a volunteer firefighter in Iowa City, Iowa, and his son Jonathan moved to Sydney, Australia, and is attending acupuncture school.

John enjoys hiking, juggling and fixing old stuff. He and Mary completely restored their 1925 home themselves.

About the recipe...
"It's a quick and easy recipe. Try it, you'll like it."

Ovea Thai Kitchen

Ovea Thai Kitchen is family owned and operated Thai restaurant which is fast making a name for itself in hometown Sarasota. Born in Bangkok, owners "Cookie and Woody" have made the business a family affair, by employing their son, Ekawee, and daughter, Awika, when they are not in school. The restaurant opened a year ago seating up to 45 patrons and is quaintly adorned with authentic Thai decor.

The family prides themselves in serving their best Thai family recipes. By using the best quality ingredients to make their food dishes, moderate prices, and warm and friendly service, they seem to have found the right combination to keep customers coming back.

If you're interested in tantalizing your Thai tastebuds, drop in and sample their mouth watering Thai soups, salads, entreés, and desserts.

Spicy Basil Noodles with Beef

Ovea Thai Kitchen

Ingredients:

1/2 cup sliced beef
1/2 dried rice noodles soaked in warm water to soften
1 teaspoon finely chopped garlic
3 tablespoons vegetable cooking oil
2 tablespoons soy sauce
1 tablespoon fish sauce (or to taste)

1/2 tablespoon sugar (or to taste)
1 few basil leaves
2-3 roughly chopped red chilies (or to taste)
2 tablespoons sliced onions
2 tablespoons bell pepper
1 tablespoon celery

Directions:

1 – Heat cooking oil in wok and sauté garlic until golden brown.

2 – Add beef until cooked, and then add noodles with soy sauce and all vegetables.

3 – Stir fry for 2-3 minutes, mix well and add fish sauce, sugar, and chilies to taste.

4 – Add basil leaves and serve hot.

Ovea Thai Kitchen

941-365-7799

**501 N. Beneva Rd., #250
Sarasota
Tuesday – Sunday
Lunch 11:30 AM To 2:30 PM
Dinner 5:00 AM To 9:30 PM**

Real Thai Cooking

Family Operated With Friendly Atmosphere

"Purple's" Tetrazzini

Gerry "Purple" Haisley — Firefighter/Paramedic

Ingredients:

1/2 pound sliced mushrooms
6 tablespoons butter
8 ounces spaghetti (thin, cooked)
5 tablespoons flour
1 teaspoon salt
1 cup canned chicken broth

2 cups heavy cream
1/2 cup white wine (not cooking wine)
1/2 cup Parmesan cheese
4 cups cooked chicken
2 tablespoons everglades seasoning

Directions:

1 – Season and cook the chicken on stovetop in non-stick pan.

2 – Sauté mushrooms in a teflon pan with 2 tablespoons butter and 2 tablespoons wine.

3 – Add to the spaghetti and set aside.

4 – Add the chicken broth and cream, cook, stirring until thickened.

5 – Cook on low and stir constantly.

6 – Add the remaining wine, 1/2 of cheese and the chicken and mix.

7 – Fold the mixture into the cooked spaghetti and turn into a greased baking dish.

8 – Sprinkle the remaining cheese over the mixture and bake at 350 degrees for 40 minutes or until browned and bubbly.

9 – My personal recommendation is to use a little more cheese and be heavy-handed with the white wine. I also suggest serving with a crusty bread and tossed salad.

Makes 4 Servings.

Gerry "Purple" Haisley
Firefighter/Paramedic
SCFD

Gerry Haisley is a firefighter/ paramedic assigned to Station #1-C, the busiest station in the Sarasota County Fire Department. The ole' guys say he gets his nickname "Purple" from the Jimmy Hendrix song "Purple Haze." With thirteen years under his belt he has established himself as team player both on duty and off. He loves to coordinate our brothers and sisters team effort in the Firefighter Olympics Competitions as well as participate. He enjoys cooking about as much as the crew enjoys eating his dishes, of which their favorite is "Purple's Tetrazzini." This married father of three has hobbies, which include restoring classic autos and becoming a couch spud. When asked what he loves most in life he proclaimed: "The pursuit of retirement."

Café on the Bay

Nestled in the Longboat Key Moorings, along beautiful Sarasota Bay, sits Longboat Key's Hidden Gem...Café on the Bay. Elegant yet casual, her charm beckons seafarers and landlubbers alike for breakfast, lunch or dinner. You will delight in an offering of extraordinary cuisine. Enjoy the indoor dining room or the covered outdoor terrace, both featuring spectacular marina and bay views. Or you may simply wish to enjoy your favorite cocktail or one of our own exotic creations at our Marker 15 Lounge. This is one "Port of Call" you will wish to visit over and over again! Inquire about our sunset special and the pre-fixed dinner offering.

Breakfast Saturday
8:30 AM – 10:30 AM
Sunday Breakfast Brunch
9:00 AM – 1:00 PM
Sunday Lunch
1:00 PM – 3:30 PM
Lunch 11:00 AM – 3:00 PM
Dinner 4:30 PM – 10:00 PM
In the Longboat Key Moorings Marina behind Publix – right out of guard gate, second left.

Veal Meatloaf

Café on the Bay

Ingredients:

1 1/2 pounds ground veal
1 egg
1/4 cup mushroom cooked
1/4 cup bread crumbs

1/2 cup cooked spinach
10 cloves roasted garlic
1 teaspoon tarragon
1/8 cup Marsala wine

Directions:

1 – Mix all ingredients in a bowl.

2 – Form into a loaf and cook at 325 degrees until temperature of meat is 160 degrees.

3 – Serve with mushroom gravy.

Makes 4 Servings.

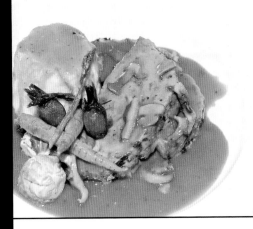

941-383-0440

**2630 Harbourside Dr.
Longboat Key, FL 34228**

Breakfast Saturday
8:30 AM To 10:30 AM

Sunday Breakfast Brunch
9:00 AM To 1:00 PM

Sunday Lunch
1:00 PM To 3:30 PM

Lunch 6 Days
11:00 AM To 3:00 PM

Dinner 7 Days
4:30 PM To 10:00 PM

Extraordinary cuisine served in a truly exquisite waterfront setting.
Come by land or sea.
Casual attire is welcomed.

Firehouse Beefeater's Enchiladas

Merv Kennell – Fire Lieutenant/Paramedic

Ingredients:

2 lbs. lean ground beef
1/2 cup onion (chopped)
3/4 cup mushrooms
3/4 cup green peppers (chopped)
1 can cream of mushroom soup
1/4 teaspoon Lawry's season salt

1 clove garlic clove (minced)
1 can tomato soup
10 oz can enchilada sauce
2 cups cheddar cheese (shredded)
8 tortillas (flour, 10")
16 oz. sour cream

Directions:

1 – Cook hamburger, season salt, onions, mushrooms, peppers, and garlic in a skillet, and drain.

2 – Combine 1 1/2 cups of cheddar with the hamburger mixture, and set aside.

3 – In a bowl, mix enchilada sauce with soups.

4 – Top each tortilla with 4 heaping Tbs. of hamburger mixture.

5 – Place seams side down in a 13' x 9" glass baking pan.

6 – Pour sauce mixture over top and sprinkle remaining cheese.

7 – Bake in oven @ 350 deg. for 30 minutes.

8 – Remove from oven and let cool 10 minutes before serving

9 – Serve with a Tbs. of sour cream on each enchilada.

Merv Kennell
Fire Lieutenant /Paramedic
SCFD

My love of the fire service began at 15 years old when I would go to the fire station to visit my brother Mark, a paramedic/firefighter. I volunteered until 3/30/78 when I was hired. I loved the challenges the fire/rescue service offered me and in 1979, (while attending Sarasota Fire Academy) I became the first 18-year old state certified paramedic in Florida. Twenty-two years later the challenges remain and the experiences of my past are priceless. I thank God daily for his many blessings. The most special of which are my wife Jennie, daughter Linde' and son Travis. This ones for my crew..."Isn't it a Great Day to be Alive!"

*About the recipe...
I found this recipe in a Mennonite Cookbook one night when I was trying to make something different for supper. My family loved it, so I tweaked it a little, tried it out on my crew and they love it as well.*

123

Robert M. Harris III

Sterne Agee Asset
Management

Robert M. Harris III has more than 30 years of experience in the financial planning industry. His success is probably gauged best by his satisfied clients. One can easily detect the passion Harris has for his work when he says, "I roll out of bed at 6 A.M. and turn on my computer. I'm constantly connected to the business."

Harris is the executive vice president and equity strategist for Sterne Agee Asset Management in Sarasota. Managing more than 200 million in assets for his clients, Bob says, "we use the most sophisticated technology and research to find companies that have demonstrated the ability to outpace the market." When asked what the secret of his success was, Bob says he has two rules: 1) Don't lose money for your customers and 2) Don't forget rule No. 1.

Bob's Low Country Crab Cakes

Sterne Agee Asset Management
This is a 75-year old family recipe from Virginia.

Ingredients:

1 pound fresh crabmeat –
  "lump or backfin"
2-3 tablespoons mayonnaise

1/2 tablespoon dijon mustard
1 1/2 cups crushed corn flakes
3 – 4 tablespoons butter

Directions:

1 – Be sure crabmeat is "fresh."

2 – Mix all ingredients in a bowl, EXCEPT butter, and then form 3-4 ounce patties.

3 – Melt butter in skillet and then brown patties over medium heat.

4 – Suggested sides: Smithfield cured ham, thinly sliced on side.

Makes 3 To 4 Servings.

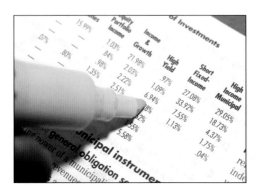

Chicken Marasala

Arty Josten — Firemedic

Ingredients:

4 boneless chicken breasts
1/4 flour
1/2 teas. salt
1/2 teas. oregano
4 tbs. cooking oil

4 tbs. butter
1 cup fresh sliced mushrooms
1/2 cup Marsala wine (red)
1 box (12 oz.) Ronzoni fettucini

Directions:

1 – Combine flour, salt, pepper, oregano blending well.

2 – Heat oil and butter in a skillet, until bubbling lightly.

3 – Dunk chicken in seasoning mixture, and then cook on medium heat about 2 minutes on one side until light brown.

4 – Turn chicken over , add mushrooms and cook approx. 2 minutes or until golden brown.

5 – Once second side has been lightly browned, add wine.

6 – Cover and simmer for approx. 10 min.

7 – Suggestions: Serve with Italian bread and a glass of chilled red wine.

Makes 4 Servings.

Arthur "Arty" Josten
Firemedic
SCFD

Arty grew up the oldest of six children in Brooklyn New York. Four days after he graduated from high school he entered the Navy. He was assigned to the John F Kennedy aircraft carrier as an aviation structural mechanic

After four years in the service, he moved to Sarasota where he was introduced to the fire service as a volunteer. He was hired by South Trail Fire Department in 1975 and his first assignment was at what is now Station #1 of SCFD

Arty met a gal named Chris while volunteering at a football game. They've been married 22 years and have two children. His daughter Jennifer, has competed in National Skating Competition and his son, Aric, is a "skuller" at Riverview High School

Potato Crusted Grouper

Café on the Bay

Ingredients:

4 thin grouper filets
flour
3 cups shredded potato
4 eggs whipped

salt and pepper to taste
4 tablespoons olive oil
2 cups heavy cream
1/8 cup grainy mustard

Directions:

1 – Flour and season grouper.

2 – Roll in egg.

3 – Heat oil in large sauté pan.

4 – Place shredded potato on top of grouper.

5 – Place grouper potato side down in oil.

6 – Cook potato until golden brown.

7 – Place shredded potato on grouper and flip over to brown.

8 – For sauce, reduce cream and add mustard.

Makes 4 Servings.

Keith Daum
Executive Chef
Café on the Bay

Keith Daum started in the restaurant business at age 28 to help out a friend during the holiday season. To his surprise, he loved the business so much he enrolled in the C.I.A. and it became his lifelong career. Keith went on to open two 4 star hotels and three other fine dining restaurants in the Rochester, New York area. He became a certified Executive Chef and won two silver medals at the A.C.F. food shows. In September of 1999 he vacationed to Sarasota to visit an old friend, Bill Herlihy. Keith was offered a job as an Executive Chef at Café on the Bay. Not sure about living in Florida, Keith went back home to New York. The rain and snow quickly made up his mind and he is presently with Café on the Bay.

"Scooter's Chili"

Scott Hansen — Lieutenant

Ingredients:

1 pound hot or mild sausage
   (skinned & scrambled)
1 pound ground chuck
1 large yellow onion (diced)
2 large garlic cloves (minced)
1 1/2 tablespoons chili powder
6 ounce can tomato paste
2 cups water
1 tablespoon instant coffee

1 tablespoon sugar
1 tablespoon paprika
1 tablespoon oregano
1 teaspoon salt
1 teaspoon pepper
1 teaspoon cumin
1 cup dark kidney beans (drained)
1 cup refried beans

Directions:

1 – Brown sausage, ground meat, onion and garlic in a pot.

2 – Add remaining ingredients, except beans.

3 – Bring to boil, cover and simmer for 1 1/4 hours.

4 – While meat mixture is cooking, combine kidney and refried beans.

5 – After meat is cooked, add beans and stir.

6 – Top with grated cheese (of choice) and finely chopped green scallion onions. Enjoy!

Scott "Scooter" Hansen
Lieutenant
SCFD

Fresh out of a five year stint with the Navy, this "Golden Shellback" left the excitement of life aboard the USS Longbeach to join the Fruitville Fire Department (now part of SCFD). Scott got his nickname, Scooter, by hustling about doing his duties. Although a 20 year veteran, he's still highly motivated as a Fire Lieutenant at Station #12-B. Raised in Wisconsin, Scott proudly proclaims, "I'm a Cheesehead." Scott spent seven years as a Big Brother before his children, Brian and Brianna, entered the picture. He and Brenda say, "the most important thing in life is knowing God is in control."

Recipe

Heat to boiling
Simmer five minutes
Stir occasionally

Save instantly.

127

NFPA Factoids And Kitchen Fire Safety Tips

Question:
At what rate did vehicle fires occur in 1999?

Answer:
One every 85 seconds.

"Microwave Safety"
If your microwave has had a fire inside of it,(even if it appears to be undamaged), don't use it again until it's been serviced.

Information Courtesy of NFPA

The Munroe family
Susan, Max, Rick, Ashley.

Linguine with Snapper and Pesto
Munroe's Restaurant

Ingredients:

4 ounces cooked linguini
1 red bell pepper grilled
seeded & julienne
3 ounces basil pesto
2 sun dried tomatoes chopped
1 teaspoon fresh basil minced

1/2 teaspoon salt & pepper
6 ounces red snapper fillet
1/2 teaspoon minced garlic
1 tablespoon pine nuts toasted
3 ounces olive oil

Directions:

1 – Sear the snapper in a pan and finish in a 350-degree oven.

2 – Heat linguini in olive oil – toss in basil, sun dried tomatoes, garlic, salt & pepper.

3 – Place the snapper in the middle of a large pasta bowl, cover with bell peppers then roll pasta on a fork and place on top. Garnish with the pesto and pine nuts.

"The Cheaper The Better — Pot Roast"

Emilio Carlesimo — Firemedic

Ingredients:

1/2 – 1 lb. / man beef roast
(inexpensive cut)
1 pkg. onion soup mix
2 lbs (or 2/man) small potatoes

16 oz. peeled carrots
1/2 lb. snow peas
16 oz. jar pearl onions

Directions:

1 – Select an inexpensive pot roast 1/2 per person....increase to 1 lb. per firefighter.

2 – Place in roasting pan, and add 1/4" of water to pan.

3 – Sprinkle 1 to 2 packets of dry onion soup mix over meat (depending on size of roast).

4 – Place in oven @ 350 deg. for 1 1/2 to 3 hrs. (approx. 1/2 hour per 1 lb.).

5 – Add small peeled potatoes, carrots and small onions 1 hour before you estimate meat will be done.

6 – 30 minutes before meat is done add snow peas to the pan and reduce the water level to no more than 1/4" to 1/2".

7 – Save the broth poured off for gravy.

8 – Do not place vegetables on top of meat (except onions).

9 – Roast is done when meat can be penetrated easily with fork.

10 – You can thicken gravy or an au jus may be served.

11 – Suggestions: Serve with a colorful salad and French bread.

Emilio Carlesimo
Firemedic
SCFD

Emilio cut his teeth as a firefighter in his home town of Detroit, Michigan, at age 22. Twenty seven enjoyable years later, he retired from Detroit as a Fire Lieutenant. He owned a condo in Venice, so they moved here with plans to relax and enjoy retirement. At age 52 he joined SCFD as a rookie firemedic, and now eight and a half years later, he's looking forward to completing his remaining 18 months till his second retirement. His firehouse antics will be sorely missed.

He and his wife, Brenda Lee, have been married 38 years and have two daughters and three grandchildren, all out of town. Emelio says when the grandchildren are in town they can't miss the trip to the fire station to visit Grandpa.

About the recipe...
"It's a colorful, tasty, and the aroma sets one's mouth to watering."

S.C.T.I. firefighter students fighting a gas fire.

Julius Halas

Fire Chief
Longboat Key

Julius began his aggressive career in the Fire Service in 1974 at the age of 20. During his tenure he served as a firefighter, EMT, paramedic, instructor, and fire officer before achieving the position of Fire Chief of the City of Sarasota in 1992. He was instrumental in the merger of the City and County Fire Departments in 1996, and served as the Deputy Chief of the 400+ personnel consolidated department until 3/01/99 when he accepted the position of Fire Chief for the Town of Longboat Key.

He and his wife Maureen have a 17-year old son "Justin." Julius' hobbies include golf, softball, and riding his "Harley."

About the recipe...
"The recipe is a modification of a Beef Stroganoff I use to make while employed as a "cook" (in my teen years). The heavy paprika reminds me of my Hungarian grandparent's dishes."

Hungarian Style Beef Stroganoff
Julius Halas — Fire Chief

Ingredients:

2 pounds choice beef
  (ex. sirloin or filet mignon, for tender meat) cut into bite size chunks
1 large or 2 small onions diced
1 teaspoon seasoning salt
1 teaspoon pepper
2 teaspoons Adolph's meat tenderizer
2 teaspoon paprika to taste

1 teaspoon garlic powder
6 ounces fresh mushrooms
1 – 10 3/4 ounce can cream of mushroom soup
1 cup sherry or burgundy cooking wine
1 cup sour cream
wide egg noodles (enough for 6-8 servings)

Directions:

1 – Sauté meat in cooking oil until brown with diced onions.
2 – Season with seasoning salt, pepper, meat tenderizer and paprika (by taste).
3 – Place meat, onions and drippings in large casserole dish. Cover with water to just above the top of the meat.
4 – Add 1 teaspoon garlic powder and 1 teaspoon additional paprika.
5 – Preheat oven to 350 degrees.
6 – Place casserole dish with a tightly fitting lid, in oven for 1 hour.
7 - Test meat for tenderness and cook additionally if needed.
8 – While meat cooks, cut 6 ounces of fresh mushrooms into bite size pieces and sauté. Add to meat.
9 – Stir in cream of mushroom soup until well blended. If too thick add a little water to maintain liquid quality.
10 – Add 1 cup cooking wine. Stir and place back in oven for about 15 minutes to allow wine to cook down and for mixture to heat thoroughly.
11 – Cook egg noodles and drain.
12 – Remove casserole from oven and add 1 cup sour cream. Blend well using a wire whisk and return to oven for 5 minutes.
13 – If gravy is too thin, thicken with roux (flour and water mixture).
14 – Serve immediately over egg noodles.
Makes 6 Servings.

Duckling St. Martin

Café on the Bay

Ingredients:

2 whole ducks
2 cups pepper jelly

Directions:

1 – Bone out duck by making a slit down the breastbone. Follow the rib cage and pull off breast, repeat on the other breast.

2 – Bone out leg by following the backbone. Pull out all bone except the main leg bone.

3 – Pin the leg meat together with a toothpick so the main leg bone is straight up.

4 – Roast leg off until all fat is cooked out and skin is golden brown.

5 – In sauté pan place breast skin side in pan. Sear until golden brown.

6 – Flip and cook medium rare.

7 – Heat pepper jelly and glaze duck meat.

Makes 4 Servings.

Steve Handra
Division Chief
Operations Support
SCFD

Steve grew up in Cincinnati, Ohio, the oldest of seven children. It was a fishing trip with a volunteer fireman buddy that led to his career choice. The night they were to go fishing, a tornado swept through their community, and he was drafted to ride a fire engine, running chain saws to clear debris through the night. He immediately joined Owensville Fire Department as a volunteer and spent 12 1/2 years there. In 1981, he left his position as Assistant Chief to take a rookie position with South Trail Fire Department in Sarasota, a place where he enjoyed vacationing. He worked his way up the ranks to his current position of Division Chief.

Steve enjoys outdoor activities and has recently become a civil war history buff.

About the recipe:
The Pork-n-Kraut was one of "Mom's" recipes that became a staple food which the seven of us grew up on.

Pork-n-Sauer Kraut

Steve Handra — Division Chief Operations Support

Ingredients:

2 lbs country style ribs
    (or thick boneless pork chops)
1 can French onion soup

2 lg. cans or bag kraut
2 tbs. brown sugar

Directions:

1 – Line bottom of 9" x 12" casserole dish with pork.

2 – Drain kraut and layer on top of pork.

3 – Sprinkle brown sugar on top of pork.

4 – Pour can of onion soup evenly over top of mixture.

5 – Cover dish and bake for 2 1/2 hrs @ 300 deg.

Makes 4 Servings.

Mom's Baked Chicken

Dutch Haus Family Restaurant

Ingredients:

1/2 cup cornmeal
1/2 cup flour
1-1/2 teaspoon salt
1-1/2 teaspoon chili powder

1/4 teaspoon pepper
1/2 cup milk
1/2 cup melted butter

Directions:

1 – Combine cornmeal, flour, salt, chili powder, and pepper.

2 – Dip chicken in milk, then coat with flour mixture.

3 – Place chicken skin side up in large shallow baking pan.

4 – Drizzle butter over chicken.

5 – Bake for 50 –55 minutes at 350 degrees.

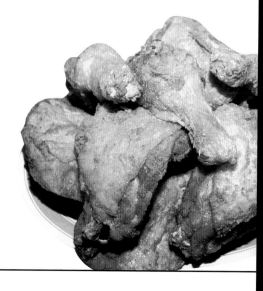

Leon and Miriam Wagler
Dutch Haus
Family Restaurant

Leon and Miriam Wagler both grew up in the Mennonite community of Hartville, Ohio. They moved from Ohio to Sarasota in 1972. Leon worked in construction but had a dream of someday owning a restaurant. The Waglers' were regular customers of Dutch Haus Restaurant from the time it opened in 1991 Then in 1995, their dream became a reality as they purchased Dutch Haus Family Restaurant. They both will tell you that the best part of owning a restaurant is meeting lots of new people

Leon and Miriam have three children and four grandchildren. The two youngest of their children bake all of the delicious desserts- pies, cakes, and cookies In their spare time, Leon enjoys hunting and fishing and Miriam enjoys cross-stitching

941-954-4287

1247 Beneva Road
(Beneva Marketplace)
Sarasota
Monday – Saturday
7 AM To 8 PM

Amish Country Cookin'

- **Family Style — All You Can Eat**
- **Carry Out Available**

**Join Us Wednesday
For All You Can Eat Fish**

1

Chris Bolds

Firefighter/Paramedic

SCFD

Chris is firefighter/ paramedic who started his career in Hillsborough County 8 years ago. He was working at Charlotte County Fire Rescue when he got the call to fill a position with the Sarasota County Fire Department. He is presently providing service county wide and taking notes on where to bid when the opportunity presents itself. He is single and enjoys physical fitness and water sports. Chris values family relationships, most importantly with his 14-year-old daughter, Tina. About the recipe Chris says, "It's not just another sauce, this comes from Mom's Kitchen!"

Bolds' Family Spaghetti Sauce

Chris Bolds – Firefighter/Paramedic

A traditional tomato sauce from Chris' family that will resuscitate any Italian dish.

Ingredients:

7 cloves of garlic
4 tablespoons extra virgin olive oil
1 pound bulk mild or hot Italian sausage
35 ounce can peeled tomatoes
28 ounce can crushed tomatoes
35 ounce water
1 tablespoons oregano
2 bay leaves

1 tablespoon basil, fresh chopped
1 tablespoon black pepper
1 tablespoon fennel seed (wrapped in cheese cloth)
1 tablespoon salt
1 tablespoons sugar
1 1/2 pounds for your favorite pasta

Directions:

1 – In a medium pan put olive oil and cloves of garlic that are sliced in half on low to medium heat.

2 – Cook garlic until you see light brown edges.

3 – Add sausage and cook until done, (careful not to burn the garlic).

4 – In a 5-6 quart pot put peeled tomatoes in and mash them.

5 – Add the rest of the ingredients and cook over low to medium heat for 15 minutes.

6 – Add sausage/garlic mixture and cook uncovered, stirring occasionally for 1 to 2 hours.

7 – Tip: 2-3 tablespoons of Pecorino romano (Locatelli) adds a nice touch.

8 – Serve hot over your favorite pasta, with plenty of garlic bread.

Makes 4 – 6 Servings.

4

Curry Painted Sea Bass

Café L' Europe

Ingredients:

6 – 8 ounce sea bass fillets
1/2 cup honey
2 tablespoons curry powder
3 tablespoons olive oil for sautéing
flour for dredging

2 cups shaved cabbage
3 apples cored and sliced thin
1/2 cup olive oil
1/4 cup raspberry vinegar
salt and pepper

Directions:

1 – Season sea bass with salt and pepper and dredge in flour.

2 – Sauté in hot olive oil on one side until brown.

3 – Turn fish and place in a 350 degree oven for about 10 minutes.

4 – Combine cabbage, apples, olive oil, vinegar in a bowl and season with salt and pepper.

5 – Pull sea bass from oven.

6 – Combine curry and honey and glaze the top of the sea bass.

7 – Place apple, cabbage, and salad on plate and fish on top.

Makes 6 Servings.

Michael Garey
General Manager
Café L' Europe

Michael Garey was born and raised in Buffalo, New York. He moved to Sarasota, Florida as a teenager and began in the restaurant business as a busboy in 1977. In 1979 he started as a busboy at the Café L' Europe. Moving up the ladder, he became a dining room captain in 1981 and assistant manager in 1982. In 1984, he left Café L' Europe to help open and manage Mr. Wong's Chinese restaurant. Michael came back to Café L' Europe in 1986 as General Manager, the title that he holds today. Mr. Garey is currently President of the St. Armands Merchants Assoc. and conceived and organized two events for the Florida Wine Festival, the Wine Marker's Dinner, and Sip and Shop. He is married to his wife, Catherine and has three daughters, Alexandra, Jenna and Amelia.

13

Raylene Hill
Firefighter/Paramedic
Sarasota County
Fire Department
Station 31, C Shift

I was raised in a large family of eight and was a prep cook for my mom for as long as I can remember. Growing up with good-hearted parents meant we always had a house full of strays. We took in dogs, cats, hamsters, birds, and even people. Early on, I got my training in emergency first aid from my Dad who had been a medic in the army. There was never a shortage of injured children and pets to practice on. I learned compassion from my dad. Today I am a firefighter/paramedic and have served with Sarasota County Fire Department since 1989. I love my job, and I receive great personal satisfaction when I have helped someone in need. On my days off I enjoy painting, sculpture, woodworking, cooking gardening and spending time with friends and family.

Mom's Swiss Steak

Raylene Hill — Firefighter/Paramedic

Ingredients:

1 whole round steak (top and bottom)
   about 3 lbs., tenderized*
1 cup flour
salt and pepper
2 cans stewed tomatoes (14.5 ounce cans)
2 tablespoons Worcestershire sauce

1 medium onion sliced very thin
vegetable oil

TIP: Meat must be tenderized. Either have the butcher run the meat through a meat tenderizer machine or tenderize it yourself by pounding it with a meat mallet.

Directions:

1 – Cut meat into individual portions. (About 10 – 12 pieces).

2 – Pour flour into a shallow dish and coat tenderized meat with flour.

3 – Pour enough vegetable oil into a frying pan to cover the bottom.

4 – Brown floured meat in frying pan over medium high heat; add oil as needed to keep it from sticking.

5 – Place all pieces of browned meat into a 9 x 13 baking pan, sprinkle with salt and pepper.

6 – Cover meat with thin slices of onion.

7 – Mix stewed tomatoes and Worcestershire sauce in the frying pan, stir until warm.

8 – Pour stewed tomato sauce over the meat and onions.

9 – Cover with foil and bake in oven at 350 degrees for about 1 1/2 hours or until meat is fork tender.

Serve with white rice or hot mashed potatoes. Enjoy!

Makes 6 Servings.

Grilled Pork Chop with Cilantro Cream Sauce and Herbed Basmati Rice

Michael's On East

Ingredients:

12 to 14 ounce double bone pork chop
1 cup Basmati rice
1/4 teaspoon fresh chopped basil
1/8 teaspoon fresh chopped oregano
1/8 teaspoon fresh chopped parsley
3 cups chicken stock
1 cup heavy cream

1 bunch cilantro
2 gloves whole garlic
1 shallot
1/8 teaspoon black peppercorns
1/2 cup white wine
salt & pepper to taste

Directions:

1 – Place rice in pot with 2 cups of 1 stock. Cover, place on low flame until done.

2 – While rice is cooking, place 1 cup stock in another pot with garlic, shallot roughly chopped, peppercorns and wine.

3 – Reduce until 1/4 cup of liquid.

4 – Add 1/2 bunch of cilantro and heavy cream. Reduce by 1/2. Season to taste.

5 – Strain sauce before serving.

6 – When rice is finished add all herbs. Mix in well.

7 – Grill pork chop until desired temperature.

Michael's On East

Sarasota's most celebrated restaurant is dazzling guests with its vibrant decor - reminiscent of a 1930's private dining club. The look is matched by the restaurant's impeccable service, just what you would expect from this recipient of nine golden spoon awards as one of Florida's Top 20 restaurants.

Michael's
On East

941-366-0007

1212 East Avenue South
Sarasota

Monday – Saturday
Lunch 11:30 AM To 2:00 PM
Dinner 5:30 PM To 10:00 PM

Recipient of
Nine Consecutive
Golden Spoon Awards
by *Florida*
Trend Magazine.

Glenn Poole
Battalion Chief
Bradenton Fire Department

Glenn Poole is a Battalion Chief with the City of Bradenton Fire Department and has been in the fire service for 14 years. He is married with two children and has a bird named Pumpkin. His hobbies include boating, fishing and weightlifting. When asked about his recipe, Glenn says, "all the men on his shift always ask for the peppers!"

Stuffed Peppers

Glenn Poole — Battalion Chief

Ingredients:

6 large peppers
3 pounds ground turkey
1 egg
1 box white rice
2 large cans (29 ounces) tomato sauce

2 teaspoons garlic pepper
1/4 cup ketchup
3 teaspoon Worcestershire sauce
16 ounce package mozzarella cheese

Directions:

1 – Cut and clean out peppers.

2 – Mix turkey, egg, rice, pepper, ketchup, and Worcestershire sauce.

3 – Add 1/4 cup of tomato sauce and mix.

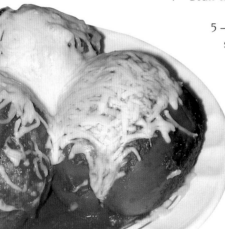

4 – Stuff the peppers.

5 – Place in deep dish and pour remainder of tomato sauce over top and in bottom of dish.

6 – Bake 350 degrees for 45 minutes.

7 – Sprinkle mozzarella cheese on top and bake again until cheese has melted.

8 – Serve with garlic bread.

Makes 6 Servings.

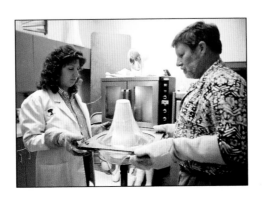

Olive Pizza

Manatee Memorial Hospital

Ingredients:

DOUGH:
1-3/4 cups warm water
 (110 degrees)
1 tbls dry yeast
1 tbls salt
1 tbls sugar
1/4 cups olive oil

2 cloves minced garlic
1/2-3/4 cup fresh basil
6 cups flour

TOPPING:
1-1/2 cups green olives
 (pitted no pimentos)

1/2 cup large black olives
1 lemon, juice of
3 cloves minced garlic
1-1/2 anchovy
1/4-1/2 cup olive oil
16 oz shredded mozzarella

Directions:

DOUGH:
1 – Dissolve sugar in water and add yeast. Let yeast proof (until it bubbles).
2 – Add olive oil, salt, garlic, basil, and 3 cups flour and mix. After 4/5 minutes add remaining flour and beat.
3 – Roll out on floured surface and knead about 5 minutes (add flour to prevent sticking, sparingly).
4 – Place in oiled large bowl and cover with clear wrap. Let rise 1 hour
(until dough doubles in size). Cut dough in 2 pieces (freeze one or double topping recipe for 2 pizza's).
5 – Pizza can be found or square on a cookie sheet. (sprinkle corn meal in pan or pizza stone before rolling out).

TOPPING:
1 – Blend all ingredients (except cheese) in food processor until mixture forms thick paste.
2 – Spread over dough, sprinkle cheese evenly on top of mixture
3 – Place pizza in a pre heated 475-degree oven on lowest rack for 15-20 minutes. If crust gets too dark after 5 minutes, reduce heat to 450 degrees.

MANATEE MEMORIAL
Hospital & Health System

746-5111
206 Second Street East
Bradenton, Fl 34208

First in the Hearts of Manatee County

"Best Hospital" 6 years in a row —
Bradenton Herald Readers
Preference Poll

47 years of quality family healthcare, committed to:
• innovative technology
• compassionate care
• experienced leadership
• community outreach

Michael Marquez
Manatee Memorial Hospital

Mike Marquez is the Chief
Executive Officer of Manatee
Memorial Hospital and
Health System in Bradenton,
Florida. He is a graduate of
Florida International
University with a B.S. in
Business Administration and
earned an MBA from Nova
Southeastern University. He
is a Diplomat of the American
College of Healthcare
Executives, Immediate Past
Chairman, Board of Trustees
of the Florida League of
Health Systems, Inc., serves
on the Board of Governors
Florida Hospital Association
and is a member of the Board
of Governors and CEO
Committee of the Federation
of American Health Systems
He is Past President and
Chairman of the Board of
Directors of the United Way
of Manatee County and
current Chairman of the
United Way Foundation
Mike and his wife Terese live
in University Park and have
two sons and a granddaughter
He is an avid golfer, has an
extensive CD collection, has a
black belt in Tai Kwon Do
and is a great cook

1

Richard Brenner
Firefighter/EMT
Bradenton Fire Department

Richard Brenner was born in Wilkinsburg, Pennsylvania, in 1959. His family moved to Bradenton that same year, and he's lived there ever since. Richard was a boat builder for 15 years before entering the field of firefighting. He was a volunteer with Whitfield Fire Department for three years before being hired at Bradenton Fire Department in 1993. His firehouse nickname is "Yul,"(as in Brenner). Leave it to firefighters to be so original.

Richard and his wife, Maria, have been married 13 years and are boat and car racing enthusiasts. In his off duty hours, Richard owns and operates Brenner Boat Hoists who provided a boat hoist for Bradenton's Fire Boat.

About the recipe...
"My recipe is worked up to eat on shift for $5.00 per person and still have leftovers."

City of Bradenton Vintage American La France.

Blackened Chicken
Richard Brenner — Firefighter/EMT

Ingredients:

4 pounds boneless skinless chicken breast
2 red bell peppers
4 onions
1 jar Chef Paul Predonne blacken seasoning
1/2 pound butter
4 – 6 ounce Crystal Hot sauce

20 ounce yellow rice
3 – 32 ounce cans Goya black beans
3 boxes Jiffy corn bread mix
2 teaspoons sugar
1 – 16 ounce cream corn white

Directions:

1 – (Be sure to use a black iron skillet when blackening.) Blacken chicken in chunks with blacken seasoning. Add butter, red pepper, and onions while blackening. Add Crystal hot sauce to spice up.

2 – Cook rice separately.

3 – Cook black beans separately with 2 ounces of hot sauce.

4 – Make cornbread according to box, adding cream of corn and sugar to mix. Serve cornbread on the side.

5 – Chop 2 onions and serve on the side for top of black beans.

Makes 8 Servings.

Dover Sole

Café L' Europe

Ingredients:

4 whole Dover sole
2 tablespoons olive oil
1 cup seasoned flour for dredging
12 asparagus spears
24 red grapes
8 morel mushrooms

1/2 cup chicken stock
4 ounces Vermouth
4 ounces Ver Jus (white grape juice)
4 ounces butter
salt and pepper

Directions:

1 – Cut asparagus into 2 inch tips, then quarter them.

2 – Cut grapes in half and slice morels.

3 – In a hot pan simmer all in chicken stock until tender. Keep warm.

4 – In a separate pan reduce Vermouth with ver jus by one half. Remove from heat and stir in softened butter. (Do not put back on the stove.)

5 – Season with salt and pepper and keep in a warm place.

6 – Skin and filet Dover sole. (If Dover is not available other sole filets such as lemon sole can be used.)

7 – Fold filets in half, dredge in seasoned flour and sauté in olive oil in a hot skillet.

8 – Brown on one side, turn and place in a 350 degree oven for 5 minutes until done. (Length of time may depend on thickness of filets.)

9 – Place asparagus mixture down on the plate and fish filets over the top of it.

10 – Lightly sauce over the top of the filets.

Makes 4 Servings.

Café L' Europe

Now celebrating its twenty seventh anniversary, Café L' Europe continues to be one of Sarasota's most beautiful and popular restaurants. A multitude of awards have been received over the years from such publications as The Wine Spectator, Sante' Award of Excellence and Florida Trend as well as the prestigious DIRONA award; bearing witness to the high quality of food. Pleasing aromas and beautiful presentations preview the finest of Continental Cuisine and New European Cuisine from elaborate appetizers to elegant entrees and truly decadent desserts. Completing the scene is a superb selection of wines from the finest vineyards of Europe and California. The final ingredient essential to fine dining is the high level of professional service. The warm welcome on arrival hints at the care taken by every person at Café L' Europe to ensure your dining pleasure.

William "Bill" Costello

Battalion Chief of Training, SCFD

Bill was born in Brooklyn, New York, with his three sisters and six brothers. He was drafted into the Army following high school, and became a communications specialist in Germany. After a tour in Vietnam, he exited the military in 1973.

On his way to California, Bill detoured through Sarasota to visit his brother and never left. Bill was hired by Fruitville Fire District in 1977 as a firefighter. He became a paramedic the following year, and in 1984 accepted the position of training officer. Through several mergers, he oversees the training of 500+ personnel as Battalion Chief of Training for SCFD.

Bill and his wife, Melinda, enjoy spending their free time with their four daughters and visiting beaches.

Bill's Meatball and Tomato Sauce

Bill Costello — Battalion Chief of Training

Ingredients:

TOMATO SAUCE:
28 oz can crushed tomatoes
2 - 12 oz cans tomato paste
2 - 29 oz cans tomato sauce
28 oz can tomato puree
1/2 cup romano cheese
2 tbs. chopped dried onions
pinch caribbean jerk seasoning
1 tbs. basil

4 whole garlic cloves
1 1/2 tsp. garlic powder
1/2 tsp. salt
1/2 tsp. black pepper
1/4 tsp. sugar
1 lb. pkg. hot sausage
1 lb. pkg. mild sausage

MEATBALLS:
2 lb. beef ground chuck
6 large eggs

1 cup Italian style bread crumbs
2 tbs. chopped dried onions
1 tbs. basil
1 cup romano cheese
1 1/2 tbs. garlic powder
1/2 tsp. salt
1/2 tsp. black pepper
1/4 tsp. caribbean jerk seasoning

Directions:

SAUCE:
1 – Mix all the sauce ingredients into a large pot. Add 84 oz of water.
2 – Add 2 pkgs. of sausage and heat on medium high heat on stove.
3 – Bring to boil, stirring to avoid sauce burning to pan.
4 – Once sauce begins to boil, turn down heat to low.

MEATBALL:
1 – Add all ingredients for the meatballs into a large bowl and mix.
2 – Roll meat into golf ball size. (makes about 20 meatballs)
3 – Add meatballs to sauce, and simmer for 2 hrs., stirring occasionally.
4 – Taste the sauce occasionally and add salt or garlic to taste.
5 – Serve over spaghetti noodles and with plenty of garlic bread.

Makes 8–10 Servings.

Pizza

Verona Pizza & Italian Restaurant

Ingredients:

2 cups flour
1/2 ounce of yeast
1/2 cup water
1 ounce sugar
1/2 ounce salt
1 teaspoon olive oil

2 spoons of pizza sauce
1 pound mozzarella
pinch Romano cheese
pinch oregano
any toppings desired (peppers, olives, pepperoni, etc.)

Directions:

1 – Sieve the flour into a large bowl with the salt, leave covered in a warm atmosphere.

2 – Activate the yeast by mixing water with dissolved sugar at hand hot temperature and allow to ferment.

3 – Make a well in the center of the slightly warmed flour and pour in the liquid with the yeast and oil. Mix the dough until soft and pliable.

4 – Knead the dough for about 10 minutes and place in a bowl covered with a clean cloth. Leave in a warm place to double in size.

5 - Knead back the dough and make into round pizza base.

6 – Spread pizza sauce over dough and top with mozzarella & Romano cheese, oregano, and any other toppings you like.

Makes one pizza.

Joseph Gerac[i]

*Verona Pizza &
Italian Restauran[t]*

Born in Palermo Sicily i[n] 1948, Joseph Geraci, move[d] to the United States in 1973 His passion has been cookin[g] top quality food for 20 years Verona's is family owned an[d] run by Joseph, the owner, hi[s] wife of 29 years, Josephine and their three children. Al[l] the food served is made b[y] one of the family members Come enjoy some of our excel-lent Italian food, in a GREA[T] family atmosphere a[t] VERONA'S

VERONA PIZZA & ITALIAN RESTAURANT

941-753-7008

**5257 33rd Street East
State Road 70
Bradenton**

Mon – Thur • 11 AM To 10 PM
Fri – Sat • 11 AM To 11 PM
Sunday • Closed

Straight From Italy

**Personally Prepared by
Joe & Josephine Geraci
Palermo, Sicily**

Rich Bucci
Firefighter/EMT
SCFD

Rich was born in New Jersey and admits it! He moved to Sarasota in 1977, "fresh out of high school," and began working in the restaurant industry waiting tables and ultimately managing. Rich joined Sarasota County Fire Department in 1986 and continues to work enthusiastically as a Firefighter/EMT. He is currently assigned to Station #11 ("the Hub") on B-shift. There he enjoys spending some of his time on the 110 foot E-ONE Ladder Truck, which allows him to police the ever-problematic overtime callback procedures.

Rich and his wife, Brenda, have a son Kyle, and their hobbies include softball, fishing, camping and visits to Tennessee. Rich says of his family, "our priority is to serve the Lord." Rich also holds the title "Driver-Engineer," but when asked which title he cherishes the most, he replies, "Dad."

Bucci's Firehouse 11 Chili

Rich Bucci – Firefighter/EMT

Ingredients:

1/2 pound mild or hot sausage
2 pounds ground beef
2 cups chopped onion
1 cup chopped green pepper
4 cloves garlic, minced
2 – 16 ounce cans tomatoes, cut-up or crushed tomatoes
2 – 8 ounce cans tomato sauce

2 – 16 ounce cans dark red kidney beans (drained)
5-6 teaspoons chili powder
1 teaspoon dried basil (crushed)
1/2 teaspoon salt
1/2 teaspoon pepper
1/4 cup brown or white sugar

Directions:

1 – In a large saucepan cook ground beef, sausage, onions, green pepper, and garlic until meat is brown.

2 – Drain fat, stir in undrained tomatoes, kidney beans, tomato sauce, chili powder, basil, salt, pepper and sugar.

3 – Bring to a boil, and then reduce heat to simmer. Cover and simmer for 20 minutes or cook in a crock pot all day on low.

Makes 8 Servings.

4

Hot and Spicy Shrimp Soup (Tom Yum)

Ovea Thai Kitchen

Ingredients:

1 cup water
1 stem lemongrass
2 kaffir lime leaves
5 pieces of medium to large shrimp
1 teaspoon ground dried chilies
   (or to taste)

1/4 cup straw mushrooms
2 tablespoons lime juice (or to taste)
1/2 tablespoon fish sauce (or to taste)
1/2 tablespoon chopped cilantro leaves
4-5 pieces bell peppers

Directions:

1 – Boil water; add lemongrass and kaffir lime leaves.

2 – Add shrimp and mushrooms and bell peppers.

3 – Simmer for 2-3 minutes until the shrimp is cooked.

4 – Add ground dried chilies, fish sauce, and lime juice to taste.

5 – The soup would be spicy-sour and a little salty, then serve garnished with fresh cilantro.

Ovea Thai Kitchen

Ovea Thai Kitchen is family owned and operated Thai restaurant which is fast making a name for itself in hometown Sarasota. Born in Bangkok, owners "Cookie and Woody" have made the business a family affair, by employing their son, Ekawee, and daughter, Awika, when they are not in school. The restaurant opened a year ago seating up to 45 patrons and is quaintly adorned with authentic Thai decor.

The family prides themselves in serving their best Thai family recipes. By using the best quality ingredients to make their food dishes, moderate prices, and warm and friendly service, they seem to have found the right combination to keep customers coming back.

If you're interested in tantalizing your Thai tastebuds, drop in and sample their mouth watering Thai soups, salads, entreés, and desserts.

Mark Kennell, Jr.
Battalion Chief
SCFD

My love for the Fire Service began in the fall of 1974 when I became a volunteer firefighter at the age of eighteen. I was looking for a career in which I could express the love and compassion of Jesus Christ for the community in which I live. I was hired with Fruitville Fire Department as an EMT in 1976 and soon became their first state certified paramedic. During my career I have had the privilege of serving in various capacities including managing Code Enforcement, Fire Investigations, Public Education and the Volunteer Firefighter Program as I worked my way up the ranks to the position of Battalion Chief.

I am married to a very special lady, Elaine, and have three wonderful children: Elizabeth, Heather, and Nathaniel.

Italian-Style Stuffed Chicken Breast

Mark A. Kennell, Jr. — Battalion Chief

Ingredients:

10 oz. cheddar cheese (or Swiss cheese if you prefer)
2 eggs, lightly beaten
3 tablespoons seasoned breadcrumbs
3 tablespoons parsley (dried or fresh chopped)
1/4 teaspoon salt

1/8 teaspoon pepper
Pinch of nutmeg
6 large boneless chicken breasts (about 2 pounds) pounded thin
2 tablespoons olive (or vegetable) oil
2 cups spaghetti sauce (preferably with green peppers & mushrooms)

Directions:

1 – In a medium bowl, thoroughly mix cheese, eggs, breadcrumbs, parsley, salt, pepper, and nutmeg.

2 – Place approximately 1/4 cup of mixture in center of each chicken breast. Roll and secure with toothpicks.

3 – In a large skillet, thoroughly brown chicken on both sides in hot oil, starting with the folded edge down first (this helps keep cheese mixture inside chicken better). After browned both sides, drain off fat.

4 – Pour spaghetti sauce over center of chicken.

5 – Simmer, covered, 45 minutes or until chicken is done.

6 – When served, pour a small amount of fresh spaghetti sauce over chicken to make it look nice. May also want to provide extra sauce in container for guests or family to add per their tastes.

7 – Suggested side dishes: fresh cooked broccoli, baked potatoes, and fresh dinner rolls.

Makes 6 Servings.

Glazed Scallops with Idiazabul Cheese

Café L' Europe

Ingredients:

1 tablespoon olive oil
12 large scallops
1 shallot chopped fine
2 ounces Serano ham chopped fine
4 ounces Verdejo Spanish white wine

1/2 lemon
4 ounces butter
2 tablespoons chopped chives
4 slices toasted baguette
4 ounces grated idiazabul cheese

Directions:

1 – Heat olive oil in a sauté pan.

2 – Add scallops and shallots. Sauté for a few minutes.

3 – Add in serano, and deglaze with verdejo.

4 – When scallops are done, remove from pan and reduce the liquid in the pan down until it is almost all gone.

5 – Squeeze in lemon juice and stir in soft butter.

6 – Season with salt and pepper and add in chives.

7 – Place scallops on toast and spoon over the sauce.

8 – Sprinkle on the cheese and glaze under the broiler.

Makes 4 Servings.

Matt (Speedy) Scarbrough

**Fire Lieutenant/EMT
Sarasota County Fire
Department**

*Twenty year veteran
Matt Scarbrough is currently
a Fire Lieutenant/EMT at
Station #11-C. His friends
call him "Speedy" because he
walks so fast. Matt has worn
numerous hats over the years
including President of
Sarasota County Arson Task
Force, President Gulf Coast
Chapter of Fire Inspectors,
and Sergeant with Florida
Highway Patrol Auxiliary.
On his off duty hours
Matt owns and operates
Sportsmans Archery, providing full service turkey, deer
and hog hunts on local ranch
lands. The only thing he
loves more than hunting,
archery, fishing, taxidermy
and black labs, is his beautiful wife Julie and their two
daughters. When asked
what's most important in
life, Matt states, "My life was
never complete until I had
my two girls, Bree and Carly."*

*Don't forget to shut
off the oven!*

Matt's Venison Camp Stew

Matt "Speedy" Scarbrough

Ingredients:

2 pounds venison
2 –15 ounce cans mixed vegetables
2 – 10 3/4 ounce cans
   cream of mushroom soup

1/2 cup teriyaki marinade
16 ounce can chunky salsa
8 ounce package (2 cups)
   colby jack cheese

Directions:

1 – Slice venison into 1/2" pieces and marinade in teriyaki sauce.

2 – Turn on stove top to medium-high temperature and brown venison in sauce 5-10 minutes.

3 – In a 12 quart pan, add mixed vegetables, and salsa and mix thoroughly… turn temperature down to medium.

4 – Add cream of mushroom soup and colby jack cheese and stir. When cheese melts, it is ready to serve.

5 – Serve over a bed of rice.

6 – Feeds a crew of 6 firefighters.

7 – Prep to finish = 30 minutes.

8 – Optional: Diced cooked sausage can be used as a meat substitute.

**Matt's Favorite tabletime saying is:
If you go away hungry, it ain't my fault!**

50's Diner Meatloaf

50's Diner

Ingredients:

20 pounds of hamburger
4 cups quick oats
2 cups milk
1 cup catsup
12 eggs
2 medium onion, chopped medium
1 tablespoon black pepper
1 1/2 tablespoons Italian seasoning
3 tablespoons salt

1/2 tablespoon celery salt
1/2 tablespoon granulated garlic
1 kitchen spoon of wet mustard
4 stalks of celery, chopped

MEATLOAF SAUCE:
6 cups catsup
3 cups brown sugar
2 teaspoons wet mustard

Directions:

1 – Mix everything together by hand.

2 – Put in 3, 4" square pans.

3 – Sauce: Mix well with whip and spread on top of meatloaf.

4 – Bake at 350 degrees for 1 hour and 10 minutes.

Makes 30 Servings Of 2 Slices.

Greg Meyer
Firefighter/Paramedic
SCFD

Greg "Buddah" Meyer was born and raised in Sarasota. Fresh out of high school he joined the South Trail Area Fire Control District as a volunteer and fell in love with the Fire Service. He was hired in 1981 and began his training to become a journeyman firefighter EMT. His desire to grow in the fire service led him to paramedic school and in 1986 he received his certification as a paramedic.

Greg and his wife, Joy, are raising three children James, Justin and Holly. His hobbies include hunting, fishing, and watching Nascar Winston Cup Racing..."Go Earnhardt!"

About the recipe...
I got this Elk Stew recipe from a friend and absolutely loved it. By the way, it's much easier to make the stew than to hunt an elk.

Station 7 crew enjoying Bull Elk stew.

Sharon's – Bull Elk Stew

Greg Meyer — Firefighter/Paramedic

Ingredients:

3 lbs. (cubed) elk meat (deer is good also)
1 large onion (chopped)
1/3 cup flour
2 cloves garlic (minced)
3 cups beef stock
16 oz. beer

1 bay leaf
2 tsp. thyme
1/2 cup red wine vinegar
1/2 cup brown sugar
1 lb. bacon
2 - 4 tbs. cooking oil

Directions:

1 – Brown meat in dutch oven in 2 tbs. of cooking oil, adding additional oil as needed to finish meat. Set aside.

2 – Brown onion in pan. Then sprinkle flour on top of onion and brown.

3 – Next add beef broth, garlic and beer. Bring to a boil.

4 – Add meat and rest of ingredients, except for bacon.

5 – Bake @ 350 deg. for 2 hours.

6 – Brown bacon, and just before serving dish, crush bacon and sprinkle on top of dish.

7 – Serve over rice or noodles

SUGGESTED SIDES: Serve with fresh Mango slices and your favorite bread.

Makes 6-8 Servings.

Oven Fried Chicken

Sarasota Health Care, Nita Thompson

Ingredients:

8 pieces chicken
sprinkle lemon pepper
2 cups flour
1 cup bread crumbs

4 tablespoons seasoned salt
3 tablespoons granulated garlic
3 teaspoons black pepper
3 teaspoons salt

Directions:

1 – Wash and pat dry 8 pieces chicken.

2 – Sprinkle with lemon pepper and toss.

3 – Mix remaining ingredients.

4 – Dredge chicken in flour mixture.

5 – Put on sheet pan.

6 – Bake at 350 degrees 1 hour.

Nita Thompson
Sarasota Health Care

Nita Thompson is currently employed with Sarasota Health Care Center in the Food Service. She started cooking at age 12 and has been enjoying it ever since. Nita has one daughter and two sons and tries all her new recipes on them. She has cooked for several places including, Sugar & Spice, East Manor, and other health care facilities. She loves the elderly and takes great pleasure in working with them. "Sissy," a nickname called by Nita's two brothers, spends her leisure time working in the garden, embroidering, and reading her favorite books.

Brett "Porkchop" Pritchard

Firefighter/EMT
Cedar Hammock
Fire Department

Brett "Porkchop" Pritchard has been a Firefighter/EMT with the Cedar Hammock Fire Department for the past five years. Brett is an outdoorsy type of guy and enjoys camping and outside activities with his family. He and his wife, Kellie, have two daughters and a three-year old black spaniel, Ash. Brett treasures spending time with his wife and daughters and thanks God everyday for having them. "I also love to praise the Lord for he is my guiding light. I love my occupation and take great pride in it. Helping others and saving lives is the best feeling that words cannot describe," he says. This recipe from Kellie's kitchen is an easy and delicious one that the whole family can enjoy!

S.C.T.I. firefighter students still fighting the gas fire.

Firefighters Hot Dog Delight

Brett Pritchard — Firefighter/EMT

Ingredients:

6 medium potatoes (about 2 pounds) cooked, peeled, and diced
2 green onions, chopped
6 dinner-size frankfurters
2 tablespoons bacon drippings or salad oil
2 tablespoons sugar

1 teaspoon salt
1 teaspoon flour
1/4 cup vinegar
1 tablespoon chopped parsley
1/2 cup water

Directions:

1 – In large serving bowl, combine hot potatoes and onions, cover and keep warm.

2 – Meanwhile in large skillet over medium heat, brown frankfurters in bacon drippings. With slotted spoon remove frankfurters, reserve drippings.

3 – Add frankfurters to potatoes and onions and keep warm.

4 – Into hot drippings stir sugar, flour and salt until smooth and thick.

5 – Gradually stir in vinegar, 1/2 cup water, and cook and stir constantly, until it thickens and boils.

6 – Pour over potatoes and frankfurters. Sprinkle with parsley.

Makes 6 Servings.

"Chicken Parm Ala Millennium Crew"

Mike Mendelson — Firefighter/EMT

Ingredients:

2 pounds boneless/skinless chicken thighs
1 1/2 cups all purpose flour
1 1/2 cups Italian flavored bread crumbs
1/4 cup grated parmesan cheese

1 24 ounce jar marinara wine sauce
(Five Brothers recommended)
2 cups mozzarella cheese
vegetable oil

Directions:

1 – In a large bowl mix flour, bread crumbs and parmesan cheese together.

2 – Heat oil in a large pan or skillet. (oil approximately 1" deep)

3 – Moisten chicken pieces and coat with flour mix thoroughly.

4 – Place pieces of coated chicken in heated oil and cook until coating is golden brown.

5 – Place partially cooked pieces in a glass/corning ware bake dish making sure pieces are not touching each other.

6 – Preheat oven to 375 degrees and then place chicken in oven for 30 minutes.

7 – After baking chicken 30 minutes, remove from oven and carefully pour wine sauce IN BETWEEN chicken pieces. *Be sure NOT to cover chicken with sauce.

8 – Place back in oven and cook another 10 minutes.

9 – Remove from oven and place mozzarella cheese on top of chicken.

10 – Cook until chicken is melted.

11 – Remove from oven and serve.

Makes 4-6 Servings Normal (2-3 at the firehouse).

Mike Mendelson
Firefighter/EMT
Sarasota County Fire
Department Station #11-A

Mike is a 10 year veteran with background in Aircraft Crash Fire Rescue. He is presently assigned to Station 11-A (The Millennium Crew — as he coins it). Mike is pursuing a position as Fire Lieutenant and is presently 'hitting the books' for the upcoming test. When asked about nicknames, Mike replies, "I am called by many names; some good and some bad." Mike's hobbies include target practice, hunting, fishing, cooking and eating. You can see how one leads to the other. Mike's family is comprised of his wife, Carol, and children, Garret, Kyle and Brianna, and reportedly "one stupid dog." The recipe is one of Mike's personal creations.

153

"Bul-Go-Gi"

Richard "Rick" Hornberger — Firemedic
A Korean dish that mom made which became a firehouse favorite.

Ingredients:

2 lbs. sirloin steak
1 small onion (minced)
1 tbs.garlic salt
1 cup soy sauce
1/4 cup vegetable oil

3/4 cup sugar
3 tbs. dry sherry
1 1/4 tsp. Accent seasoning
1/2 tsp.pepper
1 tbs. sesame seeds (optional)

Directions:

1 – Slice steak onto thin strips 2" long and a 1/4" thick.

2 – Mix all ingredients together to make marinade, then add meat.

3 – Let meat soak in marinade overnight, but not less than 4 hrs.

4 – Cook meat in a hot wok or broiler pan with marinade stirring constantly. Cook until slightly pink or browning. Do not overcook.

5 – Serve over hot bed of rice with hot marinade poured over both.

Makes 4 - 6 Servings.

Rick Hornberger
Firemedic
SCFD

Rick is a 15 year veteran firemedic engineer with SCFD, working out of Station #11-B. As if life at "The Hub" isn't busy enough, Rick has a busy "off-duty" schedule as well.

Rick's wife, Mimi, has been tinting auto glass profession-ally since 1983. Rick and Mimi opened "Sunguard of Sarasota" in 1994 and have been tinting together since. Their quality tinting materials and workmanship speak for themselves, resulting in a busy shop.

In her free time Mimi enjoys diving and scrapbooking. Rick is a divemaster and enjoys diving, hunting, and camping with their daughter, Katie.

"Chicken and Dumplings"

Leigh Flynn — Lieutenant Paramedic

Ingredients:

2 - 50 oz. cans chicken broth
2 whole chickens(or 1 whole chicken and 1 pkg. of boneless skinless chicken breasts)
1 pkg. mushrooms (sliced)

3 cups baby carrots
3 cups celery (sliced)
1 bundle fresh parsley
1 box Bisquick biscuit mix

Directions:

1 – In a large stock pot combine broth, chicken mushrooms, carrots, celery, and about 2 tbs. of parsley (chopped), and simmer for about 6 hrs.

2 – Stir occasionally to prevent sticking.

3 – Strain broth back into the broth pot and de-bone chicken.

4 – Place de-boned chicken back in stock pot and simmer on low.

5 – In a mixing bowl, combine fresh chopped parsley, with dry Bisquick mix until it's lightly speckled with parsley flakes.

6 – Add milk until you have drop biscuit mix.

7 – Drop into stock pot and cover for 20 min.

*Do not take lid off, as this is the key to good dumplings.

Makes 4-6 Servings.

Warning: Dumplings tend to get bigger in your stomach!

Leigh Flynn
Lieutenant Paramedic, SCFD

Leigh is a ten year veteran of Sarasota County Fire Department having served as a firefighter/paramedic. Leigh was promoted to the rank of Lieutenant in 2000 and is proud to be the first female Lieutenant for Sarasota County.

Born in Nashville, Tennessee, and raised in the Chicago area, Leigh moved to Florida in 1983. She is married to Matthew Flynn, who also works for SCFD, and has a ten-year old step daughter, Heather. In her spare time she enjoys golfing and dabbles in home remodeling projects ranging from woodworking to setting ceramic tile.

Leigh credits her mother and her southern roots for her cooking style. She enjoys her time in the kitchen, both at the firehouse and at home.

Claiborne Moulton

Firefighter/Paramedic

SCFD

Born and raised in Cajun Country (New Orleans), Claiborne moved to Sarasota in 1990 with his wife Evie. He became a volunteer firefighter with SCFD in 1992 and served in that capacity for two years before being hired as firefighter/ EMT. Claiborne has recently become a paramedic and is working at Station #12 on the B-shift. He sees physical fitness as a lifestyle and has no problem staying fit given his three sons ages 9, 6, and 4, who keep him running and lifting as their needs dictate. He borrowed the Jambalaya recipe from his sister Anne, and it has become a firehouse favorite wherever served.

Jambalaya (Original New Orleans Recipe)

Claiborne W. Moulton — Firefighter/Paramedic

Ingredients:

1/4 cup bacon grease or vegetable oil
   whole stalk celery chopped
1 large green pepper chopped
1 large onion chopped
2 bulbs garlic minced
3 pounds boneless chicken breast cubed
1 1/2 pounds andouille sausage
2 large bay leaves

1 tablespoon thyme
8 ounce can tomato sauce
1 pound 12 ounce can of chopped
   tomatoes with juice
6-12 ounce Crystal hot sauce
1 cup fresh parsley
1 pound medium to large shrimp
2 cups cooked white or brown rice

Directions:

1 – Sauté celery, onion and green peppers in bacon grease until soft.

2 – Add garlic, chicken, sausage, parsley, bay leaves and thyme. Cook for 10 minutes until chicken is cooked.

3 – Add tomato sauce, chopped tomatoes and Crystal hot sauce.

4 – Cook for 10 minutes, simmer.

5 – Add shrimp and rice.

6 – Cook about 10 minutes until shrimp is cooked.

7 – Serve with French garlic bread.

Serves 6-8 People.

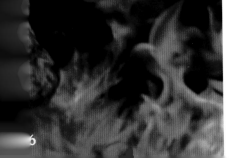

Crawfish Etouffee

King Creole

Ingredients:

1 pound package crawfish tailmeat with fat
1 cup seafood stock (warm)
1/2 cup diced green bell pepper
1/2 cup diced red bell pepper
1/2 cup diced onions

1/2 cup diced celery
2 cups cooked white rice
4 tablespoons butter
1/4 cup all purpose flour
1/4 cup green onions diced fine
2 tablespoons unsalted butter

pinch salt
pinch cayenne pepper
pinch white pepper
pinch dried basil
pinch thyme
pinch black pepper

Directions:

1 – Heat the oil in a large heavy skillet over high heat until it begins to smoke.

2 – Gradually whisk in flour stirring until smooth.

3 – Continue cooking until the roux is dark brown.

4 – Stir in vegetables and then slowly add stock.

5 – Cook on very low heat whisking constantly until the flour taste is gone.

6 – Add seasonings and crawfish then slowly stir in the butter.

7 – Serve immediately over rice.

Makes 2 Servings.

*About the recipe…Traditional Louisiana "smothered" Dark Roux.

Richard Drumgools
Executive Chef
King Creole

King Creole, Sarasota' newest addition to downtown nightlife, faithfully captures the charm and pulse of New Orleans, by recreating the look and feel of an authentic French Quarter venue. Serving up traditional Creole and Cajun fare, as well as a lively lineup of quality entertainment every night, King Creole guarantees to take you on a sensory visit to the Crescent City amid the aromas of zesty Jambalayas, Crawfish Etouffee, warm Beignets & Coffee, and the sounds of hot Jazz and cool Blues. Executive Chef, Richard Drumgools' latest challenge has proven his mettle in mastering all types of cuisines. Richard is a member of the American Culinary Federation, and has worked in many fine restaurants and clubs from Cape Cod to Florida. King Creole is open six days, featuring lunch, dinner, and a late night menu.

941-365-7474

1991 Main Street • Sarasota

Monday – Thursday
11:30 AM To Midnight
Friday • 11:30 AM To 1:00 AM
Saturday • 5 PM To 1 AM

Authentic Cajun & Creole Cuisine

- **Nightly Live Entertainment**
- **Late Night Menu**
- **Catering**
- **Private Parties**

15

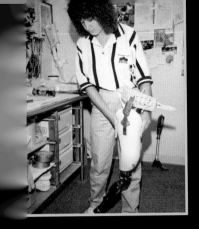

JoAnn's Delicious Fish "Everyone's Favorite"

Suncoast Brace and Limb

Ingredients:

Grouper chunks (may substitute other fish to liking)
1 quart peanut oil

1 box of "Hot-n-Spicy" Shake Bake
16 ounce bottle Ranch dressing

Directions:

1 – Heat the oil to 350 degrees.

2 - Cut the grouper into 2"x 1" chunks.

3 – Rinse well.

4 – Shake the chunks until they are coated evenly.

5 – Cook in oil until golden brown.

6 – Dip cooked fish in Ranch dressing.

JoAnn Fumerelle
President
Suncoast Brace & Limb, Inc.

Suncoast Brace & Limb, Inc. has been in business for over six years serving the orthotic and prosthetic needs of Manatee, Sarasota and South Hillsborough counties. During that time, the company has developed a reputation for professional service and care, which is sensitive to the varying needs of their patients. The goal at Suncoast Brace & Limb, Inc. is to maximize the freedom and comfort of the patient based on the patient's goals. The practitioner selects the appropriate design, material and components to fulfill a physician's prescription and then they make all of the necessary casts, measurements, model modifications and layouts for the patient. The practitioners get to know each patient and continually work with him or her on the proper care, removal and application of their device to ensure the success of the treatment plan.

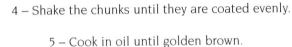

Suncoast Brace & Limb Inc.

Three Convenient Locations:

941-798-3558 • Bradenton
1878 59th Street West (Blake Park)

941-922-9797 • Sarasota
3920 Bee Ridge Rd., Bldg. A, Suite D

813-633-7232 • Sun City Center
1901 Harvorford, Suite 105

• • •

We are committed to giving people the freedom and flexibility that modern technology can provide.

8

Pan Seared Sea Bass Stuffed with an Asian Julienne

Sarasota Memorial Hospital

Ingredients:

4-6 ounces sea bass fillets
1 small carrot
1 small daikon (Asian radish)
1 small zucchini
1 small head of bok choy (Chinese cabbage)
1 small piece of fresh ginger
2 tablespoons fresh cilantro leaves
2 tablespoons fresh basil leaves

1 cup sake (Japanese rice wine)
2 tablespoons low sodium soy sauce
1/2 cup fresh lime juice
8 star anise
1/2 cup sugar in the raw
1 teaspoon Korean chili paste
1 cup rice wine
1 tablespoon sea salt

Directions:

1 – Preheat oven to 400 degrees. 2 – Rinse the fish with fresh water and pat dry with a paper towel. 3 – With a small paring knife, cut a slit in the thickest side of the filet. (Be careful not to cut all the way through the filet, just create a pocket.) Cover and place in refrigerator. 4 – Peel the carrot, daikon and ginger. Cut the carrot, daikon and zucchini into a medium julienne or matchstick shape. Combine these vegetables and put aside. 5 - Cut bok choy into thick strips and put aside. 6 - Slice ginger thinly against the grain and set aside. 7 - Slice basil leaves into very fine ribbons and mix with cilantro leaves. Set aside. 8 – Stuff the four filets with equal amounts of fresh herbs and julienne vegetables, being careful not to overstuff the fish. 9 – Seal the fish packages by placing a piece of the bok choy ribbon over the pocket and gently tucking it into the fish. Place fish back in refrigerator.

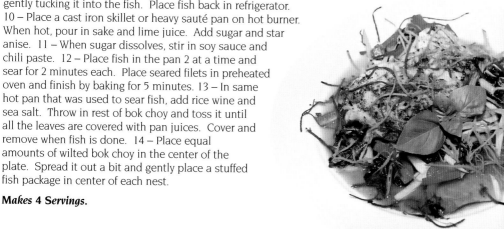

10 – Place a cast iron skillet or heavy sauté pan on hot burner. When hot, pour in sake and lime juice. Add sugar and star anise. 11 – When sugar dissolves, stir in soy sauce and chili paste. 12 – Place fish in the pan 2 at a time and sear for 2 minutes each. Place seared filets in preheated oven and finish by baking for 5 minutes. 13 – In same hot pan that was used to sear fish, add rice wine and sea salt. Throw in rest of bok choy and toss it until all the leaves are covered with pan juices. Cover and remove when fish is done. 14 – Place equal amounts of wilted bok choy in the center of the plate. Spread it out a bit and gently place a stuffed fish package in center of each nest.

Makes 4 Servings.

Candace Klemeyer
Sarasota Memorial Hospital

Sarasota became Candace Klemeyer's home at the age of seven. In 1988, Candice relocated when she attended the Art Institute of Philadelphia, the prestigious Johnson & Wales University Culinary Art Program where she graduated magna sum laude. After graduation, Candice worked in different restaurants and resorts in the Boston and Cape Cod area. She decided to return to Sarasota and became employed as a chef at Sarasota Memorial Hospital. The Food and Nutrition Services at SMH prepares, serves, and cleans up over 2300 meals per day! It is very challenging to make delicious, well-presented meals for all types of patients, particularly those on diet restrictions. The challenges do have their rewards, though. The Food and Nutrition Services recently earned the highest patient satisfaction score in the hospital!

15

Michael "Mike" Martino

Firefighter/Paramedic
SCFD

Mike was born and raised on Long Island, New York. In 1980 he married his high school sweetheart "Linda." Mike worked for the railroad and in construction until 1988 when he and Linda decided to escape the cold, frigid north, and make Sarasota, Florida, their new home.

In search of a new career path, Mike was introduced to the Fire Department by a friend who was a firefighter. Mike was hired in 1989, by Sarasota Fire Department as a firefighter. In 1994 he became a paramedic at Station #1, the busiest firehouse in the department. Since 1997 he has represented the SCFD Firefighters in collective bargaining.

Mike and Linda enjoy music, golfing, running, bicycling, and swimming, with their eight-year old son Michael.

Cheese Chicken Pasta

Mike Martino — Firefighter/Paramedic

Ingredients:

2lbs. boneless, skinless chicken breasts
2 lbs. pasta
8ozs. sharp cheddar cheese
8ozs. mozzarella cheese
4ozs. grated parmesan cheese
2 1/2 cups 2% milk

4 cloves garlic
1 lb. frozen broccoli
1 medium yellow onion
1 tsp. olive oil
salt and pepper – to taste

Directions:

1 – Dice up onion and garlic.

2 – In small fry pan add 1 tsp. olive oil and sauté onions and garlic.

3 – Boil water for pasta and cook.

4 – Grill chicken breasts on barbecue.

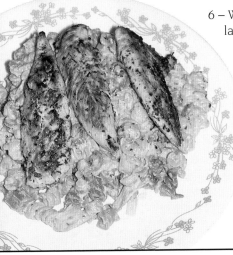

5 – Cook broccoli in microwave for 8 minutes.

6 – When all ingredients are cooked combine in a large pot over medium heat.

7 – Add the drained pasta, broccoli, sautéed onions and garlic in large pot.

8 – Add the mozzarella, cheddar, parmesan and milk.

9 – Place cooked breasts in oven to keep warm.

10 – Stir ingredients over heat until cheese has melted and has good consistency.

11 – Serve with chicken breast over the pasta.

Braised North African Snook

Café L' Europe

Ingredients:

4 - 8 ounce Snook fillets
2 ounces olive oil
flour for dredging
salt and pepper

2 tablespoons herbs d' provençe
8 ounces Riesling
2 tablespoons honey
4 ounces butter

Directions:

1 – Dredge and season snook fillets with flour, salt and pepper, and herbs d' provençe.

2 – Sauté in olive oil until brown on one side.

3 – Turn and finish in a 350-degree oven for 5-8 minutes.

4 – Return pan to stove and deglaze with Riesling.

5 – Add honey and allow to simmer for two minutes on low heat.

6 – When almost all the liquid has been reduced add the butter and swirl in.

7 – Serve on pasta.

Makes 4 Servings.

Michael Garey
General Manager
Café L' Europe

Michael Garey was born and raised in Buffalo, New York. He moved to Sarasota Florida as a teenager and began in the restaurant business as a busboy in 1977. In 1979 he started as a busboy at the Café L' Europe. Moving up the ladder, he became a dining room captain in 1981 and assistant manager in 1982. In 1984, he left Café L' Europe to help open and manage Mr. Wong's Chinese restaurant. Michael came back to Café L' Europe in 1986 as General Manager, the title that he holds today. Mr. Garey is currently President of the St. Armands Merchants Assoc. and conceived and organized two events for the Florida Wine Festival, the Wine Marker's Dinner, and Sip and Shop. He is married to his wife Catherine and has three daughters, Alexandra, Jenna and Amelia.

Mike Rezac

Firemedic
Sarasota County
Fire Department

Mike is a 10 year veteran Firefighter/EMT currently working out of Station 5 on B-shift. Mike was born in Czechoslovakia and speaks fluent Czech, Polish, and English. Before becoming a firemedic, he followed in his father's footsteps as a jeweler. He still works on his off days in their family jeweler business. His hobbies are skiing, diving, and art. He has two grown children, Angela and Michael Jr., and a nine month old grandson Cameron. He and his wife Giovanna, are expecting a baby in June. When asked what he values most in life, Mike said, "Faith in God, and family."

Tangerine Chicken Stir-Fry

Mike Rezac — Firemedic

Ingredients:

1 pound boneless chicken
3 tablespoons peanut oil
2 tablespoons soy sauce
1 tablespoon & 2 teaspoons cornstarch
1 large red or green bell pepper
1 bunch scallions

4 slices fresh ginger
2 tablespoons ketchup
1 can (11 ounce) mandarin oranges
3/4 cup beef broth

Directions:

1 – Cut chicken into 2" wide strips and cross cut into 1/4" slices. Place chicken in a bowl.

2 – Add 1 tablespoon each of soy sauce, oil, cornstarch, and mix.

3 – Cut bell pepper, scallions, and any other optional veggies (ie…water chestnuts) into squares. Slice ginger.

4 – In a bowl, stir together beef broth, ketchup, and remaining 2 teaspoons cornstarch and 1 tablespoon of soy sauce.

5 – In a large skillet or wok, heat 1 tablespoon oil until very hot.

6 – Once hot, add chicken with marinade and stir-fry until it is almost done. Take out and set aside.

7 – Add 1 tablespoon oil, bell peppers, scallions, ginger, and any other veggies you may be using. Stir-fry until scallions wilt.

8 – Return chicken to skillet and stir in broth.

9 – Bring liquid to a boil. It will start to thicken when done.

10 – Add drained oranges.

11 – Before serving, discard ginger slices.

Makes 4 Servings.

Sweet Potato Crusted Snapper

Sarasota University Club

Ingredients:

2 – 6 ounce snapper filets
2 tablespoons oil
1 sweet potato washed and grated
4 ounces crawfish (you may substitute shrimp or lobster)
1 small yellow pepper diced
1/2 small red bell pepper diced
1 small red onion diced
4 ounce can stewed tomatoes roughly chopped with liquid
2 cloves garlic smashed and chopped
2 tablespoons chili seasoning mix heaping
1/4 cup black beans cooked, washed and drained
2 dashes Tabasco
pinch red pepper flakes
salt and pepper to taste
2 ounces Brandy

Directions:

1 – Cover snapper with grated sweet potatoes, about 1/4'" thick.

2 – Sear potato side down in a hot sauté pan with oil, until golden brown. Turn over and cook for 1 minute. Take off heat and place in baking pan. Set aside until chili sauce is complete.

3 – In the same pan as snapper was sautéed in, place onions, peppers, and garlic. Sauté until translucent.

4 – Add crawfish, black beans and brandy. Flame off alcohol.

5 – Add stewed tomatoes and liquid, Tabasco, chili seasoning and red pepper flakes, bring to boil, then to simmer.

6 – Add salt and pepper to taste, set aside.

7 – Finish potato crusted snapper in a 350 degree oven for approximately 10 minutes.

8 – Separate chili onto two plates and place snapper on top of chili.

Makes 2 Servings.

Frank Hagaman, Jr.
Line Chef
Sarasota University Club

Joining the University Club kitchen team in Spring 2000, Frank brings strong culinary skills to satisfy a quality demanding membership. Frank's background includes a degree in Culinary Arts from the New England Culinary Institute and over eight years of practical restaurant experience. If you're looking for a recipe to truly impress friends, this Sweet Potato Crusted Snapper is it. Easy to prepare and a visual temptation, even your finicky fish eaters will not turn this down.

Dan Rankin
Firefighter/EMT
SCFD

After serving three years with the Nokomis Fire Department as a volunteer, Dan Rankin, was hired by Sarasota County Fire Department and has been serving as a Firefighter/EMT for two years. Dan loves the fire service and is greeted warmly wherever he rides. His culinary talents were put to the test in his first few shifts winning the heart of his peers via their tummies. Dan says his greatest challenge in firehouse cooking is to create five-bugle meals at rookie pay prices! Dan is married to his wife of three years, Monica. He enjoys art, playing guitar and bagpipes, paintball, trail biking, and martial arts in his off duty hours.

Italian Stuffed Meatloaf

Dan Rankin — Firefighter/EMT

Ingredients:

6 pounds ground chuck
3/4 pound capicola (sliced very thin and diced)
2 tablespoons oregano
1 teaspoon salt
1 teaspoon basil
1 teaspoon garlic powder
1 teaspoon black pepper
2 tablespoons olive oil
4 cups marinara sauce

1 cup diced white onion
1 1/2 cups diced green & red pepper
2 cups sliced mushrooms
1/2 cup red cooking wine
5 large eggs
1 pound shredded mozzarella cheese
2 cups Italian bread crumbs
1 tablespoon chopped parsley
1 teaspoon paprika

Directions:

1 – Heat 2 tablespoons of olive oil in a medium sauté pan.
2 – Add diced white onions, mushrooms, and bell peppers.
3 – Bring to a simmer and add oregano, garlic, basil, and black pepper and cook completely. Let stand.
4 – Next, in a large mixing bowl, beat 5 large eggs. Add ground beef, 1 1/2 cups of marinara sauce and 2 cups of Italian breadcrumbs. Mix well. (Add more breadcrumbs if needed to give a workable texture).
5 – Place ground beef on a large cookie sheet and form into a loaf. Form a pocket in the loaf by cutting a line lengthwise down loaf, approximately 1" from bottom. Fillet out from center to the left and right.
6 – Combine peppers, mushrooms, onions and capicola with 3/4 pound shredded cheese. Fill loaf with ingredients. (Set some aside to garnish).
7 – Fold sides in and pinch together.
8 – Lay another cookie sheet on top of loaf and flip over so the seam is down.
9 – Cook for 45 minutes to 1 hour @ 350 degrees. (Cook time may vary with different ovens) Check loaf after 45 minutes until done using a meat thermometer.
10 – When loaf has cooked completely, top with remaining sauce, cheese and sprinkle with paprika and parsley. Heat until cheese melts.

Beachnut Grouper

Beach House Restaurant

Ingredients:

2 – 8 ounce filet of fresh grouper
1 ounce chopped cashews
1 ounce chopped peanuts
1 ounce chopped pecans
Basic egg wash consisting of 1 part
    eggs to 3 parts milk – whisked
Flour for dusting
3 ounces olive oil or peanut oil

FRUIT SALSA:
1/2 cup pineapple, diced
1/2 small red onion, diced
1/2 cup mango or papaya, diced
3 pieces scallions, diced, mostly green
1 teaspoon fresh chopped cilantro
1/4 cup red bell pepper, diced
1 teaspoons olive oil
1/2 lime, zested and juiced
1 teaspoon salt (optional)

Directions:

FRUIT SALSA:
1- Mix all ingredients in a mixing bowl and chill.

BEACHNUT GROUPER:
1 – In a large sauté Pan, heat the oil.

2 – Dust the fish in the flour, dip in the egg wash and roll in the mixed nuts.

3 – Gently place in the hot skillet and lightly brown on one side. Turn over and place in a 400 degree pre-heated oven for approximately 8-9 minutes.

4 – Remove from pan and pat dry.

5 – Top with the fruit salsa and serve with your favorite starch and vegetable.

6 – "Bon Appetite"

Makes 2 Servings.

Will Manson
Kitchen Manager
Beach House Restaurant

Will Manson, Kitchen Manager at the Beach House is a native of Bradenton where he and his family have strong ties to the community. Will first worked for the Sandbar in 1986 as a Line Cook and by then the art of great cuisine was in his blood. He took a three-year hiatus to attend The Culinary Institute of America where he earned an Associates Degree in Occupational Studies in Culinary Arts. Will rejoined the Chiles Restaurant Group in 1997, currently at the Beach House, and is really showing off his skills with fresh native seafood.

Marc Hassard
Fighterfighter/EMT
SCFD

Marc has been in the fire service for over 12 years and has spent all of that time with the Sarasota County Fire Department, loving every minute of it. "To have a career where you can personally make a difference is tremendously rewarding," he says. He also has enjoyed working part-time for the Suncoast Communities Blood Bank for the past 10 years. Between the two professions, he says he has the satisfaction of knowing he's helping and protecting the citizens of Sarasota County. When asked about life Marc replies, "God has truly blessed me with my wonderful wife, Lisa, two great daughters, Amy and Alison, and two careers that give a sense of purpose and fulfillment."

"Hassard-ous Italian Fish Fillets"

Marc Hassard – Fighterfighter/EMT

Ingredients:

4 – fillets flounder fillets
   (or choice of fish)
16 oz. Italian bread crumbs
4 tbs. butter or margarine
2 tbs. parmesan cheese

2 tbs oregano
1 tbs. Italian seasoning
pinch garlic salt
pinch salt
olive oil

Directions:

1 – Thoroughly dry off fillets, and set aside.

2 – In a mixing bowl, combine all ingredients except butter and olive oil, and mix thoroughly by hand.

3 – Take dry fillets and spread butter onto both sides.

4 – Then place fillets into the bread crumb mixture and press firmly on both sides (to assure even coating).

5 – Using a non-stick frying pan, pour enough oil in bottom of pan to completely cover it.

6 – Heat pan to just boiling point of oil.

7 – Place fillets in heated oil until breading is golden brown (thicker fillets will take a little longer to cook thoroughly).

8 – Serve hot with your favorite rice dish and vegetable.

Makes 4 Servings.

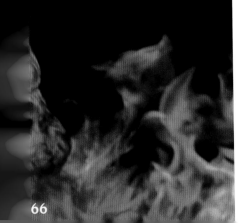

Asian Pasta Cake

The Colony Restaurants

Ingredients:

1 pound angel hair pasta, cooked
2 eggs (4ounces), beaten
2 teaspoons ginger, minced
1/4 cup scallions, minced

2 teaspoons garlic, minced
2 ounces sesame oil
2 ounces soy sauce
1/2 cup shiitake mushrooms, sliced

Directions:

1 – Combine all ingredients except the eggs and
let flavors incorporate into pasta.

2 – For service, mix 3 ounces of pasta with a small amount
of the egg mixture and toss.

3 – Place on a hot griddle and sauté on both sides.

Tom Klauber
Food & Beverage Director
The Colony Restaurants

The Colony's Director of Food & Beverage Operations Tom Klauber is also Chef/Proprietor of Longboat Key's popular Pattigeorge's restaurant. Tom began his culinary career by working at his family's resort, later attending the University of Houston's Hotel & Management School, and earning a degree from the Culinary Institute of America. He then traveled and studied abroad, receiving his diploma from La Varenne's Ecole de Cuisine in Paris, France. He gained experience in fine restaurants in Paris, Florence and Amsterdam before returning to The Colony, where he worked as executive chef and food and beverage director from 1982 to 1992. Prior to opening PGs in 1998, Tom was chef/owner at Gieusseppi Wong in Aspen.

Tom Klauber has received numerous accolades, including being recognized in "Chefs in America" as one of the outstanding chefs in the United States, and receiving the James Beard Foundation "Rising Stars of American Cuisine" Award.

the Colony Restaurants

Monday – Saturday
Lunch: 11:30 AM To 2:30 PM
Dinner: 6:00 PM To 10:00 PM
Sunday Brunch:
10:00 AM To 2:00 PM

941-383-5558
1620 Gulf of Mexico Drive
Longboat Key

• • •

Enjoy an award-winning dining experience complemented by an unparalleled wine list with *spectacular* views of the Gulf of Mexico.

- **Prestigious DiRoNA Award**
- **The Wine Spectator's Award of Excellence**
- **Five Star Diamond Award for outstanding hospitality from the American Academy of Hospitality Sciences**
- **Member of Nation's Restaurant News Fine Dining Hall of Fame**

Joe Patek
Dive Rescue Team, Instructor, Last Original Haz Mat Team Member
Venice Fire Department

Joe was born and raised in New York City. He worked for Honeywell Protection before moving to Florida in search of more meaningful employment. Joe put himself through fire school and in his last week of class was offered a position with Venice Fire and accepted. In the 23 years he's been with Venice, he's become a member of the Dive Rescue Team, an instructor, and is the last original Haz Mat Team member. He is proud to have the responsibility of managing the "Youth Fire Setter Program." He and Eileen have enjoyed 25 years of marriage and have two children, Jami and Chris. His daughter, Jami, is heading to FAU this fall. He and his son, Chris, enjoy martial arts and both are black belts.

S.C.T.I. firefighter students getting LPG gas training.

Salmon Steaks Dinner Made Easy

Joe Patek — Dive Rescue Team, Instructor,
Last Original Haz Mat Team Member

Ingredients:

8 ounce salmon steak (per person)
2 cups onion slices
4 cups squash slices
4 cups tomato slices
salt - to taste

pepper – to taste
cilantro flakes – to taste
4 tablespoons olive oil
2 tablespoons butter

Directions:

1 – For each salmon steak 2 pieces of 12"x12" of aluminum foil is needed.

2 – Put 2 tablespoons of olive oil and 1 tablespoon of butter on sheet of foil.

3 – Place salmon steak on oiled and buttered and spiced foil.

4 – Surround salmon with onion slices, tomato slices, and squash slices.

5 – Repeat step 2 to top of salmon steak.

6 – Place 2nd sheet of foil on top and "roll seal" ends of foil to make a package.

7 – Grill on medium 5 minutes each side, or covered pan on medium, 5 minutes each side.

8 – Rice or bread can also be served with this meal if desired.

Chicken Kavala

Café L' Europe

Ingredients:

4-8 ounce chicken breast with skin on
4 ounce jumbo lump crabmeat
8 large spinach leaves
4 ounce feta cheese
2 ounce olive oil
flour for dredging
salt and pepper

1 shallot
1/2 cup Vermouth
1 lemon
4 ounces heavy cream
8 ounces soft butter
1 tablespoon chopped cilantro

Directions:

1 – Lightly pound chicken breast with meat mallet until about 1/4 inch thin. When pounding keep skin side down. Season with salt and pepper.

2 – Place 2 spinach leaves on chicken, then top with the appropriate amount of crabmeat and feta. Roll up tightly and reserve.

3 – Chop shallot fine and sauté in a small saucepan until translucent.

4 – Deglaze with Vermouth and juice in 1 lemon. Reduce by 1/2. Add in cream and reduce by 1/2.

5 – Stir in butter and add chopped cilantro. Season with salt and pepper and reserve sauce in a warm place.

6 – In a hot sauté pan drizzle in olive oil.

7 – Dredge chicken in flour and sauté on one side until brown. Turn and place in a 350 degree oven for 15 minutes.

8 – Remove from oven when done and let rest for 5 minutes.

9 – Slice and place on plate. Drizzle with sauce.

Makes 10 Servings.

Jeff Trefry
Executive Chef
Café L' Europe

Upon graduation from the prestigious Culinary Institute of America, Jeff moved west to Santa Barbara, California and worked as a pastry chef for the El Encanto Hotel. To broaden his knowledge of the culinary arts and hone his skills, Jeff moved east and spent three years at Café L' Europe in the early 1980's. Jeff's career path led him to the Five-Star Five-Diamond Ritz Carlton Resort in Naples and he was promoted to Executive Sous Chef. In 1989, promotion placed Jeff as Executive Chef in charge of culinary operations at the Ritz Carlton in Kansas City, Mo. He then worked in Bermuda and Hilton Head Island, S.C. but is now back with Café L' Europe as Executive Chef. Jeff executes New European Cuisine with his own imagination and personal style. He is married to Janet and has three children – Megan, Jack and Mike.

Debbie Calvert
Firefighter/Paramedic
SCFD

Debbie Calvert or "Sharkbait," which she is nicknamed, is like the fish she catches for this recipe! She loves the water and enthusiastically enjoys all watersports. Her nickname, Sharkbait, is for when she is spearing fish; one must watch out for that 12 foot Bull shark that is hungrier than you. An avid scuba diver, Debbie says this recipe is simple and great after a long day of diving. Friends show up out of the woodwork when they know Debbie had a good day on the boat. Her friends are familiar with her blackened fish delight! When not on duty as a firefighter/-paramedic with Sarasota County Fire Department, Debbie loves renting sailboats. She is quite the adventurer, also, taking pleasure in traveling to exotic places and exploring islands that most people don't know exist.

Blackened Fish with Mango Salsa
Debbie Calvert (Hunter/Gatherer) — Firefighter/Paramedic

Ingredients:

1 boat
1 scuba gear
1 spear gun (hunter)
1 filet knife
1 seasoned cast iron skillet
fresh fish of your choice
   (grouper, snapper, flounder)

1 stick butter
Chef Paul Prudhomme's red fish magic
1 unripe mango-off neighbor's tree (gatherer)
1 small onion
2-3 tablespoons sugar
salt
pepper

Directions:

FISH:1 – Fish must be fresh. (I like to spear my own.)
2 – Melt 3/4 stick of butter and dip fish in butter.
3 – Sprinkle Paul Prudhomme's blackening seasoning over fish. (Generously sprinkle seasoning if you like it spicy.)
4 – Be sure to cook outside. Heat skillet until it is almost white with heat. Throw fish on skillet (very smoky). When you see white on the side of the fish, approximately 4 minutes, flip the fish with a spatula. Depending on the thickness of the filet, fish will be done when flaky and white throughout. Do not overcook.

MANGO SALSA: 1 – The sweetness of the salsa compliments the spicy fish. Peel and chop a mango into small cubes.
2 – In small sauté pan, melt 1/4 stick of butter.
3 – Chop 1 small onion.
4 – Add onion and mango to pan. Add a dash of salt and pepper.
5 – When onion starts to become transparent, add 2 tablespoons sugar. This will make it start to be sticky.
6 – When mango is tender yet still slightly firm and sweet, the salsa is done.
7 – Serve blackened fish with a large drop of salsa on top.

Fish and salsa serves 4.

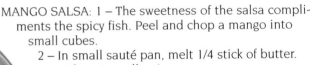

Mussels a la Provencal

Sarasota University Club

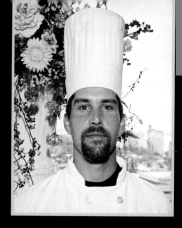

Ingredients:

1 Medium Red Bell Pepper, diced
1 Medium Yellow Bell Pepper, diced
2 Large Vine Ripe Tomatoes, diced
4 Green Onions, chopped
4 Cloves Garlic, chopped
1/2 cup White Wine
4 ounces Whole Butter, cubed 1/2 inch

2 Pinches of Sea or Kosher
  Salt or Pepper to Season
20 Blue or Common Mussels, about
  11/4-11/2 pounds. (Be sure all are closed
  and fresh.) Available year round from
  your local fish market. (New Zealand
  green mussels may be substituted.)

Directions:

1 – In medium saucepan, add 1 cube butter, chopped garlic and the red and yellow peppers. Sauté on high for 2 minutes.

2 – Reduce heat to medium, add mussels first. Then add onions, tomatoes, lemon juice and white wine.

3 – At this point, you can add your favorite seafood to create your own "fruits of the sea"

4 – Cover and cook for 10 minutes or until all mussels are open (discard any unopened mussels).

5 – When all mussels are open, stir in remaining cubed butter and season with salt and pepper. Serve from pot it was cooked in.

6 – You may also ladle the seafood and mussels over your favorite pasta.

Makes 2-4 Servings.

John R. Halling
Executive Chef
Sarasota University Club

Recently taking charge of the Sarasota University Club kitchen, Chef John brings a combination of classic French, International cuisine and traditional Florida cooking styles. Formerly of Francoise et Henri, Cape Codder Hotel in Cape Cod, and Bayou Bills, Treasure Island Florida. These and other Chef positions have allowed Chef John a wide range of experience to please many different palates. The recipes that Chef John presents are some of his personal favorites. Chef John finds them easy to prepare and very flavorful. The Sarasota University Club hopes you enjoy these recipes and they provide many enjoyable dining experiences.

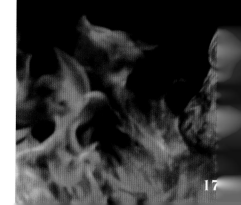

(Page number)

Dave Edmonds
Battalion Chief, S.C.F.D.

Dave was born in Eagle River, Wisconsin. He moved to Sarasota, Florida, and was in construction work when the recession nearly stopped building. He applied with the Sarasota Fire Department in 1974 and was hired. Dave fell in love with the job and teaching. He became a respected instructor who taught new recruits at the Sarasota County Vo-Tech Fire Academy for more than 20 years. Dave worked his way up through the ranks to the position of Battalion Chief.

Dave is looking forward to another challenge as he nears retirement with Sarasota and begins as Fire Chief of Boca Grande in November of 1999.

Dave has two grown children and a stepdaughter. He enjoys spending his free time with his wife, Lynn, and fishing.

2000 E-One 95' Elevating platform assigned to station 1; pictured with Keith's nephew, Daniel Durrance, in the "ladder" part of the day.

Spicy Shrimp
David R. Edmonds — Battalion Chief

Ingredients:

1/2 pound butter (2 sticks)
1/2 cup onion, chopped
1 cup mushrooms
3 cloves garlic, chopped
1/2 teaspoon red pepper
1/2 teaspoon black pepper
1/2 teaspoon white pepper
1/2 teaspoon thyme

1/2 teaspoon rosemary, crushed
1/2 teaspoon whole oregano
1 teaspoon parsley
1 tablespoon Worcestershire sauce
1 pound peeled and deveined
   medium shrimp
1/2 cup chicken broth
1/2 cup red wine or beer

Directions:

1 – Melt one stick of butter in a large skillet.

2 – Sauté onion until clear, then add the next 10 items, cook 1 minute, stirring continually.

3 – Add shrimp and cook 2 to 3 minutes, stirring constantly.

4 – Add remainder of butter and chicken broth, and cook 2 minutes or until hot.

5 – Stir in wine or beer and cook 1 minute.

6 – Remove from heat.

7 – Serve with yellow rice or linguine pasta. Garlic bread and peas accompany this quite well, also.

Makes 2 – 3 Servings.

Penne A La Vodka

Café on the Bay

Ingredients:

1 pound penne pasta cooked
12 ounces tomato sauce
8 ounces heavy cream

6 ounces diced prosciutto
8 ounces Asiago cheese
4 ounces Vodka

Directions:

1 – In large sauté pan, heat tomato sauce and vodka.

2 – Toss pasta in sauce until hot.

3 – Add heavy cream and prosciutto.

4 – Finish with cheese.

Makes 4 Servings.

941-383-0440

**2630 Harbourside Dr.
Longboat Key, FL 34228**

Breakfast Saturday
8:30 AM To 10:30 AM

Sunday Breakfast Brunch
9:00 AM To 1:00 PM

Sunday Lunch
1:00 PM To 3:30 PM

Lunch 6 Days
11:00 AM To 3:00 PM

Dinner 7 Days
4:30 PM To 10:00 PM

Extraordinary cuisine served in a
truly exquisite waterfront setting.
Come by land or sea.
Casual attire is welcomed.

Café on the Bay

Nestled in the Longboat Key
Moorings, along beautiful
Sarasota Bay, sits Longboat
Key's Hidden Gem…Café on
the Bay. Elegant yet casual,
her charm beckons seafarers
and landlubbers alike for
breakfast, lunch or dinner.
You will delight in an offering
of extraordinary cuisine.
Enjoy the indoor dining room
or the covered outdoor terrace, both featuring spectacular marina and bay views.
Or you may simply wish to
enjoy your favorite cocktail or
one of our own exotic creations at our Marker 15
Lounge. This is one "Port o'
Call" you will wish to visit
over and over again! Inquire
about our sunset special and
the pre-fixed dinner offering.
Breakfast Saturday
8:30 AM – 10:30 AM
Sunday Breakfast Brunch
9:00 AM – 1:00 PM
Sunday Lunch
1:00 PM – 3:30 PM
Lunch 11:00 AM – 3:00 PM
Dinner 4:30 PM – 10:00 PM
In the Longboat Key
Moorings Marina behind
Publix – right out of guard
gate, second left.

1

Millie Bradley

Fire Training Secretary - SCFD

Millie was born in New York City. As an only child, she was very close to her father. She credits him with her love for the outdoors, fishing, and hunting. One of her favorite memories dates back to a 1966 morning when she shot a 7-point Whitetail at 7:30 A.M.

Millie and Edward were married 37 years ago and have two grown daughters, Christine and Diane), and two poodles (Cindy and Snoopy).

Millie's family relocated to Florida in 1982, and in 1985 she joined S.C.F.D. as a secretary. She is right hand to the Chief of Training and nothing gets to him unless it goes by her. Millie is affectionately nicknamed "Chief Millie" by the firefighters she's helped raise.

Veal Chops Hungarian

Millie Bradley — Fire Training Secretary, SCFD

Ingredients:

6 Veal chops, rib or loin, cut 3/4" thick
1/4 cup flour
1 teaspoon salt
1/2 teaspoon Accent
1/4 teaspoon pepper
2 –3 tablespoons fat
1/2 cup onion, chopped
1/2 teaspoon paprika
1/2 cup hot water

3 cups (about 4 ounces) broad noodles

FOR GRAVY:
1 cup sour cream
2 tablespoons water
1 tablespoon paprika
1/2 teaspoon salt
1/2 teaspoon Accent
1/8 teaspoon pepper

Directions:

1 – Set out a large, heavy skillet having a tight fitting cover.
2 – Wipe with a clean, damp cloth the veal chops.
3 – Coat chops evenly with a mixture of flour, salt, Accent, and pepper.
4 – Heat 2-3 tablespoons of fat in the skillet over medium heat.
5 – Add the chops and brown evenly on both sides.

6 – Spoon onion over chops, sprinkle with paprika and add hot water to skillet.
7 – Cover skillet tightly. Simmer over low heat 45 minutes or until chops are tender when pierced with a fork.
8 – Meanwhile, cook and drain noodles.
9 – Remove chops to hot platter. Remove skillet from heat.
10 – For Gravy: mix together sour cream, water and a mixture of paprika, salt, Accent, pepper. Pour into skillet and set over low heat. Heat thoroughly, stirring constantly. Do not boil.
11 – Toss the drained noodles with butter or margarine.
12 – Arrange noodles around chops. Spoon the gravy over the chops. Serve at once.

Makes 6 Servings.

Penne with Pork Loin and Celery Sauce

Munroe's Restaurant

Ingredients:

4 ounces cooked penne pasta
4 ounces roasted pork loin, sliced
1 stalk celery, sliced
4 ounces celery root, sliced
2 ounces onion chopped
1 teaspoon whole grain mustard

1 teaspoon capers
1 lemon, juice of
1 tablespoon olive oil
1/2 teaspoon minced garlic
1/2 teaspoon salt & pepper

Directions:

1 – Sauté pork loin and celery root in olive oil to heat.
Add onion and celery.

2 – Add all other ingredients and toss well,
cook approximately 2 minutes.

3 – Finish with fresh lemon juice.

Richard Munroe
Chef/Proprietor
Munroe's Restaurant

Locals and seasonal visitors alike enjoy the bistro setting of Munroe's Restaurant. Proven to be Sarasota's favorite restaurant with casual elegance, friendly service, and creative, American foods.

Whether you start off your meal with one of our famous appetizers or finish with one of our colorful desserts, you won't go away disappointed.

For the late night guest, we offer live entertainment upstairs, with a late night menu and premium bar.

177

Will "Big Will" Hartley

Fire Lieutenant
SCFD

Will is a 13 year veteran who has spent nearly his entire career in two of the busiest stations in Sarasota County Fire Department. Since becoming a Firefighter/EMT, Will has learned to cook quite well. The "Big-House Enchiladas" has become a B-shift favorite when he cooks. Interestingly enough, with his recent promotion, Will has taken the helm at Station #11-B "The Big House" as Fire Lieutenant. Seldom does a member of a crew become its leader. He enjoys spending his off-duty time with three ladies...his wife, Kathy, and daughters Erika and Caitlin. Will is an avid hunter and kingfisher. He savors attending "Buccaneer's" home games. GO BUCS!

Will's "Big House" Chicken Enchiladas

Will Hartley – Fire Lieutenant

Ingredients:

8 – 10 ounce boneless, skinless chicken breasts
2 – 32 ounce jars of salsa (prefer Chi-Chi's or Pace)
2 – 12 ounce bags Mexican 4-cheese blend, shredded
10 – 12 large flour tortillas

2 tablespoons cooking oil
2 teaspoons seasoning salt (to taste – prefer Lawry's)

OPTIONAL:
hot sauce (to taste)
16 ounce sour cream

Directions:

1 – Rinse chicken and cube.
2 – Heat cooking oil in 12" non-stick frying pan.
3 – Sauté chicken in pan, adding seasoning to taste.
4 – When chicken is cooked, add 3/4 of 1 bottle of salsa to chicken and heat on a medium heat.
5 – Add 1 bag of cheese to mix and stir in until melted. Remove from heat.
6 – Grease 2 large oven safe baking dishes (approximately 9"x14").
7 – Spoon remaining salsa from first jar on bottom of baking pans. Lay out tortillas and spoon enchilada mix onto tortillas evenly.

8 – Roll up tortillas and place in baking dish seam side down. 5-6 enchiladas per pan, centered.
9 – Pre-heat oven to 350 degrees.
10 – Divide remaining jar of salsa, pouring 1/2 over each pan of enchiladas. Divide remaining cheese and sprinkle 1/2 over each pans content.
11 – Place in oven and bake 20 minutes, or until cheese is melted. Remove from pan with spatula and serve with sour cream and hot sauce, if desired.
TIPS: Don't be afraid to use too much salsa or cheese on top or below enchiladas, it helps keep enchiladas from drying out.

Makes 10 Servings (Or 5 – 6 Firemen).

Scallops Mar Vista

Mar Vista Dockside Restaurant & Pub

Ingredients:

7 – 8 medium to large sea scallops
1 ounce sliced butter Mushrooms
2 ounces artichoke hearts
1 – 2 ounces dry white wine
1/4 teaspoon fresh chopped parsley
1/4 teaspoon fresh chopped garlic
1-1/2 ounce Olive oil
1/2 ounce garlic butter (see recipe)

GARLIC BUTTER:
1 stick softened butter
1/4 ounce chopped or pureed garlic
1/4 ounce chopped or pureed shallots
1 teaspoon salt
1 teaspoon white pepper
1 small bunch chopped parsley

Brian Miner

Kitchen Manager & Chef
Mar Vista Dockside
Restaurant & Pub

Brian Miner has seen a great deal of our country for a young man of 26. He was born and raised in Anchorage, Alaska and attended college at Mesa State in Grand Junction, Colorado. He moved to Florida in 1994 and shortly thereafter began as a Server with the Beach House Restaurant eventually becoming a Bartender and Server at the Sandbar Restaurant. Brian's interest quickly turned to the creative side of food preparation and many of his skills have been self-taught. When his cooking skills were discovered, Mar Vista was fortunate to be able to put them to use. Brian's goal is to return to school for a degree in Culinary Arts. In the mean time he enjoys fishing the local waters and most of all his hobby of photography.

Directions:

GARLIC BUTTER:

1 – Soften butter in mixing bowl, add remaining ingredients and mix with a wire whip until smooth.

2 – Reserve in room temperature or refrigerate. You may freeze remaining butter.

SCALLOPS:

1 – In medium sauté pan heat oil. When almost smoking, add scallops turning once when brown.

2 – Add mushrooms and toss with scallops approximately 1 minute.

3 – Add artichoke hearts and white wine. Reduce the wine and finish with the garlic butter.

4 – Place in serving dish or bowl with pasta (optional), and serve.

Makes 1 Serving.

941-383-2391

**760 Broadway
Longboat Key**

**Lunch 11:30 AM To 5 PM Daily
Dinner 5 PM To 10 PM Sun-Thurs
Dinner 5 PM To 10:30 PM Fri & Sat**

A Taste of Old Florida

Indoor & Outdoor Dining on the Water!

Grilled Lobster with Key Lime Butter

Chad Gamble — Firefighter/EMT

Chad Gamble (right)
Firefighter/EMT
Braden River Fire Department

Friend & Co-worker, Goose (left)

This is Chad Gamble's first year as a Firefighter/EMT with the Braden River Fire Department. He enjoys water sports, especially fishing, diving, and underwater photography. Family, his girlfriend, Jimmy Buffet and the sea are what Chad loves most in life.

About the recipe he says, "This recipe is an easy way to make a meal at a campsite or on the boat in the Florida Keys. It seems to even taste better in the keys, listening to Jimmy Buffet of course."

Ingredients:

4 Florida spiny lobster tails
4 sprigs fresh basil leaves
1 tablespoon Old Bay seasoning

4-5 key limes
4 tablespoons salted butter

Directions:

1 – Cut tails down the middle with flippers on the bottom.

2 – Sprinkle with Old Bay and cover meat with basil leaves to seal in flavor.

3 – Melt butter with juice of one key lime.

4 – Grill lobster on medium heat with fins down on a baking pan for 8-10 minutes, depending on size of tails once meat is opaque all the way through. Remove from heat.

5 – Serve with fresh lime and lime butter.

Makes 4 Servings.

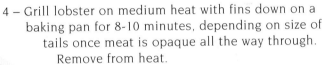

Porchetta Osso Bucco

Café L' Europe

Ingredients:

4 – 1 pound pork shanks
1/2 cup olive oil
5 cloves slivered garlic
2 sprigs fresh rosemary
1/4 cup paprika
2 tablespoons salt
2 tablespoons black pepper
1/4 cup orange zest

2 carrots diced small
4 celery stalks diced small
1 onion diced small
1 cup red wine
1/4 cup tomato paste
4 cups chicken stock
1 cup cooked orecchiette pasta

Directions:

1 – Rub pork shanks with olive oil, garlic, rosemary, paprika, salt, pepper, and orange zest.

2 – Allow to set overnight in the refrigerator.

3 – The next day in a large braising pan, sear the shanks until brown on all sides.

4 – Deglaze the pan with red wine. Stir to dissolve. Add carrots, onion, celery and chicken stock.

5 – Cover with foil tightly and cook in a 350-degree oven for 2 1/2 hours or until tender.

6 – Remove from pan and season pan juices.

7 – Place in large bowls with pasta and pour pan juices over the top.

Makes 4 Servings.

Café L' Europe

Now celebrating its twenty seventh anniversary, Café L' Europe continues to be one of Sarasota's most beautiful and popular restaurants. A multitude of awards have been received over the years from such publications as The Wine Spectator, Sante' Award of Excellence and Florida Trend as well as the prestigious DIRONA award; bearing witness to the high quality of food. Pleasing aromas and beautiful presentations preview the finest of Continental Cuisine and New European Cuisine from elaborate appetizers to elegant entrees and truly decadent desserts. Completing the scene is a superb selection of wines from the finest vineyards of Europe and California. The final ingredient essential to fine dining is the high level of professional service. The warm welcome on arrival hints at the care taken by every person at Café L' Europe to ensure your dining pleasure.

Wayne A. Welsh
Fire Lieutenant/Paramedic
Special Operations Team
SCFD

Wayne A. Welsh is a Lieutenant/Paramedic with the Sarasota County Fire Department and is on the Special Operations team. He's been with the fire service for 18 years and definitely knows his history when it comes to the Sarasota Fire Department. He is the published author of *Buckets and Brawn; The History of Sarasota and Its Fire Department*! However, more important to him is his 15-year old daughter and family. On his off-duty days, Wayne is an outdoors adventurer and enjoys scuba diving and wilderness backpacking. When asked about this recipe, he replies, "My mother always cooked our favorite dinner on our birthday and this was mine!"

"Millennium Boot drive."

Chinese Pepper Steak
Wayne A. Welsh — Fire Lieutenant/Paramedic

Ingredients:

1 tablespoon soy sauce
1 clove garlic or garlic salt
1/4 cup vegetable oil
1 pound round steak cut into 1" cubes
1 green pepper cut into 1" cubes

1 large onion coarsely chopped
1/2 cup celery diced
1 tablespoon cornstarch
1/2 cup water
2 tomatoes cut into eighths

Directions:

1 – Mix soy sauce, garlic, and vegetable oil together: pour over steak cubes and let stand 1 hour in refrigerator.

2 – Pour into deep pot and allow meat to thoroughly brown on all sides.

3 – Add green pepper, onion, and celery.

4 – Cover and cook 10 minutes over low heat or until vegetables are tender.

5 – Dissolve cornstarch in water and stir into pot.

6 – Add tomatoes, cover, and cook 5-10 minutes more or until meat is tender.

7 – Serve over boiled white rice.

Makes 4 Servings.

Stuffed Filletto with Lobster & Prosciutto

Osteria Northern Italian Restaurant

Ingredients:

8 ounces Filet Mignon
4 ounces Lobster tail
2 slices of Prosciutto (paper thin)
2 ounces Brandy

4 ounces demiglace
2 ounces Chicken stock
salt & pepper
1 ounce heavy cream

Directions:

1 – Portion 2 filets to 4 ounces.

2 – Use paring knife to cut a star shape in the center of the filet.

3 – Blanche lobster meat in boiling salted water.

4 – Cook lobster meat and stuff in center of the filet.

5 – Wrap the filet with prosciutto and secure with toothpicks.

6 – Season filet with salt & pepper in hot pan.

7 – Sear the filet for 2 minutes on each side.

8 – Finish in 350 degree oven to desired temperature.

9 – Remove pan from oven, deglaze with brandy, add demiglace, chicken stock and cream.

10 – Reduce 5 minutes.

Makes 2 Servings.

Lee Guidry
Chef
Osteria Northern
Italian Restaurant

The Casadio family has consistently served the very best in authentic Northern Italian cuisine for over 15 years. Pasta, seafood, veal, chicken and lamb are amongst the specialties along with fine wines. This charming St. Armands restaurant is also known for the impeccable attention that is given towards their customers. Amidst the intimate atmosphere, finish off your meal with an espresso or cappuccino and delicious desserts. This will be the perfect ending to a delightful experience at Osteria's.

941-388-3671

**29 1/2 N. Blvd. of the Presidents
Sarasota
Serving Dinner 7 Days A Week
4:30 PM To 10:30 PM Daily**

Served the very best in authentic Northern Italian cuisine for over 15 years.

18

James "Jim" Costa
Firemedic
SCFD

Jim grew up in the small town of Falmouth, Massachusetts in a family of firefighters. His father served 22 years as a "callman" in Falmouth, where his "Uncle Charlie" (who lived with them) was a paid firefighter and firehouse cook for 28 years. Jim followed in their footsteps and served three years as a volunteer before joining the Navy for a four year stint as a radarman.

Jim met his wife, Martha, while working as a civilian CFR Firefighter at a military base in the Bahamas. They enjoy boating, camping and fishing tournaments. Jim is an avid collector of firefighting memorabilia, including a restored 1952 Maxim pumper from Ogunquit, Me.

Jim has enjoyed working the past nine years with SCFD and looks forward to retiring there.

Boston Tofu Chili (AKA Fake 'em out Chili)
James "Jim" Costa — Firemedic

Ingredients:

1 pound tofu crumbles (politely hot or other variety)
30 ounce jar spaghetti sauce, garden style
14.5 ounce can kidney beans
2 – 14.5 ounce cans Boston baked beans
14.5 ounce can diced tomatoes

1 medium-large onion chopped
1 medium-large green bell pepper chopped
chili powder to taste
red pepper to taste
OPTIONAL (FOR MEAT LOVERS):
1 pound slices of linguica Portuguese sausage

Directions:

1 – Add all ingredients to 10-quart pan, cover and bring to simmer for 1 hour or more. (Remove the chunk of bacon from beans)

2 – Serve with bread or crackers and salad.

Makes 6 + Servings.

*They will think it's real meat unless you spill the beans!

Brandied Blue Cheese Steak

Sun 'N Fun RV Resort

Ingredients:

2 12 oz. T-bone steaks (New York Strip Steaks or Tenderloin Steaks)

1 1/2 cups of demi glace (brown gravy; prepare ahead of time)

4 oz. blue cheese

1 tablespoon heavy cream

2 oz. butter

1 1/2 oz. brandy

dash multi purpose seasoning (or other seasoning salt)

Spiro Paizes
Peggy Sue's Fifty's Diner
Sun 'N Fun RV Resort

Manager of Peggy Sue's Fifty's Diner, Spiro Paizes, has a management and culinary degree as well as an extensive background in restaurants. Spiro has owned many restaurants in the USA and currently owns operations in South Africa. Spiro also owns Safari Joe's Publications and Food Products and is the author of "Men Only Cooking, No Women Allowed" which can be purchased off the internet at www.safarijoes.com.

Directions:

1 – Season two steaks with multi purpose seasoning or similar seasoning (salt and pepper.)

2 – Melt the butter in a sauté pan. Cook steaks on medium heat evenly on both sides.

3 – In a separate pan heat the demi glace (brown gravy) and cream together.

4 – When the steaks are done to your liking, add the brandy to the steaks, then the demi glace and incorporate the blue cheese. Heat, allowing the cheese to get warm and almost melted.

5 – Pour the balance of sauce over the steaks until just covered. You can also do steaks on the grill and add the sauce.

6 – Serve and enjoy!

Makes 2 Servings.

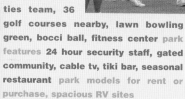

John Elwood
Training Captain
SCFD

John is a Captain with Sarasota County Fire Department and has over 18 years of fire service experience. Captain Elwood is currently assigned to the training division where he oversees the training of new employees. His past assignment was in special operations serving as company officer. For the past eleven years he has served as a lead instructor with Sarasota County Technical Institute's Fire Academy where he instructs on subjects ranging form minimum standards to special operations. John instructs at the state and national level in technical rescue disciplines. He is currently seeking a Bachelors degree in public administration. John was born in Fairfax, Virginia, and moved to Sarasota in 1972. His hobbies include scuba diving, rock climbing, and weight training.

Poached Chicken & Figs with Curried Corn & Dried Fruit Chutney

Munroe's Restaurant

Ingredients:

1 ear yellow corn shucked and peeled
3 ounces dried cherries
1 small carrot julienne
3 ounces blackberries
1 lemon juice of
1 tablespoon curry powder
1/2 teaspoon cumin

1/2 teaspoon granulated garlic
1/2 teaspoon nutmeg
1/2 teaspoon cinnamon
2 tablespoons olive oil
4 dried figs
8 ounce skinless, boneless chicken breast

Directions:

1 – Poach chicken breast in water until fully cooked, add figs towards the last two minutes of poaching.

2 – To make the chutney – sauté corn kernels, onion and carrot in olive oil in a sauté pan for 2 minutes, add cherries and black berries – sauté for one more minute. Add spices and lemon juice, stir well and remove from heat.

3 – To plate – fan slice the poached chicken breast in four, alternate the figs and chicken centered on the plate – cover liberally with the chutney. Garnish with fresh mint and lemon zest.

"Grilled Chicken Penne"

Cosimo's Brick Oven Trattoria & Bar

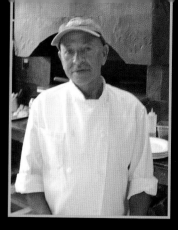

Ingredients:

6 to 8 oz. Grilled Chicken Breast (sliced)
2 Tbs. Diced Tomatoes
2 oz. Chicken Stock
2 Tbs. Pitted Calamata Olives
1/4 cup Basil Pesto Sauce
4 oz. Pesto

8 leaves Arugula
2 Tbs. Fresh Mozzarella
1 tsp. Olive Oil
pinch each Salt and Pepper
4 oz. Penne Pasta

Directions:

1 – In olive oil, sauté chicken, olives, and tomatoes.

2 – Add chicken stock, then Pesto, Arugula and heat.

3 – Just before serving, add mozzarella (being careful not to melt cheese).

4 – Season with salt and pepper.

5 – Toss with fresh cooked penne pasta and serve.

Makes 1 Serving.

Giovanni (Gigi) Mauri

Executive Chef
Cosimo's Brick Oven
Trattoria & Bar

Born and raised in the Piedmont Region of Italy, Executive Chef Giovanni (Gigi) Mauri has been in the restaurant business for over four decades, with stops in Switzerland, London, and Washington, D.C. before arriving in Southwest Florida in 1990.

At Cosimo's Brick Oven, Chef Gigi and his staff skillfully combine "Old World" Italian Cuisine with New World flavors and techniques to create an unforgettable dining experience.

If you're in the mood for a wood-fired pizza, specialty salad, signature pasta, or the famous calamari, you must try Cosimo's Brick Oven! And don't forget the daily specials or the extensive and affordable wine list!

Winner, Best New Restaurant, Sarasota Herald Tribune, 1999

Jean Vessel
Firefighter/Paramedic
SCFD

Jean was an active volunteer with the Fruitville Fire Department at age 17. She vividly recalls the day Chief Nutter came through her check out line at the grocery store and asked when she was going to come to work for the department. She replied, "how about tomorrow?" It's been 20 years since she became the first female to be hired by Fruitville to be a firefighter. Presently she is certified as a firefighter, paramedic, arson investigator, and instructor.

Her husband Dennis is also a firefighter. She has twin 12-year old sons, Chris and Jon, and a three-year old daughter, Selena. They enjoy boating and fishing on their 22' Grady White "Dvessel," and playing with their 140 pound rotweiler appropriately named "Bigun."

Crab Stuffed Flounder

Jean Vessel — Firefighter/Paramedic

Ingredients:

2 lbs. flounder fillets
1 lb. imitation crab meat
7 oz pkg. herb stuffing
salt
pepper

paprika
dillweed
Miracle Whip
fresh parsley
fresh lemon

Directions:

1 – Cook stuffing according to package instructions.

2 – Then mix broken up crab meat into it and set aside.

3 – Rub Miracle Whip on baking pan where fillets will rest and place half of fillets on pan.

4 – Scoop "stuffing and crab mix" onto fillets.

5 – Sprinkle with fresh lemon juice.

6 – Place other half of fillets on top and rub top of fillets with Miracle Whip.

7 — Salt and pepper to taste.

8 — Dust with paprika and dillweed.

9 — Place in pre-heated @ 350 deg for 25 - 30 minutes.

10 — Garnish with parsley and serve.

Makes 4 Servings.

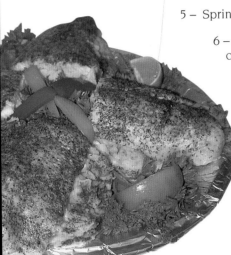

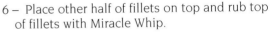

Fettuccini con Tartufo

Café L' Europe

Ingredients:

1 pound egg fettuccine
3 teaspoons white truffle oil
1 cup heavy cream
1 cup mascarpone cheese

salt and cracked black pepper
1/4 cup grated grana padana cheese
sliced truffle

Directions:

1 – Bring heavy cream to a boil.

2 – Whisk in mascarpone and remove from heat.

3 – Season with salt and pepper.

4 – Cook pasta to al dente.

5 – Remove from water, drain and toss with truffle oil.

6 – Dress with sauce, cheese and sliced truffle.

Makes 6 Servings.

Jeff Trefry
Executive Chef
Café L' Europe

Upon graduation from the prestigious Culinary Institute of America, Jeff moved west to Santa Barbara, California and worked as a pastry chef for the El Encanto Hotel. To broaden his knowledge of the culinary arts and hone his skills, Jeff moved east and spent three years at Café L Europe in the early 1980's. Jeff's career path led him to the Five-Star Five-Diamond Ritz Carlton Resort in Naples and he was promoted to Executive Sous Chef. In 1989, promotion placed Jeff as Executive Chef in charge of culinary operations at the Ritz Carlton in Kansas City Mo. He then worked in Bermuda and Hilton Head Island, S.C. but is now back with Café L' Europe as Executive Chef. Jeff executes New European Cuisine with his own imagination and personal style. He is married to Janet and has three children – Megan, Jack and Mike.

Michael's On East

Sarasota's most celebrated restaurant is dazzling guests with its vibrant decor - reminiscent of a 1930's private dining club. The look is matched by the restaurant's impeccable service, just what you would expect from this recipient of nine golden spoon awards as one of Florida's Top 20 restaurants.

Michael's Famous Bowtie Pasta

Michael's On East

Ingredients:

1 lb. Cooked Farfalle (cooled and drained)
2 oz. Snow Peas
1/4 c. Parmesan Cheese
1 Large Red Pepper (Julienned)
1/4 c. Chopped Sundried Tomatoes
6 Cloves Garlic (minced)

8 Basil Leaves (chopped)
3 Bacon Strips (chopped)
2 8 oz. Chicken Breasts Marinated & Grilled
2 Tbsp Rosemary Infused Olive Oil
6 Large Shiitake Mushrooms (Julienned)
1 1/2 cup Cream

Directions:

1 – Add two tablespoons of Infused Oil to a large sauté pan on medium high heat.

2 – Add Bacon, Peppers, Mushrooms and sauté for approximately one minute.

3 – Add Garlic and Sundried Tomatoes and sauté for another minute.

4 – Add Cream, Basil, Cheese, Chicken and Pasta.

5 – Cook until slightly thick. Salt and pepper to taste.

Makes 4 Servings.

941-366-0007

1212 East Avenue South
Sarasota

Monday – Saturday
Lunch 11:30 AM To 2:00 PM
Dinner 5:30 PM To 10:00 PM

**Recipient of
Nine Consecutive
Golden Spoon Awards
by *Florida*
Trend Magazine.**

Shepherd's Pie

Charles Tomeo, D.M.D.

Ingredients:

1 pound ground beef
1 pound Italian sausage
1/2 cup onion chopped
1 can sweet corn
salt & pepper to taste
4 large potatoes

1 1/2 - 2 cups milk
1/2 stick butter
1/2 cup shredded cheddar cheese
2 packages brown gravy mix
1 teaspoon parsley

Directions:

1 – In large skillet, brown beef, sausage, onion, salt and pepper.

2 – Drain fat and pour into baking dish.

3 – Prepare gravy according to instructions and pour over meat mixture.

4 – Layer the corn on top of meat and set aside.

5 – Peel potatoes, cut into halves and boil until soft.

6 – Place potatoes in large bowl. Add milk, butter, salt & pepper to taste, and mix with electric mixer.

7 – Spread potatoes over beef mixture. Sprinkle parsley and cheese on top and bake in the oven at 350 degrees for 30 minutes.

Charles Tomeo, D.M.D.

Dr. Charles Tomeo attended the University of Maryland Dental School, spent two years in the U.S. Army and in 1979 completed his residency at Albert Einstein Hospital in New York. Dr. Tomeo moved to the Bradenton-Sarasota area where he opened the surgical practices he still operates today. As a skilled oral surgeon, he thoroughly enjoys seeing smiles on his satisfied patients' faces. Known for his big heart and love for kids, it is little wonder that Dr. Tomeo founded the Manatee Wildcat Football Youth League program in 1986 and remains president today. Dr. Tomeo has two sons and six daughters. He and his wife, Ruth, enjoy traveling, including occasional jaunts to Key West. Dr. Tomeo has a passion for the skies and finds piloting his Cessna twin engine aircraft to be the ultimate stress reliever.

Bernie Vandersweet

Fire Lieutenant/Paramedic

SCFD

Bernie was 19 year old, Air Force "door gunner" when he met his wife, Linda, in New Mexico. They were married 27 years ago, and moved to Florida where they raised their three children, Kimberly, Alicia and Michael. He joined the South Trail Fire Department upon moving to Sarasota and has 23 years of service at present. His current assignment is Lieutenant/Paramedic at Station 13-C. He is also a member of the Swat-Medic Team. Bernie enjoys cooking and the Spicy Wet Burritos is a recipe he created as the chef of his family owned restaurant in New Mexico.

Spicy Wet Burrito

Bernie Vandersweet — Fire Lieutenant/Paramedic

Ingredients:

2 pounds ground round
1 large Spanish onion diced
1 jalapeno pepper diced
1 poblano pepper diced
2 packages of dry taco seasoning
1 teaspoon salt
1 teaspoon cumin
1 teaspoon garlic powder

1 tablespoon chili powder
1 16 ounce can refried beans
5 – 8 ounce cans of enchilada sauce
1 1/2 cups of water
3 cups shredded lettuce
4 cups grated cheddar cheese
12 – 10 inch size flour tortilla shells
1 box Spanish rice

Directions:

1 – Brown beef; add onions, diced peppers, dry ingredients, water and bring to a boil.

2 – Simmer uncovered for 10 minutes.

3 – Remove from heat.

4 – Spread refried beans on each flour tortilla shell, sprinkle with cheese.

5 – Add 1/2 cup of meat mixture across center portion of tortilla shell.

6 – Roll shell up like you would an egg roll and place each shell in a greased baking pan with seam side down.

7 – Cover burritos with enchilada sauce and cover the top with the remaining cheese.

8 – Bake at 375 degrees for 30 minutes, until bubbly.

9 – Remove each burrito from pan and place on serving plate.

10 – Garnish with Spanish rice and lettuce.

11 – Place a heaping of sour cream to the top of the burrito and enjoy!

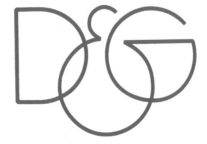

Chicken & Yellow Rice – Arroz con Pollo

Columbia Restaurant

Ingredients:

3 pound chicken fryer, cut in quarters
2 onions, chopped
1 green pepper, chopped
2 medium tomatoes, peeled, seeded and chopped
2 cloves garlic, minced
1/2 cup olive oil
1 bay leaf

4 cups chicken broth
2 cups long-grain white rice, uncooked
1/2 teaspoon saffron
1/2 tablespoon salt
1/2 cup small green peas (cooked)
4 asparagus tips
2 roasted red peppers, cut in strips
1/4 cup white wine

Directions:

1 – In a skillet, sauté chicken in heated oil until skin is golden.

2 – Remove chicken and place in casserole.

3 – In same oil, sauté onion, green pepper, tomatoes, and garlic for 5 minutes.

4 – Pour over chicken.

5 – Add chicken broth, saffron, salt, bay leaf and rice.

6 – When mixture begins to boil, cover casserole and bake in oven at 350 degrees for 20 minutes or until chicken is done.

7 – Sprinkle with wine and garnish with peas, roasted red peppers, and asparagus tips.

Makes 4 Servings.

Richard, Adela and Casey Gonzmart
Owners
Columbia Restaurant

Our family has been creating some of Florida's favorite Spanish cuisine for nearly 100 years. We feature the freshest seafood and steaks as well as our won tradition family recipes. Through the years we have received some of the highest awards in the restaurant industry, but our highest praise comes from our loyal customers who dine with us again and again

Join us daily for lunch or dinner, and take in the beautiful sites of St. Armands Circle while enjoying the delicious dishes our chef prepares especially for you

The Gonzmart family looks forward to welcoming you to the Columbia Restaurant

Since 1905

941-388-3987

**411 St. Armands Circle
Sarasota
Monday – Saturday
11 AM To 11 PM
Sunday
12 Noon To 10 PM**

The Columbia Restaurant is truly a part of Florida's experience.

Come and enjoy one of our traditional family recipes.

1

Jason Wilkins
Firemedic
SCFD

Jason Wilkins was hired by SCFD as a Firefighter / EMT in April of 1996, after spending approximately three years as a volunteer. He was pleased to get his first assignment at Sta.#11-A , and he's been there ever since. His light hearted, jovial spirit is enjoyed by his peers.

When asked about his role in the crew, Jason replied: "I'm simply the guy that's being looked at whenever there is a practical joke in the station. I've spent a lot of my time behind closed doors in the Lieutenant's office because of my sense of humor, but it's worth it. The job we do is stressful, so I try to provide the laughs. It makes the world a better place."

Christmas Eve, Station #12-B
"Fully Involved."

J-'s Stuffed Chicken

Jason Wilkins — Firemedic (Motorcycle Enthusiast)

Ingredients:

6 skinless
boneless chicken breasts
1 box stuffing
1 pound of sausage
(Italian, polish, whatever you desire)

1 cup chopped mushrooms
1 cup chopped onions
4 tablespoons minced garlic
(5 or 6 if you're a garlic lover)
1 stick butter

Directions:

1 – Make stuffing according to box.

2 – Sauté sausage, mushrooms, onions and 2 tablespoons garlic (or more if you desire).

3 – Mix everything with the stuffing.

4 – Cut a pocket into the chicken breast or just cut in half, and add stuffing mix inside chicken.

5 – Place the chicken in a 10"x14" glass casserole dish.

6 – Melt stick of butter and add remaining garlic to make a garlic butter sauce.

7 – Pour 1 tablespoon garlic butter on the breast and place in an oven at 350 degrees for 45 minutes.

8 – Add remaining garlic butter and broil chicken for another 5-10 minutes until lightly brown on top.

Note: You can add or delete veggies to your liking. Suggested sides are roasted garlic mashed potatoes and a veggie of your choice.

Coconut and Almond Shrimp

Café on the Bay

Ingredients:

16 Jumbo shrimp
3 Egg whites
1/4 cup Flour
1 teaspoon Baking powder
1/4 cup Coconut

1/4 cup Sliced almonds
2 cups Salad oil
1/8 cup Horseradish
1/2 cup Orange marmalade

Directions:

1 – Butterfly and clean shrimp.

2 – Mix egg and flour in batter and baking powder. If too thick, add water.

3 – Dip shrimp in flour and then batter.

4 – Roll battered shrimp in coconut and almonds.

5 – Heat salad oil in pan.

6 – Fry shrimp in hot oil until golden brown.

7 – Serve with sauce of horseradish and orange marmalade.

Café on the Bay

Nestled in the Longboat Key Moorings, along beautiful Sarasota Bay, sits Longboat Key's Hidden Gem…Café on the Bay. Elegant yet casual, her charm beckons seafarers and landlubbers alike for breakfast, lunch or dinner. You will delight in an offering of extraordinary cuisine. Enjoy the indoor dining room or the covered outdoor terrace, both featuring spectacular marina and bay views. Or you may simply wish to enjoy your favorite cocktail or one of our own exotic creations at our Marker 15 Lounge. This is one "Port of Call" you will wish to visit over and over again! Inquire about our sunset special and the pre-fixed dinner offering.
Breakfast Saturday
8:30 AM – 10:30 AM
Sunday Breakfast Brunch
9:00 AM – 1:00 PM
Sunday Lunch
1:00 PM – 3:30 PM
Lunch 11:00 AM – 3:00 PM
Dinner 4:30 PM – 10:00 PM
In the Longboat Key Moorings Marina behind Publix – right out of guard gate, second left.

941-383-0440

**2630 Harbourside Dr.
Longboat Key, FL 34228**

Breakfast Saturday
8:30 AM To 10:30 AM

Sunday Breakfast Brunch
9:00 AM To 1:00 PM

Sunday Lunch
1:00 PM To 3:30 PM

Lunch 6 Days
11:00 AM To 3:00 PM

Dinner 7 Days
4:30 PM To 10:00 PM

**Extraordinary cuisine served in a truly exquisite waterfront setting.
Come by land or sea.
Casual attire is welcomed.**

Chris House
Firefighter/Paramedic
SCFD

With a bachelor's degree in history and education from Boston University in hand, Chris started his professional career as an educator. After six months of teaching derelicts, he decided he was in the wrong business and began looking for a new career. He joined the Fire Service and became a firefighter/paramedic for the city of Sarasota. He has worked there for the past 25 years.

Chris enjoys golf, fishing, and snow skiing in the Rockies, travel and Russian studies. He met his wife of five years, Lara, in Russia. When asked what gives him satisfaction, Chris replies, "living life to its fullest and helping others along the way."

Station 3 returns from a pump test.

Cheese Meat Lovers Dream

Chris House – Firefighter/Paramedic

Ingredients:

2 cups ricotta cheese
8-10 ounces provolone cheese
10-12 ounces mozzarella cheese
10 ounces Romano cheese
2 eggs
1/4 cup milk
1/8 teaspoon cayenne pepper
2 tablespoons chopped garlic
1 tablespoon basil
1 tablespoon oregano
1/2 pound grated parmesan cheese

1 1/2 packages lasagna noodles
MEAT SAUCE:
1/2 pound ground veal
1/2 pound ground pork
1/2 pound ground beef
2 cups chopped onions
1 cup chopped green pepper
1/2 cup chopped celery
1/2 cup chopped carrots
3 tablespoons chopped garlic
2 cups eggplant, skinned & diced

1 can tomato paste
2 – 28 ounce cans of diced canned tomatoes
1 tablespoon thyme
2 bay leaves
2 teaspoons oregano
2 teaspoons basil
4 cups water
2-3 ounces parmesan cheese
2-3 tablespoons olive oil
pinch of salt & pepper

Directions:

MEAT SAUCE
1 – Heat olive oil in large non-stick pan. Combine meats and brown.
2 – Place browned meat in a large kettle and add onions, peppers, celery, carrots, salt and pepper. Cook 4-5 minutes or until veggies are soft.
3 – Add garlic and tomatoes and cook 2 minutes.
4 – Add tomato paste, water, and rest of spices and then simmer for 1 hour.

LASAGNA:
1 – Pre-heat oven to 350 degrees.
2 – Mix cheeses, eggs, milk, salt, pepper, basil, and oregano.
3 – Place approximately 2 cups of meat sauce on bottom of deep lasagna pan.
4 – Sprinkle 1/4 of cheese mix on sauce.
5 – Layer with dry noodles.
6 – Cover noodles with 1/4 cheese mix.
7 – Then cover thinly with meat sauce.
8 – Then another layer of noodles.
9 – Then layer with cheese, then meat sauce, then noodles.
10 – Remaining sauce on top.
11 – Bake 45 – 60 minutes.
Tips: Let cool 10-15 minutes before serving.
Serve with garlic bread and "house salad."

Makes 8 - 10 Servings.

Grouper Provencal

Phillippi Creek Restaurant

Roy LaLone
Owner
Phillippi Creek

Ingredients:

2 cups prepared rice of choice
4-5 ounce grouper
8-10 (each) small to medium shrimp
1 tablespoon chopped garlic

8-10 (each) black olive
2 cups chopped fresh tomato
1/4 cup sliced mushroom
3 tablespoons butter

Directions:

1 – Grill grouper until fully cooked.

2 – Sauté butter, garlic, tomatoes, olives, mushrooms, and shrimp until cooked.

3 – Spread rice over dinner plate.

4 – Place grouper over bed of rice.

5 – Pour Provencal sauce and shrimp over grouper.

Makes 1 Serving.

Experience casual waterfront dining at "the place to go" for seafood. Located in a tropical setting, this family restaurant features a multiple choice of fresh local seafood daily. Outdoor and indoor waterfront dining. Open 11 a.m. daily, serving lunch and dinner on the waterfront.

Dan Rankin
Firefighter/EMT
SCFD

After serving three years with the Nokomis Fire Department as a volunteer, Dan Rankin, was hired by Sarasota County Fire Department and has been serving as a Firefighter/ EMT for two years. Dan loves the fire service and is greeted warmly wherever he rides. His culinary talents were put to the test in his first few shifts winning the heart of his peers via their tummies. Dan says his greatest challenge in fire-house cooking is to create five-bugle meals at rookie pay prices! Dan is married to his wife of three years, Monica. He enjoys art, playing guitar and bagpipes, paintball, trail biking, and martial arts in his off duty hours.

Chimichanga

Dan Rankin — Firefighter/EMT

Ingredients:

1 cup water
2 pounds ground beef
2 1/2 ounce package of taco seasoning
1 cup salsa
1 3/4 cup taco sauce

16 ounce can refried beans
1/2 pound shredded cheddar & jack cheese
24 ounce bottle vegetable oil
8-10 large tortilla shells

Directions:

1 – On medium high, brown 2 pounds ground beef. Strain.
2 – Add taco mix and 1 cup water to beef. Stir mixture and beef and continue to cook until beef is coated evenly and most of water has evaporated.
3 – Add 1 cup salsa and stir. Set aside to cool.
4 – Heat refried beans.
5 – Lay out tortilla shells.

6 – Place 1/2 cup of ground beef mix just below center of shell and add 1 tablespoon of refried beans.
7 – Fold the bottom of the shell over the beef and beans and pull back gently to make a tight roll. Fold the sides in about 1"-1 1/2". Roll the rest of the way to the top. Continue to roll the rest of the shells this way.
8 – In a large skillet, heat about 1/2"-3/4" of oil. When oil is heated (about 350 degrees) place tortilla roll in heated oil (folded side down) and cook until golden brown.
9 – Remove from oil and set on a plate covered with paper towels.
10 – Allow the excess oil to drain and salt if desired.
11 – Place on a cookie sheet and top with taco sauce and cheese.
12 – Place in oven and cook at 350 degrees until cheese is melted.
13 – Serve with Spanish rice.

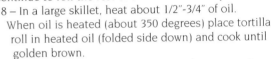

Penne with Portobello Mushroom and Mushroom Sauce

Munroe's Restaurant

Ingredients:

4 ounces cooked penne pasta
1 large portobello mushroom cap, peeled
2 ounces dried mushrooms reconstituted
1/2 teaspoon salt & pepper
1/2 teaspoon minced garlic

3 ounces olive oil
2 ounces onions julienne
1 lemon juice of
1 teaspoon parsley minced
1/2 teaspoon fresh thyme

Directions:

1 – Sauté mushroom cap in a pan with olive oil. Remove the cap when cooked.

2 – Add onions to the oil – cook until tender, add dried mushrooms, lemon juice, garlic and herbs.

3 – Toss in pasta and season with salt & pepper.

4 – Garnish with scallions and tomatoes as pictured.

Steve Cantu
Firefighter Paramedic, SCFD

Steve was born in Winterhaven, Florida. He grew up working as a bee keeper in his family's business Cantu Apiaries in Wauchula. The primary business is renting bee's to farmers for cross pollination of crops. Steve says they have a couple thousand hives, and each hive has approximately 50,000 bees.

Steve grew weary of being gone with the bees for six months at a time and was looking for a stable job where he would not have to travel. A friend introduced him to the Fire Service, and he began volunteering for Hardee County, who hired him in '95 as a firefighter. He became a paramedic in '96, and was hired by SCFD in '97.

Steve and his wife, Lisa, enjoy mountaineering as their hobby.

Engine 81 pulls lines for possible attic fire.

197

Pepper Dietz
Firefighter/Paramedic

Pepper Dietz is a firefighter/ paramedic with the Sarasota County Fire Department. He has been in the fire service for nine years. He is married to wife, Debbie, a labor & delivery nurse, has one daughter, Cricket, and a Siberian husky, Whaler. Pepper says, "the quiche is an excellent quick dinner that gives remarkable Mexican flair to quiche." I guess Pepper should know since he says his most important thing in life is food! His Siberian husky loves it, too!

Mexican Fiesta Quiche
Pepper Dietz — Firefighter/Paramedic

Ingredients:

3/4 pound pork sausage (or 8 links vegetarian sausage – in frozen breakfast foods section)
6 – 6" Corn tortillas
1 cup (4 ounces) monterey jack cheese
1 cup (4 ounces) cheddar cheese

1/4 cup canned chopped green chilies
7 – 8 beaten eggs
1/2 cup whipping cream
1/2 cup small curd cottage cheese
1/2 teaspoon chili powder
4 teaspoons minced parsley or cilantro

Directions:

1 – Cook sausage.

2 – Place 5 tortillas in 9" pie pan overlapping and extending 1/2" beyond rim.

3 – Place remaining tortilla in center.

4 – Layer bottom with sausage, cheeses and chilies.

5 – In a bowl, combine eggs, whip cream, cottage cheese, chili powder, and whip together.

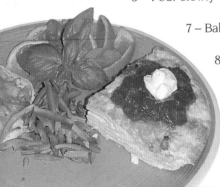

6 – Pour slowly over the ingredients already in pie pan.

7 – Bake at 350 degrees for 50 minutes or until center is set.

8 – Sprinkle with parsley or cilantro.

Makes 6 Servings.

Scampi Mediteraneo

Osteria Northern Italian Restaurant

Ingredients:

12 medium shrimp
2 ounces white wine
2 cloves garlic crushed

1 ounce Gorgonzola cheese
touch of heavy cream
touch of olive oil

Lee Guidry
Chef
Osteria Northern
Italian Restaurant

Directions:

1 – Sauté garlic until brown in olive oil.

2 – Add shrimp and reduce heat.

3 – Add white wine and Gorgonzola cheese.

4 – Reduce until thick.

5 – Garnish with baby greens.

The Casadio family has consistently served the very best in authentic Northern Italian cuisine for over 15 years. Pasta, seafood, veal, chicken and lamb are amongst the specialties along with fine wines. This charming St. Armands restaurant is also known for the impeccable attention that is given towards their customers. Amidst the intimate atmosphere, finish off your meal with an espresso or cappuccino and delicious desserts. This will be the perfect ending to a delightful experience at Osteria's.

Ted Lang
Lieutenant, SCFD

Ted grew up in Miami, Florida, in family of five kids hoping someday to be a firefighter. He moved to Sarasota in 1980 as a 19-year old mechanic and was employed as such for Toyota and then Sarasota County Area Transit.

In 1982, his childhood wish became reality when he was hired by Sarasota Fire Department. In the past 8 years he's become a firefighter, EMT, special Op's/ Haz Mat team member, inspector, and fire investigator. His most recent accomplishment was promotion to the position of Fire Lieutenant in 1998.

Ted and Susan have been married five years and have three children: Zachary, Katelyn, and Rebekah. Ted prioritizes his life as Faith, Family, Fire Department, and Fun. For "fun" he enjoys fishing and diving.

About the recipe...
The "Chicken and Rocks" recipe came from and old Sarasota firefighter who used to cook this for the crews. He shared the recipe with me before he retired.

Ted carefully sampling the famous "Chicken & Rocks" recipe.

Chicken & Rocks

Ted Lang — Lieutenant

Ingredients:

2 whole chickens
4 1/2 cups all purpose flour
1 cup shortening

1 teaspoon salt
2 1/4 cup warm water
butter

Directions:

1 – Boil 2 chickens (cut into pieces) for approx. 1 hour. (Water barely covering chicken.)

2 – In a mixing bowl, mix 4 1/2 cups flour to 1 cup shortening to consistency no bigger than a pea. Mix in 1 teaspoon salt and 2 1/4 cups warm water, adding water slowly. Mush together into a ball.

3 – Cover counter top with flour and flatten out with a rolling pin, approximately 1/8 inch. Use butter and cut into strips 1" wide and 3" long.

4 – Take chicken out of pot.

5 – Bring water to a boil.

6 – Add dumplings and bring to a boil again.

7 – Stir in 1 cup flour and 2 1/2 cups warm water or more until consistency is thick.

8 – Season and serve over chicken.

Makes 6 Servings.

I assume no responsibility for any discomfort caused by this meal!

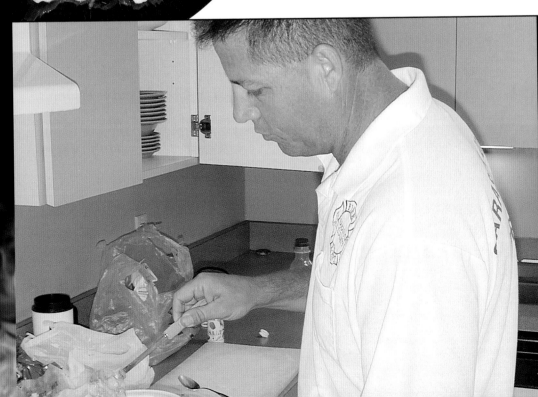

Chicken Coca-Van

Troy Pittman — Firefighter Paramedic

Ingredients:

4 - lg. breasts boneless/skinless
chicken breasts
1/2 lb. bacon
2 - lg. onions

8 oz. mushrooms (sliced)
3 cups chicken stock
3 cups beef stock
1/2 tsp. each garlic, salt, pepper (to taste)

Directions:

1 – Sauté the onions, mushrooms and then brown bacon (not crispy) and set aside.

2 – Seer chicken in bacon dripping and garlic powder.

3 – Heat the beef and chicken stock and thicken with cornstarch to make gravy.

4 – Place chicken oven pan and layer with sautéed onions and mushrooms and bacon.

5 – Sprinkle with salt and pepper.

6 – Pour gravy over the top of all the ingredients.

7 – Preheat oven to 375 and place dish in oven for 1 hour.

8 – When cooked, serve over large egg noodles or mashed potatoes.

Makes 4 – 6 Servings.

Troy Pittman
Firefighter Paramedic
SCFD

Troy was born in Sarasota in 1964. As a child he was fascinated with emergency medicine and hoped to become a paramedic someday. In high school he was introduced to the fire department by some buddies who were volunteers at the time. He was "hooked" from that day forward. He was accepted as a volunteer in 1983 with the Fruitville Fire Department and was hired six months later.

Troy's father, Willy, loved to fly and build small aircraft in his free time. As a member of Pittman Aviation, there's no doubt it rubbed off on Troy who enjoys flying as a private pilot as well.

Troy and his wife, Heidi, have their hands full with four young children in the house: Seth, Wyatt, Cheyenne, and one-year old Sierra.

About the recipe... Troy learned how to make this recipe as a "prep cook" in his teens. It's been a firehouse favorite since the first time he made it for the crews.

Station 12-C crew trying a little Coca-Van.

201

Garlic Scallops with Pasta

Herb Blumenthal — Firefighter/Paramedic

Ingredients:

1 cup olive oil
1/2 (or more) head garlic
1 small onion
1/2 cup loosely packed cilantro

1 pound bay scallops
1 pound linguini
1/2 cup fresh grated parmesan cheese
salt & pepper to taste

Directions:

1 – Finely chop the garlic and onion, coarsely chop the cilantro.

2 – Cook the pasta per package directions.

3 – Heat the oil, add the garlic and onions and cook until opaque, NOT BROWN.

4 – Rinse the scallops and add to the oil, constantly stir until the scallops are all white.

5 – Add the cilantro and stir until it wilts.

6 – Pour this mixture over the pasta and mix well.

7 – Sprinkle grated cheese on top and enjoy.

*Be sure to use fresh garlic, onion, cilantro and cheese or you may not enjoy it.

Serves 4 average people or 2 firefighters.

Herb Blumenthal
Firefighter/Paramedic
SCFD Station #1-A

Herb was born in Israel. At the age of five, his family moved to Miami. Upon graduating from high school, Herb moved back to Israel for a few years. In 1973, after serving two years in the Israeli Army, he decided to move back to the U.S. His job search led him to the classifieds where he found an ad for an EMT with a private ambulance service. It's been 27 years, several different employers, and a lot new technology since those early days; but Herb has stayed the course and is working as a firefighter/paramedic at the busiest station in SCFD.

Herb has been married 26 years to Roberta. They have three children: Adam, Sydney, and Ben. He's easily recognized by his classic handlebar mustache.

Chicken or Grouper Martinique

Sarasota University Club

Ingredients:

2-6 ounce Chicken Breasts or
Grouper Filets

4 ounce Button Mushrooms,
medium chopped

2 ounce Fresh Grated Parmesan Cheese

2 cloves Fresh Garlic, Smashed
and chopped

1 clove Shallot, chopped finely

2 ounce White Wine

2 ounce Melted Butter

1 ounce Lemon Juice

1 teaspoon Old Bay or Florida
Bay Seasoning

1/4 cup Fresh Basil, chopped

Directions:

1 – Preheat oven to 375

2 – Place chicken breasts or grouper in a broiler pan with sides at least 1 inch high.

3 – Mix all remaining ingredients together until it is able to form in your hand.

4 – Divide the mixture in two, and completely cover the chicken or grouper.

5 – Bake in pre-heated oven at 375 degrees for 15 minutes until chicken is fully cooked or grouper is fork tender and golden brown.

6 – Retain juices in broiler pan and drizzle over the top before serving.

Makes 2 Servings.

Floral Arrangement
Sarasota University Club

"Perched high atop the Bank of America building in downtown Sarasota for thirty years, the Sarasota University Club has a long tradition of providing graceful service to its membership and local community. With commanding views of Sarasota and the keys out to the Gulf of Mexico, the club offers a majestic dining experience The Sarasota University Club is a private dining club created for the benefit and enjoyment of its membership."

SARASOTA UNIVERSITY CLUB

941-366-5400

**1605 Main St.
Sarasota
Monday – Saturday**

**Sarasota's
only private
metropolitan club,
providing ambiance
and gracious
hospitality for
your enjoyment.**

Rocco Salvatori
Firefighter/EMT
Bradenton Fire Department

This is Rocco Salvatori's first year as a Firefighter/EMT with the City of Bradenton Fire Department. He is single and enjoys fishing and weightlifting. Spending time with his family and friends is what Rocco loves the most. This recipe is one of his mother's and one of her favorites!

Chicken Parmesan
Rocco Salvatori — Firefighter/EMT

Ingredients:

4-6 skinless/boneless chicken breasts (split)
2 eggs
8 ounces bread crumbs

30 ounce jar spaghetti sauce
1 cup grated parmesan cheese
1 cup grated mozzarella cheese
2 pounds spaghetti

Directions:

1 – Scramble eggs together to make egg wash. Place bread crumbs in a separate bowl.

2 – Dip chicken into eggs then into breadcrumbs.

3 – Put a generous amount of oil into a cast iron skillet over medium heat. Fry chicken until breadcrumbs are crisp.

4 – Pour spaghetti sauce on a shallow cookie sheet to cover bottom.

5 – Place chicken on cookie sheet and smother with sauce. Mix together parmesan and mozzarella cheese. Sprinkle cheese mixture over chicken.

6 – Place chicken in oven at 325 degrees for approximately 20 minutes. (Remove when chicken is cooked through. The time will vary; depending on how long the chicken was fried.)

7 – Serve over a plate of spaghetti with garlic bread.

Makes 4-6 Servings.

1928 Sanford on display at J.P. Igloo.

Grouper Imperial
Sandbar Restaurant

Ingredients:

4 –5 ounces of grouper (chunks)
 or any other firm fish
5 small sliced mushrooms
2 ounces white wine (dry)
3 ounces heavy cream

1 tablespoon capers
1 ounce chopped shallots or red onions
1 ounce cooking oil or olive oil
Flour for dusting fish

Directions:

1 – Heat oil in a medium sauté pan.

2 – Lightly dust fish pieces and drop in oil. Brown slightly on all sides and add shallots or onions, mushrooms and capers.

3 – Deglaze your pan with the wine and reduce until almost no liquid remains.

4 – Add heavy cream and reduce 1/2 or until thickened.

5 – Toss with your choice of a pasta or steamed rice.

6 – As an option, you may add 1 teaspoon of Dijon mustard and tarragon leaf.

Makes 1 Serving.

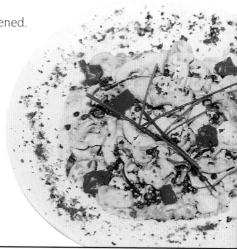

Ed Chiles
Owner
Chiles Restaurant Group

Ed Chiles graduated from the University of Florida in 1978 with a degree in Political Science. He worked at Joe's Stone Crab, the venerable Miami Institution for a year and then joined a partnership to purchase and operate the Sandbar Restaurant in 1979. This partnership included Lawton Chiles, Ed's father and past Governor of Florida along with Wilbur Boyd, and Dennis Fecteau. In 1990 Chiles purchased the Mar Vista Dockside Restaurant and Pub and again in 1993 purchased the former Harbor House now known as the Beach House Restaurant. Ed and his wife Anne take great pride in their development of the three restaurants. Their daughters Ashley and Christin have also began to get their feet wet in the business by filling in as hostesses and bussers whenever needed.

James Homick
Firefighter Paramedic
SCFD

Jim grew up in Indiana in a farming community. After a brief stay in St.Louis, he moved back to Indiana where he attended college in pursuit of a degree in crop dusting. He enjoyed flying and was even involved in some aerobatics. He moved to Florida in 1978 and soon became a volunteer with the Ruskin Fire Department. He attained his state certification as a firefighter and later paramedic before being hired by the SCFD in 1985. Jim is currently assigned to station #7-C.

Jim works as an account manager for a court reporting service in Hillsborough County during his off duty hours. Between both jobs, Jim says he doesn't have much free time but enjoys cooking and relaxing when he gets a chance.

Retired Chief, Tom Chase, helps collect money for Jerry's Kid's.

Chicken Paprakcosh
James Homick — Firefighter Paramedic

Ingredients:

3 1/2 pound chicken thigh and legs
oil (your choice)
2 large onions chopped
1 green pepper chopped

1 1/2 tablespoons paprika or more
1 cup or more sour cream
salt and pepper to taste

Directions:

1 – Brown chicken lightly in oil. Add onions and green pepper and cook until soft.

2 – Sprinkle paprika over chicken and stir.

3 – Pour in broth; add salt and pepper to taste.

4 – Cover and simmer until chicken is tender.

5 – Mix sour cream and some of the liquid from the pan.

6 – Cover and reheat briefly.

7 – Serve in soup plate.

*This recipe tastes better if refrigerated overnight.

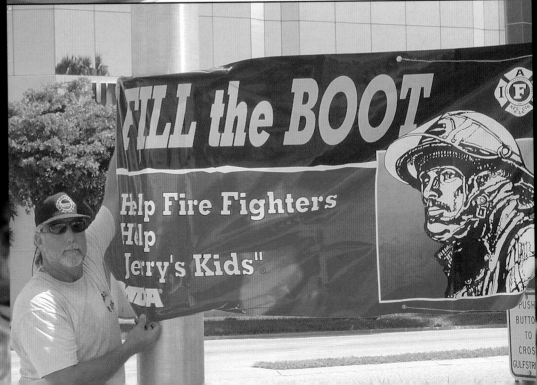

"Iowa River Stew"

Curt Bowen — Firemedic

Ingredients:

1 lb. ground beef
1 medium green pepper (chopped)
1 large onion (chopped)

32 oz. can tomatoes (whole)
32 oz. can chili or red beans
salt and pepper to taste

Directions:

1– Brown meat, pepper, and onion. Season while cooking.

2 – Cook until meat is done.

3 – Add canned tomatoes and beans.

4 – Simmer for 20 minutes.

Curt Bowen
Firemedic, SCFD

Curt was the youngest of nine kids in his family. He was raised on a farm in Oskaloosa, Iowa. In 1983 he struck out on his own in search of a new home and ended up in Sarasota. He rented a house next to the Northeast Fire Department (currently Station #6 of SCFD). He joined the volunteers and was hired by Metro-Sarasota 13 years ago.

He began diving for fun upon his arrival in Florida and today is certified as a Technical Instructor Course Director (the highest certification possible as a diver). He is known around the world for his underwater cave mapping (cartography). He is developer, owner, and publisher of his own magazine, "Advanced Diver Magazine."

Curt and Linda have been married 10 years.

About the recipe... "We used to eat this recipe while camping along the river in Iowa as kids. That is how it got its name. It brings back memories each time I eat a bowl."

Chief Stulce collecting cash during MDA 2000 Boot drive.

Grilled Venison (Backstrap)
Shawn Carvey — Firefighter/EMT

Ingredients:

1 section venison backstrap
8-10 ounces Kraft Italian dressing
1 tablespoon Everglade seasoning
salt and pepper to taste
1 tablespoon Luzianne Cajun season

1-2 tablespoons fresh minced garlic
4 pieces/strips bacon
2 tablespoons butter
aluminum foil

Directions:

1 – Cut backstrap into 1 inch butterflies about 2/3 of the way through.

2 – Marinate in Italian dressing for 2-3 hours.

3 – Place on sheet of aluminum foil.

4 – Add butter, everglades, salt and pepper, Cajun seasoning.

5 – Smear garlic on and make sure to get in between the butterflies.

6 – Place bacon in between each butterfly.

7 – Wrap in aluminum foil, be sure to leave air pocket in foil and cook on grill for 45 minutes – 1 hour at medium heat.

8 – Serve with mashed potatoes and biscuits.

Serves 4 firemen or 6 people.

Shawn Carvey
Firefighter/EMT
Venice Fire Department

Shawn comes from a long line of Florida "Crackers" dating back to his great great grandfather. Born in Sarasota Memorial, his community ties are strong. He grew up working for his father in their 26-year old family-owned cabinet business "Stylecraft." After high school he headed to St. Thomas College in Miami on a baseball scholarship, seeking a degree in sports medicine. He became an EMT and volunteered for three years with Englewood Fire Department where his brother-in-law is a firefighter. He was hired by Venice Fire Department in 1996 and enjoys being a member of the Haz Mat and Dive team.

He and his wife Marcie have a daughter, Brooke, and a nine-month old son, Austin. He loves hunting on his father's 80-acre parcel in Alabama.

About the recipe...
Venison Backstrap has long been a "huntin' camp" favorite and a real treat for firefighters in my station.

City of Venice Vintage American La France.

8

Penne with Salmon and Caviar

Munroe's Restaurant

Ingredients:

4 ounces fresh salmon cubed
3 ounces frozen peas thawed
1 ounce domestic sturgeon caviar
1 ounce mesculin salad mix
2 ounces white wine
1/2 teaspoon garlic minced

1/2 teaspoon shallots minced
2 ounces water
1 ounce olive oil
2 ounces red onion julienne
4 ounces penne pasta cooked

Directions:

1 – Poach the salmon in water and wine.

2 – Add peas, onions, garlic, shallots and olive oil – bring to a boil.

3 – Add pasta, toss to heat.

4 – Place in a large pasta bowl and sprinkle with caviar to finish.

NFPA Factoids And Kitchen Fire Safety Tips

Question:
How many fire deaths occurred in the home in 1999?

Answer:
2895

"Oven Fires"
If a fire starts in your oven, keep the door closed and turn off heat. Call fire department if fire doesn't go out quickly.

Information Courtesy of NFPA

Top Photo:
Marianna Haluska taste testing her first cookie.

Bottom Photo:
The Chef teaching the little Chef's.

Olivier "Ollie" Grangeon
Firefighter/EMT
SCFD

Olivier Grangeon has been with the Sarasota County Fire Department for two years. Even though it's only been two years, he has been very busy educating himself to enhance his career. His certificates include firefighter/EMT, pump operator, hazardous materials I & II, confined space and trench rescue. If that's not enough, Olivier, can also be called Pilot Grangeon. On his off days, he takes to the skies and flies planes for a charter company. "Frenchy," Olivier's nickname, is married, has one daughter and just loves life! When asked about his recipe he says, "It's a great excuse to have a chilled glass of white wine."

Sarasota County crews search for victims in Homestead during the aftermath of "Hurricane Andrew."

Veal Scaloppini A La Créme

Olivier "Ollie" Grangeon — Firefighter/EMT

Ingredients:

5 – 4 ounce veal scaloppini
1 pound mushroom of your choice
3 cups heavy cream
11/2 cup Swiss cheese

flour
salt
pepper
cognac

Directions:

1 – Rub scaloppini in flour, salt, pepper, and fry in a medium size pan.

2 – Put some cognac and light up.

3 – Put scaloppini in oven topped with the shredded Swiss cheese in the juice left over in the pan, add water, let some evaporate and add butter. Mix to make a sauce and when it thickens add heavy cream and mushrooms.

4 – Top the scaloppini with the sauce.

5 – Serve with white rice and a white wine, like chablis.

Makes 5 Servings.

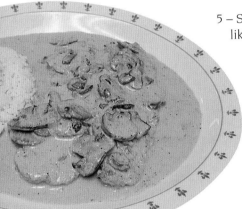

210

Pad Khing with Chicken

Ovea Thai Kitchen

Ingredients:

1/2 cup sliced chicken
1/4 cup vegetable cooking oil
2 teaspoons finely chopped garlic
2 tablespoons baby corn
2 tablespoons sliced mushrooms
1 tablespoon shredded ginger
2 tablespoons sliced carrot
2 tablespoons chopped cabbage

2 tablespoons snow peas
1 tablespoon oyster sauce
1 tablespoon soy sauce
1 1/2 teaspoon sugar
2 tablespoons bell peppers
2 tablespoons sliced onions
1/2 tablespoon water chestnuts

Directions:

1 – Heat wok and add the oil.

2 – When hot, add garlic and stir well.

3 – Add chicken, stir until just cooked.

4 – Add all vegetables and stir for 3-4 minutes.

5 – Add oyster sauce, soy sauce and sugar.

6 – Mix well for 1 minute.

7 – Serve with accompanied rice.

Ovea Thai Kitchen

Ovea Thai Kitchen is family owned and operated Thai restaurant which is fast making a name for itself in hometown Sarasota. Born in Bangkok, owners "Cookie and Woody" have made the business a family affair, by employing their son, Ekawee, and daughter, Awika, when they are not in school. The restaurant opened a year ago seating up to 45 patrons and is quaintly adorned with authentic Thai decor.

The family prides themselves in serving their best Thai family recipes. By using the best quality ingredients to make their food dishes, moderate prices, and warm and friendly service, they seem to have found the right combination to keep customers coming back.

If you're interested in tantalizing your Thai tastebuds, drop in and sample their mouth watering Thai soups, salads, entreés, and desserts.

Mike Hawkins
Fire Lieutenant
Cedar Hammock
Fire Department

Mike grew up in the small town of Ripley, New York, near Buffalo). Both his father and grandfather served as volunteers with Ripley Fire Department in his childhood. He was nine years old when they moved to the Bradenton area. His father became a firefighter for the city of Bradenton. With firefighting in his blood, he sought and attained a position with Cedar Hammock Fire Department and has remained with them since. During his 14 year tenure he attained certification as H.O.T." instructor, NAFI fire/explosion investigator, and has been a Fire Lieutenant for seven years. Mike and Denise have been married 11 years, and they have two sons, Clinton – 8 and Travis – 5. They enjoy baseball and ice hockey.

About the recipe...
Mike remembered fondly the fund-raiser chicken BBQ's held for the Ripley Volunteer Fire Department and after a lot of persuasion was able to obtain the recipe for this tasty BBQ marinade.

Chicken BB-Q White Sauce

Mike Hawkins — Fire Lieutenant

Ingredients:

1 cup white vinegar
1/2 whole egg
2 tablespoons salt

1 teaspoon poultry seasoning
1/2 teaspoon black pepper
1/2 cup vegetable oil

Directions:

1 – Blend/mix all ingredients in a shakable container. (Mix very, very, very well.)

2 – Pour over chicken and marinate in refrigerator at least one hour.

3 – Place on grill like normal and use remaining sauce to baste.

Osso Buco

Ophelia's

Ingredients:

6 – 2 inch cuts out of center of veal shank
6 shallots
6 cloves of garlic
4 leaves of fresh sage
2 bay leaves
1 teaspoon thyme

4 cups veal stock
2 pounds Portobello mushrooms
2 cups dry red wine
1 cup flour
1 cup olive oil
2 cups cream

2 cups water
salt & pepper
1 cup grated asiago cheese (add to finish)
1 cup polenta flour (add and stir gradually for 20 minutes)

Directions:

1 – Dredge shanks in flour, salt & pepper in braising pan, brown off shanks approximately 10 minutes per side.

2 – Take out of pan and sauté shallots, garlic, mushrooms and herbs in same pan.

3 – Add wine and veal stock, reintroduce shanks to liquid, cover with foil and bake at 300 degrees for 2-2 1/2 hours.

Francesco Manzone
Ophelia's

Francesco Manzone was born in Sicily, Italy. His family soon relocated to Milan. As a child, Francesco spent a lot of time in the kitchen with his mother and admired her cooking skills. In 1993, he decided to make his hobby his profession and to begin his training as International Chef in Switzerland. At this time Francesco had no knowledge of the German language. Today he speaks four languages proficiently. Francesco was hired as a Saucier in a four-star hotel. In 1997 he moved to Florida and worked at Nick's on the Water and Café Baci. Presently he is an intragral part of the creative staff at Ophelia's. Francesco is married and the proud father of a new baby boy.

Ophelia's
on the bay

941-349-2212
9105 Midnight Pass Road
Siesta Key
Open 7 Days A Week
5 AM To 10 PM

Beautiful Bay Front View From Our Elegant Dining Room

2

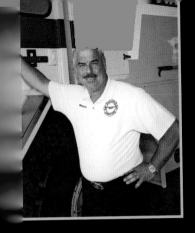

Wally Sharpe
Training Officer
Sarasota Bradenton
Airport C.F.R.

Wally was working for Grumman Aerospace when he got a call from a high school buddy who was a firefighter in Sarasota. His friend urged him to come down for a visit. In 1975, Wally left his Long Island, New York, home for a trip that led to a new home, "Sarasota."

Seeking employment as a firefighter, he was hired by Northeast Fire Department. After two and a half years with Northeast, he moved to Sarasota Bradenton Airport C.F.R. as a firefighter. Twenty-two years later, he enjoys his duties as the Training Officer for his department.

Wally and Peggy have been married five years and have 13 1/2-year old twin boys, Benjamin and Clayton. His hobbies include archery, fishing, diving, and watching his boys play soccer.

About the recipe...
"Their's one thing better than this chicken recipe, and that's the end of my shift!"

Aircraft Rescue firefighters at work.

Mandarin Chicken
Wally Sharpe — Training Officer

Ingredients:

3 lbs. chicken thighs
2 small boxes orange jello

2 small cans mandarin oranges
1 small box white rice (instant)

Directions:

1 – Arrange chicken in a large 2" pan.

2 – Bake @ 350 deg. for 20 minutes...remove from oven and drain grease.

3 – Bring water and Jello powder to boil. (Do not add cold water)

4 – Arrange mandarin oranges on chicken.

5 – Pour juice from orange can into heated jello mixture.

6 – Pour Jello mixture over Chicken and orange slices.

7 – Bake 20 more minutes @ 350 deg, and baste to moisten.

8 – Cook rice by box directions.

9 – Place chicken on rice and add juice to taste.

Snapper Livornese

Cuoco Matto Restaurant

Ingredients:

4 6-8 ounce red snapper filets
Extra virgin olive oil
1 cup chopped tomatoes
1/4 cup capers
18 calamata olives pitted

1/2 cup white wine
1/2 cup fish fume
salt & pepper to taste
flour

Directions:

1 – Season red snapper with salt and pepper, then lightly flour.

2 – Sauté in a hot pan, which is coated with olive oil, until golden brown on both sides.

3 – Add chopped fresh tomatoes, capers, and olives to pan.

4 – Finish with wine and fish stock, let sauce reduce and serve over fish filets.

Makes 4 Servings.

Frank Bologna
Executive Chef & Co-Owner
Cuoco Matto Restaurant

In Italian "cuoco" means cook or chef and "matto" means crazy. Frank Bologna is the Executive Chef and co-owner of this "Crazy Chef Italian Restaurant." Guests can dine or enjoy a drink at the bar, amongst the warm and entertaining ambiance of an open kitchen with an authentic wood-burning oven. The splendid tastes of Rosticceria Cucina Toscana (rustic Tuscan cuisine) are featured along with a distinct wine list at reasonable prices. Warm delicious Foccacia bread with a tangy balsamic vinegar and oil dipping sauce, is served promptly with every meal. Everyone will enjoy the personable, attentive service superb food, and cozy atmosphere found at Cuoco Matto.

Cuoco Matto
Rosticceria Cucina Toscana
RISTORANTE

941-365-0000

1603 N. Tamiami Trail
Sarasota
Daily
11:30 AM To 11:00 PM

Serving
Lunch & Dinner
7 Days A Week

• • •

Catering available
on or off premise

2

Keith Cromwell
Firefighter/EMT
Bradenton Fire Department

Keith started life in the opposite corner of the country. Born in Portland, Oregon, his family moved to Bradenton when his was in his teens. He graduated from Southeast High School in '72, and landed a job with Winn Dixie. During a six month lay-off, he heard about the Fire Department through some firefighters at his church. He applied at the Bradenton Fire Department and was hired. It's been 24 years since that wheel was set in motion, and Keith is thankful for the lay-off that led him to this career.

Married 18 years, Keith and Kathleen have four sons and four grandchildren. Keith's hobbies include his grandchildren, reading, and raising trees. He has donated over 100 hand raised oak trees to Manatee County Schools.

Baked Corn Beef

Keith Cromwell — Firefighter/EMT

Ingredients:

CORNED BEEF:
4-5 1/2 pounds corned beef
4 bay leaves
2 tablespoons whole cloves
1 teaspoon garlic powder or garlic pieces

SAUCE:
4 tablespoons butter
2/3 cup packed dark brown sugar
2 tablespoons yellow mustard
1 cup ketchup
4 tablespoons white vinegar

Directions:

1 – Place corned beef in deep pot and cover completely with cold water. Add garlic, bay leaves and cloves.

2 – Cover pot and bring to a boil.

3 – Lower heat and simmer 4-5 hours or until fork tender.

4 – Just before done, start oven at 350 degrees and make sauce.

5 – In small saucepan, combine butter, brown sugar, mustard, ketchup, 1 tablespoon cooking liquid from beef, and vinegar.

6 – Mix well over heat until blended – do not boil.

7 – Place tender corn beef in baking pan. Pour sauce over meat.

8 – Bake 30 minutes uncovered, basting with sauce occasionally.

9 – Let stand 5 minutes to set juices.

Makes 6 large servings.

Pecan Crusted Crab Cake

Café on the Bay

Ingredients:

2 pounds crab meat
1/8 cup diced celery
1/8 cup diced red and green peppers
1/8 cup mayonnaise
1/4 cup bread crumbs
1 teaspoon old bay spice

2 eggs whipped
1/4 cup flour
1/4 cup ground pecans
1/2 cup mayonnaise
1 lime juiced
1 teaspoon diced jalapeno

Directions:

1 – Mix celery, peppers, 1/8 cup mayonnaise, bread crumbs and old bay spice.

2 – Fold in crab meat.

3 – Form into 8 cakes.

4 – Mix flour and pecans.

5 – Dip cakes in egg.

6 – Roll cake in flour and pecan mix.

7 – Sauté in oil until golden brown on both sides.

8 – For sauce, mix 1/2 cup mayonnaise, limejuice, and jalapenos. Serve on top of cakes.

Makes 4 Servings.

Keith Daum
Executive Chef
Café on the Bay

Keith Daum started in the restaurant business at age 28 to help out a friend during the holiday season. To his surprise, he loved the business so much he enrolled in the C.I.A. and it became his lifelong career. Keith went on to open two 4 star hotels and three other fine dining restaurants in the Rochester, New York area. He became a certified Executive Chef and won two silver medals at the A.C.F. food shows. In September of 1999 he vacationed to Sarasota to visit an old friend, Bill Herlihy. Keith was offered a job as an Executive Chef at Café on the Bay. Not sure about living in Florida, Keith went back home to New York. The rain and snow quickly made up his mind and he is presently with Café on the Bay.

941-383-0440

2630 Harbourside Dr.
Longboat Key, FL 34228

Breakfast Saturday
8:30 AM To 10:30 AM

Sunday Breakfast Brunch
9:00 AM To 1:00 PM

Sunday Lunch
1:00 PM To 3:30 PM

Lunch 6 Days
11:00 AM To 3:00 PM

Dinner 7 Days
4:30 PM To 10:00 PM

Extraordinary cuisine served in a truly exquisite waterfront setting. Come by land or sea. Casual attire is welcomed.

Millie Bradley
**Fire Training Secretary
SCFD**

Since September of 1985, Millie "Chief Bradley" has worked for the Sarasota County Fire Department. She is currently the Senior Secretary for Battalion Chief Costello. She was nicknamed "Chief Bradley" in her early years at SCFD by the guys at Station #5 for keeping things running and organized all the time! Celebrating her 37th year of marriage, Millie has two daughters, one grandson and two poodles. She is a beanie baby collector with over 200 at home. Her other favorite past times include fishing, hunting, refinishing furniture and playing with her dogs. She calls her 30-year-old Meatball recipe, very rich and filling and a real winner! You can't eat too many of these meatballs, for sure, unless you are one of those big appetite firefighters! Millie says the most important things in life to her are "My husband, my dog, all animals and my job. Joining the fire department has been the best thing that ever happened to me. There are no finer people to work with, and I wish I had done it sooner!"

Bayflight coming in for a landing.

Norwegian Meatballs & Gravy
Millie Bradley — Fire Training Secretary, SCFD

Ingredients:

4 tablespoons butter
1/3 cup finely chopped onion
1 pound ground beef
1/4 pound ground lean pork
1/2 cup (1/2 slice) soft bread crumbs
1/2 cup milk
1 egg beaten
3 teaspoons sugar

1 3/4 teaspoon salt
3/4 teaspoon Accent
1/2 teaspoon nutmeg
1/4 teaspoon all spice
3 tablespoons flour
1/4 teaspoon pepper
1 cup water
3/4 cup cream

Directions:

1 – Heat in a large, heavy skillet over low heat 2 tablespoons butter. 2 – Add and cook over medium heat until onion is transparent, stirring occasionally 1/3 cup finely chopped onion. 3 – Mix together lightly the onion and 1 pound ground beef, 1/4 pound ground lean pork, 1/2 cup (1/2 slice) soft bread crumbs, 1/2 cup milk, 1 beaten egg AND a mixture of 2 teaspoons sugar, 1 1/4 teaspoons salt, 3/4 teaspoon Accent, 1/2 teaspoon nutmeg, 1/4 teaspoon allspice. 4 – Shape meat mixture into 1-inch balls. 5 – Heat in the skillet over low heat, 2 tablespoons butter. 6 – Add the meatballs and brown over medium heat. Shake pan frequently to obtain an even browning and to keep balls round. Reduce heat, cover skillet and continue to cook about 10 minutes, shaking pan occasionally. Remove meatballs to warm serving dish; set aside and keep warm. 7 – Blend into the fat in the skillet, 3 tablespoons flour, 1 teaspoon sugar, 1/2 teaspoon salt, and 1/4 teaspoon pepper. 8 – Heat until mixture bubbles and flour is lightly browned. Remove from heat. Add gradually, stirring in a mixture of 1 cup water and 3/4 cup cream. 9 – Bring rapidly to boiling, stirring constantly; cook 1-2 minutes longer. Pour gravy over meatballs in dish. 10 – Serve at once.

Makes 6 Servings.

Optional – I like to add a box of MBT instant broth, 8 packets, to the gravy. It gives it a nice color and adds a little more flavor to the gravy.

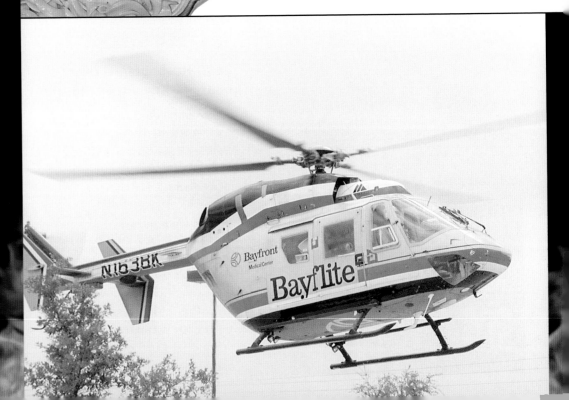

8

Mussels Steamed in Calvados

Café L' Europe

Ingredients:

4 pounds mussels
1 teaspoon olive oil
2 ounces Calvados
1 ounce Ver Jus (white grape juice)
2 stems fresh thyme

1 apple sliced thin
2 shallots sliced
1 teaspoon curry powder
4 ounces butter
salt and pepper

Directions:

1 – Clean mussels very well by allowing to purge overnight in salt water.

2 – Add olive oil to a large pot and heat very hot until it begins to smoke. Add mussels and stir. When you notice they are beginning to open, add calvados, shallots and thyme and cover the pot for 2 minutes. (At this time most of the mussels should be open.)

3 – Add apples, curry and ver jus.

4 – Allow to simmer for a couple of minutes.

5 – Finish with butter and season with salt and pepper.

Makes 4 Servings.

Café L' Europe

Now celebrating its twenty seventh anniversary, Café L' Europe continues to be one of Sarasota's most beautiful and popular restaurants. A multitude of awards have been received over the years from such publications as The Wine Spectator, Sante' Award of Excellence and Florida Trend as well as the prestigious DIRONA award; bearing witness to the high quality of food. Pleasing aromas and beautiful presentations preview the finest of Continental Cuisine and New European Cuisine from elaborate appetizers to elegant entrees and truly decadent desserts. Completing the scene is a superb selection of wines from the finest vineyards of Europe and California. The final ingredient essential to fine dining is the high level of professional service. The warm welcome on arrival hints at the care taken by every person at Café L' Europe to ensure your dining pleasure.

Porter Shellhammer
Battalion Chief
SCFD

Porter started his career in the fire service as a volunteer with Longboat Key Fire Rescue in 1974. His pursuit of a full time/paid position took him to the South Trail Fire Department where he began his ascent to the position he now holds. Porter was a pioneer in both paramedicine, and hazardous materials/incidents mitigation.

After 25 years of service, he has the opportunity to equip our personnel with the latest information and technologies as he heads the Training Division for SCFD.

Porter and his wife, Joan, have two daughters, a tiger cat, and a miniature schnauzer. He loves to golf, fish, and spend time with his family; however, his ultimate priority is serving the Lord.

About the recipe...
This recipe is one of Porter's favorites. His wife Joan says that he taught her how to make this dish shortly after they were married.

"Chicken Spinach Noodle Casserole"
Porter Shellhammer — Battalion Chief

Ingredients:

4 lbs. (1 hen) chicken
1 stick margarine
1 cup green pepper (chopped)
1 cup celery (chopped)
1 cup onion (chopped)
3/4 lb. Velveeta (cubed)

6 oz. stuffed green olives
6 oz. mushrooms (sliced)
1 pkg. spinach noodles
4 cups chicken stock
1 can mushroom soup

Directions:

1 – Boil chicken to provide 4 cups of chicken stock. Take meat off bones and set aside.

2 – Sauté with green peppers, celery, and onion.

3 – Stir in cubed cheese.

4 – Add olives, mushrooms, and chicken.

5 – Boil noodles in 3 cups of stock until all is absorbed.

6 – Mix soup with noodles and add rest of ingredients in a 9"x 13" glass baking dish.

7 – Remaining stock can be used to moisten if needed.

8 – Reheat in oven 300 degrees for 45 minutes. Then serve hot.

Makes 6 – 8 Servings.

20

"Easy Duty Lasagna"

Jerry Sahagian — Firefighter/EMT

Ingredients:

1 lb.ground beef
1 tbs.chopped garlic
1 med or large chopped onion
1 large carton ricotta cheese
2 eggs
1 pkg. lasagna noodles

1 can stewed chopped tomatoes (undrained)
32 oz. jar Spaghetti Sauce ("Prego")
1 tbsp.basil
1/3 cup parmesan cheese

Directions:

1 – Brown beef in pot with onion, garlic, and basil…drain fat.

2 – Add chopped tomatoes & spaghetti sauce, then simmer.

3 – In a large bowl mix ricotta cheese, eggs and parmesan.

4 – Spread thin layer of meat sauce on bottom of 9 X 13 pan.

5 – Cover with layer of noodles.

6 – Top noodles with layer of cheese sauce mixture.

7 – Repeat layers, ending with sauce on top.

8 – Bake uncovered at 350 deg. for 1 hour.

9 – Suggested sides: Garlic bread, and tossed salad.

Makes 6–8 Servings.

Jerry Sahagian
Firefighter/EMT
SCFD

Jerry, a former computer aided draftsman, started his career in the fire service as a Firefighter/EMT just seven years ago at the age of 28. He and his wife, Liz, have three beautiful daughters named Renee, Kara, and Heather, ages ten, six, and three respectively. Who says three's a crowd ?

Jerry's favorite sport is wrestling and is proud to have won the Florida Firefighter Olympics Gold Medal in that sport. This former Eagle Scout is active in his church as a youth group sponsor, and says the thing he loves most in life is : "The peace that comes only from God."

Robert Bennett
Firefighter/Paramedic
SCFD

Fifteen years ago, Robert Bennett began volunteering with the Anna Maria Fire Department. He got the "bug" for firefighting and is currently a Firefighter/ Paramedic with Sarasota County Fire Department. In 1994, Robert was honored as Paramedic of the Year for the State of Florida. He and his wife, Teri, have a daughter, Alison and one baby on the way due January of 2001. Robert loves spending his extra time around the water. Fishing, surfing and hydro sporting on the gulf are among his favorite activities. When asked about the recipe, he says, "Fast and easy to cook when you expect to get 'banged' out on the next call before you can eat!"

Headquarters to
Battalion 4 command.

222

Stuffed Pork Chops

Robert Bennett — Firefighter/Paramedic

Ingredients:

6 center cut pork chops
8 ounce box homestyle herb stuffing mix
1/8 teaspoon paprika
1/8 teaspoon sage

1/8 teaspoon oregano
1/8 teaspoon garlic
1/8 teaspoon basil
1/8 teaspoon fajita seasoning

Directions:

1 – Butterfly chops.

2 – Cook stuffing according to directions on the box.

3 – Add spices to stuffing mix, leaving a small amount for outside of chops.

3 – Stuff pork chops with stuffing mix. (Optional – Put butter on stuffing mix to make it crunchy.)

4 – Season outside of pork chops with left over seasoning.

5 – Cook pork chops for 45 minutes in the oven at 350 degrees.

Cuban Stuffed Pot Roast – Boliche Relleno

Columbia Restaurant

Ingredients:

3 pounds boliche (eye round of beef)
1 large green pepper, cut in strips
3 large onions, sliced in half-moons
2 tablespoons oregano
4 bay leaves
6 cloves garlic, minced
1/2 pound smoked ham, cut up in
    1-inch pieces

1 tablespoon salt
2 teaspoons black pepper
1 cup red wine
3 whole chorizos (Spanish sausages)
4 tablespoons paprika
3 cups beef broth
1/4 cup olive oil

Directions:

1 – Pierce a hole (about 1 inch in diameter) through the length of the boliche. Stuff with Spanish sausage and ham.

2 – Heat oil in a Dutch oven.

3 – Mix salt, pepper, oregano, paprika and rub on outside of roast until it is well covered.

4 – All onions, green pepper, and garlic.

5 – Brown boliche in Dutch oven. Add broth, red wine and bay leaves. Cover.

6 – Cook over medium-low heat for approximately 2 1/2 hours, turning several times.

7 – When done, remove from Dutch oven and process gravy in food processor until smooth.

8 – Cut boliche into 1/2 inch slices and pour gravy over it.

9 – Serves with white rice, black beans and fried ripe plantains.

Makes 8 Servings.

Richard, Adela and Casey Gonzmart

Owners
Columbia Restaurant

Our family has been creating some of Florida's favorite Spanish cuisine for nearly 100 years. We feature the freshest seafood and steaks as well as our won tradition family recipes. Through the years we have received some of the highest awards in the restaurant industry, but our highest praise comes from our loyal customers who dine with us again and again.

Join us daily for lunch or dinner, and take in the beautiful sites of St. Armands Circle while enjoying the delicious dishes our chef prepares especially for you.

The Gonzmart family looks forward to welcoming you to the Columbia Restaurant!

Dawn Wright
Firefighter/Paramedic
SCFD

Dawn Wright began her career in the EMS field in 1983. In 1987 she joined the Sarasota County Fire Department as a firefighter/paramedic and is currently assigned to station #4. Dawn is married to Jim, a Lieutenant with SCFD, and they have three boys, eight-year old Bryan, and five-year old twins, David and Stephen. They keep her very busy! Her husband, children and job are most important to her but not always in that order.

About the recipe...she says, "Diana Galan made a simpler (still great) version, Rich Nichols (who taught me a lot of what I know about cooking) added some stuff, then I added some more and now this is my most requested meal!

Chicken and Yellow Rice
Dawn Wright — Firefighter/Paramedic

Ingredients:

1 whole 3-5 pound chicken
4 cups chicken broth
1 pound package Vigo yellow rice
1 medium – large white onion
1 medium – large green pepper

4 ounce jar diced pimentos
10 ounce can Rotel brand diced tomatoes
15 ounce can very early young peas.

Directions:

1 – Place chicken in large pot, cover with water.

2 – Bring to boil then reduce heat and simmer 1-2 hours.

3 – Remove chicken to plate, refrigerate to cool. Reserve 4 cups broth.

4 – Pull cooled chicken meat from bones, discard bones and skin.

5 – Dice onion and pepper, open canned vegetables (don't drain)

6 – Place broth, meat, and veggies in large pot with lid and bring to a boil.

7 – Add rice mix and boil for 1 minute. Cover and reduce heat to simmer. Simmer covered 20 – 25 minutes until liquid is absorbed and rice cooked.

8 – Remove from heat and let stand covered 5 minutes. Stir and serve.

9 – Serve with hot bread and make sure you have Crystal hot sauce on hand.

Makes 4 – 6 Servings. (Depends on Crew)

Veal Chop with Anchovy Sauce

Munroe's Restaurant

Ingredients:

1 16 ounce veal rib chop
3 ounces olive oil
4 anchovy fillets
1 ounce baby spinach leaves

1/2 ounce fresh basil leaves
1 roma tomato diced
1/2 teaspoon minced garlic
1 lemon juice of

Directions:

1 - Pan sear veal chop in olive oil to desired temperature, remove from pan and reserve.

2 – Using the veal chop pan, add anchovy fillets, spinach and basil to the juices – toss to heat.

3 – Add remaining ingredients; toss well and spoon over the veal chop.

Richard Munroe
Chef/Proprietor
Munroe's Restaurant

Locals and seasonal visitors alike enjoy the bistro setting of Munroe's Restaurant. Proven to be Sarasota's favorite restaurant with casual elegance, friendly service, and creative, American foods.

Whether you start off your meal with one of our famous appetizers or finish with one of our colorful desserts, you won't go away disappointed.

For the late night guest, we offer live entertainment upstairs, with a late night menu and premium bar.

Munroe's

Urban Bistro - Vintage Tavern

941-316-0609

**1296 First Street
Sarasota
Lunch Monday – Friday
Dinner Monday – Saturday
5:30 PM To 10:00 PM
Closed Sundays**

Sarasota's Favorite Restaurant

- American cuisine
- Bistro setting
- Live entertainment upstairs
- Desserts • Appetizers
- Late Night Menu
- Premium Bar
- Catering Available

225

Hans Rode
Firefighter/Paramedic
SCFD

Hans is part of a Sarasota circus family whose parents relocated from Germany to work with Ringling Brothers Circus. After a few years, they began working for other independent circus's. They performed throughout the U.S., Canada, and Mexico until he was 10 years old. In 1972 his family opened the "Old Heidelberg Castle of Sarasota" where he performed as a trampoline jumper and played the "Cow Bells." As he grew older, he began cooking, baking in the restaurant, and decorating wedding cakes.

He became a firefighter in 1987 with the Sarasota Fire Department and is currently assigned to Station #4 on A-shift as a paramedic/ firefighter. His authentic German dishes are enjoyed regularly by his crew and a real treat to firefighters who are floated in to cover.

About the recipe...
"The Roulade recipe is a traditonal German dish that was served at the Heidelburg Castle."

German Roulade

Hans R. Rode — Firefighter/Paramedic
In German, this is called, "Gemuetlich."

Ingredients:

MEAT:
4 pound bottom round/
    roulade meat sliced thin
medium spicy – mustard
pinch salt and pepper
4 dill pickles, 4 slices bacon

2 small sliced onions
water to cover.

GRAVY:
3 tablespoons butter
cornstarch

1/2 teaspoon salt
1/2 teaspoon pepper
sliced mushrooms (optional)

(All ingredients in this recipe can be found at Geier's Sausage Kitchen or Publix.)

Directions:

1 – Your local butcher will have or can slice beef for roulade. To prepare the meat, pound it with a mallet on both sides and thin to approximately 1/8". This will make it tender.
2 – Lay flattened meat out; spread some mustard evenly on each piece of meat.
3 – Salt and pepper meat, lay a slice of bacon long ways and a slice of pickle across.
4 – Sprinkle on some onions, saving approximately 1/4 cup and set aside.
5 – Roll roulade up with the slice of pickle at the top in the center using a wooden toothpick to hold them together.
6 – Place roulades in 9x9 baking dish, toothpick side down. Broil top until brown.
7 – Pour 3 cups (or until roulades are mostly covered) of water on top and add remaining onions.
8 – Cover tightly with foil or lid, reduce oven heat to 325 and bake 2 hours or until tender.
9 – When done, use stock to make gravy.
10 – Melt 3 tablespoons of butter in saucepan over medium heat. Stir in cornstarch, 1/2 teaspoon salt, and 1/2 teaspoon pepper. Slowly add 2 cups of stock, stirring constantly. Bring to boil, continuing to stir. Boil one minute, stirring constantly. Add sautéed mushrooms to gravy (optional).
11 – Recommended serving with "MAGGI" Spaetzle (or boiling potatoes) and sweet and sour red cabbage. (You may add 2 slices bacon cut into small pieces and sautéed with 1/4 sliced small onion to red cabbage.)

Mishi (Stuffed) Chicken

Marty Ferris — Firefighter/EMT

Marty Ferris
Firefighter/EMT

Ingredients:

large pot
6-7 pound whole roasting chicken
1/2 pound ground round
3/4 cup rice
2 tablespoons pinenuts (if desired)

1/4 cup water
salt
pepper
cinnamon

Directions:

1 – Remove giblets and wash chicken.

2 – Mix together 1/2 pound ground round, 1/4 cup rice, 2 tablespoons pinenuts, 1/4 cup water, 1 teaspoon salt, 1/8 teaspoon pepper and 1/8 teaspoon cinnamon.

3 – Loosely stuff chicken with approximately 1/2 of the stuffing mixture.

4 – Place chicken in a large pot and cover with water.

5 – Add 1 tablespoon salt, 1/2 teaspoon pepper, and 1/4 teaspoon cinnamon. Bring to boil. Cover pot with a lid and simmer for 1 1/2 hours.

6 – Sprinkle in remaining stuffing in small drops. Add 1/2 cup rice. Bring to a boil, then simmer uncovered for 20 minutes.

7 – Remove chicken from pot, shred approximately 1/2 cup chicken into small pieces and add back into the soup.

8 – Serve with unleavened bread, yogurt, Greek olives, sliced tomatoes and cucumber.

Makes 8 Servings.

When I was small, my mother made Mishi Chicken on Sundays. I can still remember the wonderful aroma of cinnamon mingled with the smell of fresh bread and laughter. My Lebanese grandmother, my mother and her two sisters often spent all day baking piles and piles of unleavened bread in giant ovens down in the basement. Today, my children tell me this is the best soup to eat if you have a cold or flu. It has made its way into the firehouse and is enjoyed by all. Whether it is from the warm childhood memories or from the warmth it gives going down, this is definitely a dish that is soothing to my soul.

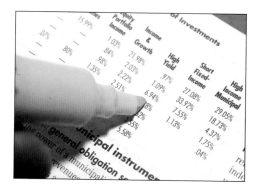

Tom Hennessy
Captain
Southern Manatee
Fire Department

Tom grew up in a family of six children in Long Island, New York. As a child he was extremely skinny, hence the nickname T-bone, which has stuck to this day. He moved here in 1979 and was hired by Sarasota Bradenton CFR in 1980. Eighteen months later, he took a position with Oneco-Tallevast Fire Department (currently Southern Manatee Fire) and has been there ever since. He was promoted to Lieutenant in 1982 and Captain in 1995.

Tom and Pamela have been married 16 years and have two sons, Brian and William. They enjoy hunting, camping, and fishing the Manatee River.

Off duty, Tom and his firefighter partner own and operate Starfire Training Systems. Their company provides OSHA safety related classes.

Tom's Cajun Redfish
Tom Hennessy — Captain

Ingredients:

2 pounds redfish fillets
1/2 cup virgin olive oil
4 tablespoons butter

2 cloves garlic
1 bottle redfish seasonings
   (Chef Prudhommes)

Directions:

1 – Coat redfish fillets generously with redfish seasonings on both sides.

2 – In large fry skillet add olive oil, butter, garlic-finely chopped, and stir.

3 – Bring to medium-high heat.

4 – Add redfish fillets to pan, cook 2-3 minutes on each side until flakey.

5 – Remove fillets, place on paper towel momentarily to drain.

6 – Serve hot with tator tots and coleslaw.

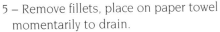

Jumbo Lump Crabcakes

Café L' Europe

Ingredients:

2 tablespoons olive oil
flour for dredging
1 pound jumbo lump crab
3 tablespoons mayonnaise
3 shakes Worcestershire sauce
1 tablespoon Dijon mustard
3 slices white bread

salt and pepper
1 sheet puff pastry
1 tablespoon herbs d' provençe
1 lemon
2 tablespoons capers
2 ounces Vermouth
8 ounces butter

Directions:

1 – Remove all shell and cartilage from crabmeat.
2 – Remove crust from bread and dice small.
3 – Add to crabmeat along with Worcestershire, Dijon, mayonnaise and season with salt and pepper.
4 – Form into 2 ounce cakes and reserve.
5 – With cookie cutter, cut 12 three inch circles of puff pastry.
6 – Sprinkle with herbs d' provençe and bake in a 400 degree oven until brown. Reserve.
7 – In a hot sauté pan drizzle in olive oil.
8 – Dredge cakes in flour and lightly brown on one side.
9 – Place in 350 degree oven for 5 minutes.
10 – Juice lemon and with vermouth reduce in a small saucepan until almost all liquid has evaporated.
11 - Remove from heat and stir in with a wooden spoon, the soft butter until it has all melted into a sauce consistency.
12 – Layer puff pastry with crab cakes and sauce around them. Garnish with capers.
Makes 4 Servings.

Paul Madden
Firefighter/Paramedic
Chaplain
SCFD

Paul was raised in Ottawa,
Illinois, the youngest of four.
In 1978, he moved to Tarpon
Springs, Florida, in search of
work and ended up making
pilings in a concrete yard. He
attended seminary school in
the early 80's and graduated
in 1984 with an A.S. degree
in pastoral training.

In 1986 he pursued a career
in emergency services and
was hired by South County
Ambulance (currently
Sarasota County Fire
Department). Paul was given
the responsibility as chaplain
shortly after arrival at South
County and through several
mergers has retained the title
he covets.

Off duty you can find Paul
working as fire science coordi-
nator for Vo-Tech or occasionally bass fishing the Myakka
and Peace rivers.

Paul has two children, James
and Christina.

Pizza Wheels

Paul Madden — Firefighter/Paramedic, Chaplain

Ingredients:

1 large egg (beaten)
1/3 cup milk
1/3 cup fine - dry bread crumbs
1/3 cup onion (finely chopped)
3/4 teas. salt

2 lbs. lean ground beef
10 oz. can pizza sauce
3 oz. can mushrooms (chopped, drained)
3/4 teas. dried basil leaves (crushed)
3 slices mozzarella cheese

Directions:

1 – Combine egg, milk, bread crumbs, onion, and salt.

2 – Add beef to mixture; mix well.

3 – Add 2 oz. of pizza sauce to mixture.

4 – In a shallow baking pan, shape 7 to 8 patties (4"- 4 1/2" diameter, by 1" thick).

5 – Combine remaining pizza sauce, mushrooms and basil.

6 – Spoon onto patties.

7 – Bake at 350 deg. for 30 minutes.

8 – Remove from oven, place thin cheese strips (spoke fashion) atop pizza.

9 – Bake for 2 min to melt cheese.

Makes 7 – 8 Servings (or 4 Firemen).

Potato Crusted Beef Medallions

Sarasota University Club

Ingredients:

4 – 2 ounce beef filet medallions
1 ounce flour for dipping
1 tablespoon olive oil
4 slices Prosciutto
1 peeled baking potato
1 egg slightly beaten

salt and pepper to season
1 teaspoon chili powder
1 large clove diced shallots
1 tablespoon olive oil
1 medium diced tomato
1 tablespoon rosemary

Directions:

1 – Wrap filet with Prosciutto, secure with a toothpick if necessary.
2 – Shred the potato with a mandolin or with the grater attachment of a food processor.
3 – First add the tablespoon of flour to the shredded potato mix. Next add the egg and chili powder.
4 – Heat a non-stick pan to medium with 1 tablespoon olive oil.
5 – Season the filets with salt and pepper, then dip one side of the filets in the flour, shake off excess flour.
6 – Divide the shredded potato into four equal portions, top each of the floured filets with a portion of the potato.
7 – In the pan, carefully lay filet, potato side down. Saute until potato is crisp and brown, turn over and cook 2 more minutes for medium rare.
8 – Remove filets from the pan, add 1 tablespoon olive oil and shallots, cook until evenly brown.
9 – Add tomato, rosemary, salt and pepper and cook until tomatoes are soft and a sauce has formed.
10 – Divide the sauce on two plates, top with two filets per plate.

Makes 2 Servings.

Timothy J. Nichol
General Manager
Sarasota University Club

Former Executive Chef of University Club, Tim was promoted to General Manager in January 2000. Tim's background includes over ten years of private club experience, an Associate degree, Restaurant Management and Bachelor's degree, dual major Marketing/Management from Northwood University, Midland Michigan.
"This is one of my favorite recipes that I would demonstrate for cooking classes held at the University Club. The potato protects the filet and the rosemary/tomato sauce transforms simple ingredients into a flavorful sauce that pairs well with different red wines." All the chefs at the University Club enjoyed being a part of the Firehouse Favorites Cookbook and hope you will enjoy the recipes.

Tom Aloisio

Firemedic
Sarasota/Bradenton
International Airport
Fire Department

Tom started fire fighting in 1971 at Northeast Fire Department at Airport Fire since 1981. He has been married 26 years and has two children and one grand-daughter. When asked about his job and family, he replies, "My family, they make it easier to do this job for as long as I have." Tom hobbies include Civil War Reenacting, collecting and selling medical antiques.

The eggplant recipe has been a longtime favorite in his family since the 1920's.

Sarasota Bradenton International Airport Crash Rescue Truck 3 is a 1996 Oshkosh which can dump 3,000 gallons of foam in one minute and forty-five seconds.

Eggplant Roteini

Tom Aloisio — Firemedic

Ingredients:

2 large firm eggplants
1 cup olive oil
1/2 cup each romano cheese and
    parmesan cheese

2 cups Italian bread crumbs
3 eggs well beaten
4 pounds part-skim ricotta cheese
1 pound grated mozzarella cheese

Directions:

1 – Wash eggplant then peel.

2 – Slice eggplant 1/4" thick lengthwise.

3 – Dip each slice in eggs, then roll in crumbs combined with Romano & Parmesan cheeses.

4 – Sauté eggplant in hot oil until golden brown on both sides and soft.

5 – Drain on paper towels, or brown paper bags.

6 – Place 1-2 tablespoons of ricotta cheese on the slice of eggplant, roll into a jelly roll shape and place in baking pan. Continue until the pan is full.

7 – Cover with your favorite tomato sauce and the mozzarella cheese.

8 – Bake at 325 degrees 30 minutes or until the mozzarella cheese is melted and bubbles.

9 – Let stand 10 minutes after removing from the oven.

*Serve with a side of pasta, salad and garlic bread.

Scrumptious Pot Roast

Charlie Russell — Firefighter/EMT

Ingredients:

3 1/2 -4 pound chuck pot roast
10 3/4 ounce can of cream of mushroom
2 packs dry onion soup mix
1/2 cup water

6 potatoes
10 carrots
1 large Spanish onion

Directions:

1 – Cut potatoes, carrots and onions into bite size pieces and put in crock pot.

2 – Mix in cream of mushroom soup.

3 – Put pot roast in next.

4 – Pour in 2 packs on onion soup mix on top of roast.

5 – Pour 1/2 cup of water over top.

6 – Cover and put crock pot on low 7 to 8 hours or until roast is done.

Makes 4 Servings.

Charlie Russell
Firefighter/EMT
Englewood Fire Department

Charlie Russell, a Firefighter/EMT, is presently with the Englewood Fire Department. Serving 17 years in the fire service to date, Charlie has been honored as the 1999 Firefighter of the Year. He is an outdoorsman enjoying hunting, fishing and sports. Back home in Mississippi is where this delicious recipe came from, straight from his mom's kitchen. When asked what he loves most in life he replies, "What I love most in life is meeting new people and helping people. Living life to the fullest each day is important because you never know what tomorrow will bring."

James "Jiggy" Mattera
Firemedic
SCFD

Jiggy moved to Sarasota as a 14-year old from Long Island, New York. His father was retiring and Jiggy had high hopes of broadening his baseball prospects.

In 1996, at the urging of a friend, became a volunteer firefighter with Braden River and subsequently SCFD. His interest peaked and he went to both fire and EMT school to become eligible for hiring. He was hired by SCFD in January 1996 and is currently assigned as a floater out of Station #5-A.

Jiggy is a 25-year old eligible bachelor who enjoys our warm beaches, as well as, playing "left wing" for the firefighters ice hockey team, "Running Hot." He has three roommates; Bowzer and Dakota (sibling Rotweilers) and Domino (his cat).

Jiggy's Chicken Fettuccini

James "Jiggy" Mattera

Ingredients:

6 skinless
boneless chicken breasts
6 portobello mushrooms (sliced-optional)
32 ounce jar (per pound of pasta) of
   Ragu alfredo or parmesan garlic
   ("white") sauce

2 pounds fettuccine pasta
   (plain or spinach)
6 slices provolone and mozzarella cheeses
oregano
garlic
basil

Directions:

1 – Heat sauce.
2 – Preheat oven to 350 degrees.
3 – Grill chicken until cooked, just slightly rare.
4 – Grill portobello mushrooms on top of grill rack (after chicken) and sear mushrooms quickly.
5 – Line sheet pan with foil.

6 – Add desired amount of spices (oregano, garlic, basil) to sauce.
7 – Cook pasta, drain and set aside.
8 – Place chicken on foil. Put 1 tablespoon of sauce on each chicken. Evenly distribute grilled mushrooms on top of chickens. Top mushrooms with a spot of sauce. Place mozzarella cheese and provolone cheese next.
9 – Put in oven until cheese melts thoroughly. Lightly brown is preferred.
10 – Fill plate with pasta, ladle sauce around pasta, and place chicken on center of pasta.
11 – Sprinkle with sauce and basil or oregano.
12 – Serve with garlic bread and caesar salad.

Pan Seared Sea Scallops with Bow Tie Pasta

Ophelia's

Ingredients:

2 pounds large Sea scallops
2 cups chiffonade of spinach
2 cups sliced shiitake mushrooms

1 cup sliced sun-dried tomatoes
1/4 cup roasted garlic oil
salt & pepper

Directions:

1 – In a large sauté pan or cast iron skillet, heat oil until it just starts smoking.

2 – Season Sea scallops and add to pan browning scallops for approximately 2-3 minutes or until golden brown on one side.

3 – Add spinach to pan, add pasta plus 1 teaspoon garlic oil to serve.

Stan Ferro
Ophelia's

Stan Ferro, a native of Massachusetts, exposure to the culinary world began in the kitchens of the restaurants his Great Aunt Ophelia owned, when he was a child. She was always the chef and he loved to help her. After moving to Cape Cod, Stan began cooking during the summer after his first year in college. Traveling in Europe on his honeymoon with Jane gave Stan exposure to European Cuisine. Upon their return, Stan worked for Marriott in Boston and was the chef at the Hasty Pudding Club at Harvard. When he moved back to the Cape, Stan mastered the art of carpentry and in 1976 renovated the Playhouse Restaurant. He was chef there for 14 years. In 1988 he renovated Ophelia's and was the chef there for five years. He now runs the business end of it. Stan is also an avid golfer and on the committee of the Siesta Key Chamber golf tournament.

235

Mike Rezac

Firemedic
Sarasota County
Fire Department

Mike is a 10 year veteran Firefighter/EMT currently working out of Station 5 on B-shift. Mike was born in Czechoslovakia and speaks fluent Czech, Polish, and English. Before becoming a firemedic, he followed in his father's footsteps as a jeweler. He still works on his off days in their family jeweler business. His hobbies are skiing, diving, and art. He has two grown children, Angela and Michael Jr., and a nine month old grandson Cameron. He and his wife, Giovanna, had a new baby in June. When asked what he values most in life, Mike said, "Faith in God, and Family."

Teleci Rizky – (Veal Cutlets)

Mike Rezac — Firemedic

Ingredients:

3 pounds leg of veal cut into 8 slices
1 teaspoon salt
9 tablespoons flour
5 eggs (beaten)

3 cups bread crumbs
1 3/4 cup butter or olive oil
1 large lemon

Directions:

1 – Pound meat and then sprinkle with salt. (Tips: May use turkey, fish, or chicken in place of veal, if preferred. Works best when meat is sliced thin.)

2 – Dip first in flour, then beaten eggs, and then in bread crumbs.

3 – Fry in hot butter or oil until golden brown.

4 – Serve hot with lemon wedges.

5 – Suggested sides: Potato salad and German style barrel pickles.

Makes 4 Servings.

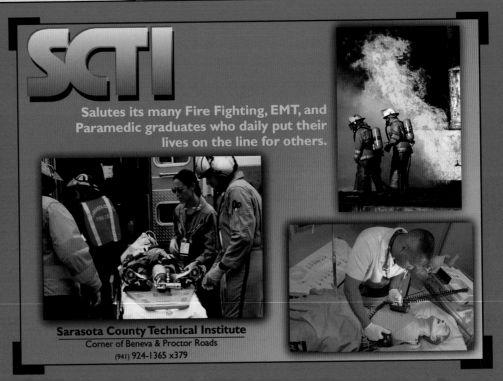

Chargrilled Swordfish

The Colony Restaurants

Ingredients:

10 Swordfish Steaks, 7-ounce each
To coat extra virgin olive oil
To taste chopped garlic
To taste salt and freshly ground black pepper
Orange segments for garnish

ORANGE PONZU SAUCE:
2 quarts orange juice
1 teaspoon tamari soy sauce
1 teaspoon chopped ginger
1 tablespoon chopped shallots
1/2 cup brown sugar
6 ounces Mirin

Directions:

1 – In medium saucepan over medium heat, reduce orange juice to one half.

2 – Add all remaining ingredients and reduce by one half. Strain and hold.

FINAL ASSEMBLY:

1 – Season the swordfish steak and rub with garlic and oil.

2 – Grill to desired doneness according to thickness of steak.

SUGGESTED SIDE DISHES:
Place pasta cake on dish and "shingle" the cooked swordfish on top. Place small amount of Asian slaw off one end of the swordfish. Ladle ponzu sauce over other end of swordfish and onto plate. Garnish with orange segments.

Makes 10 Servings.

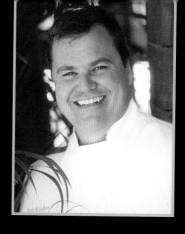

Tom Klauber
Food & Beverage Director
The Colony Restaurants

The Colony's Director of Food & Beverage Operations Tom Klauber is also Chef/Proprietor of Longboat Key's popular Pattigeorge's restaurant. Tom began his culinary career by working at his family's resort, later attending the University of Houston's Hotel & Management School, and earning a degree from the Culinary Institute of America. He then traveled and studied abroad, receiving his diploma from La Varenne's Ecole de Cuisine in Paris, France. He gained experience in fine restaurants in Paris, Florence and Amsterdam before returning to The Colony, where he worked as executive chef and food and beverage director from 1982 to 1992. Prior to opening PGs in 1998, Tom was chef/owner at Gieusseppi Wong in Aspen.

Tom Klauber has received numerous accolades, including being recognized in "Chefs in America" as one of the outstanding chefs in the United States, and receiving the James Beard Foundation "Rising Stars of American Cuisine" Award.

---

the Colony Restaurants

Monday – Saturday
Lunch: 11:30 AM To 2:30 PM
Dinner: 6:00 PM To 10:00 PM
Sunday Brunch:
10:00 AM To 2:00 PM

941-383-5558

1620 Gulf of Mexico Drive
Longboat Key

• • •

Enjoy an award-winning dining experience complemented by an unparalleled wine list with *spectacular* views of the Gulf of Mexico.

• **Prestigious DiRoNA Award**

• **The Wine Spectator's Award of Excellence**

• **Five Star Diamond Award for outstanding hospitality from the American Academy of Hospitality Sciences**

• **Member of Nation's Restaurant News Fine Dining Hall of Fame**

Tom Cook
Firefighter/Paramedic
SCFD

Tom grew up in Minneapolis, Minnesota, with the dream of being a firefighter someday. While attending college for a B.A. in liberal arts, he simultaneously attended EMT and paramedic school. After graduation, Tom moved to Florida in pursuit of our water and favorable weather.

He was hired by Manatee County EMS in 1996 as a paramedic and while working there, attained his training and certification as a firefighter. In 1998 his childhood dream came true when he was hired by Sarasota County Fire Department as a firefighter/paramedic.

Certainly a man named "Cook" would have an interest in food, and Tom is no exception. His experience as a saute` and short order cook blends well in the Fire Department.

Tom has a 15-year old daughter, Danielle. His hobbies include fishing, boating, and biking.

SCFD battles a four-alarm blaze in an office complex.

Seafood Pasta with Rosemary Lemon Sauce
Tom Cook — Firefighter/Paramedic

Ingredients:

2 lemons
1 pint heavy whipping cream
1 tablespoon dried rosemary
dash of white or black pepper

1 pound fettuccini or other pasta
1-1 1/2 pounds scallops
shrimp or other seafood

Directions:

1 – In large, uncovered saucepan, combine whipping cream and rosemary.

2 – Over medium heat, allow cream to boil and reduce, stirring as needed to prevent burning.

3 –Grate the outside zest of one washed lemon into sauce, being careful not to include any of the deeper white part of lemon rind.

4 – As sauce approaches desired thickness add the juice of 1 lemon and seafood. Add pepper to taste.

5 – Reduce heat on sauce to low and start boiling pasta.

6 – This recipe will serve 2-3 people if served as an entrée, or up to 6 if served as a side dish for large meal.

Paella Bouillibaise

Café L' Europe

Ingredients:

SAFFRON RICE:
1 cup long grain rice
1 onion finely chopped
2 1/4 cups chicken stock
1 pinch saffron

BOUILLIBAISE:
24 littleneck clams
24 mussels

1 pound bite size fish pieces (any variety)
6 large scallops
6 jumbo shrimp
2 tablespoons chopped garlic
1 head fennel thinly sliced
2 ounces Vermouth
2 cups clam juice
1 teaspoon herbs d' provençe
1/2 cup piquillo pepper puree

Directions:

1 – Prepare rice as follow: In a hot saucepan, add olive oil and rice and stir together. Add stock and stir in with saffron. Allow to simmer until all the liquid has been absorbed. Remove from heat and keep warm.

2 – In a large pot heat olive oil. When hot add in clams and mussels and allow to steam open.

3 – Add to the pot garlic, shrimp, scallops, fish pieces and sliced fennel.

4 – Deglaze with Vermouth.

5 – Add clam juice, herbs and pepper puree.

6 – Simmer for 10 minutes uncovered.

7 – Fluff up rice with a fork and ladle paella over the top.

Makes 6 Servings.

Michael Garey
General Manager
Café L' Europe

Michael Garey was born and raised in Buffalo, New York He moved to Sarasota Florida as a teenager and began in the restaurant business as a busboy in 1977. In 1979 he started as a busboy at the Café L' Europe Moving up the ladder, he became a dining room captain in 1981 and assistant manager in 1982. In 1984, he left Café L' Europe to help open and manage Mr. Wong's Chinese restaurant. Michael came back to Café L' Europe in 1986 as General Manager the title that he holds today Mr. Garey is currently President of the St. Armands Merchants Assoc. and conceived and organized two events for the Florida Wine Festival, the Wine Marker's Dinner, and Sip and Shop He is married to his wife Catherine and has three daughters, Alexandra, Jenna and Amelia

Mike Cooper
Firefighter/EMT
(Soon To Be Paramedic)
Bradenton Fire Department

Mike Cooper, or "Coop" to his firehouse peers, wasn't always a firefighter. Born in Fairlawn, New Jersey, Coop moved to Bradenton when he was five. His first job was a busboy, and he worked his way up through the ranks until he found himself cooking as a chef with the local Holiday Inn. Coop's cousin (Joe Cordasco) is the Sarasota firefighter who got him interested in a career in firefighting. He was hired by Bradenton Fire Department in 1997 and is currently nearing completion of his training as a paramedic. His prior work experience has been a bonus for his crew, as they enjoy his culinary talents when he's on shift. As 23-year old bachelor, Coop says the thing he enjoys most in life is being a firefighter.

London Broil

Mike Cooper — Firefighter/EMT

Ingredients:

2 pounds London broil
8 ounce bottle French dressing
1 teaspoon black pepper

1 teaspoon garlic powder
1 teaspoon onion powder

Directions:

1 – Season meat with pepper, onion and garlic.

2 – Pour French dressing over seasoned meat.

3 – Marinate overnight.

4 – Grill London broil 15-20 minutes.

5 – Suggested sides: green beans, baked potato and salad.

Makes 3-4 Servings.

Tolsma's Sauerbraten Meal

Bob Tolsma — Volunteer Division Chief

Ingredients:

4 - 6 lbs. beef rump roast
3 medium onions
1 cup water
6 whole black peppers
6 whole cloves

3 bay leaves
dash salt
dash pepper
5 tbs. butter or margarine
vinegar

Directions:

1 – In a large earthen ware or glass bowl, place beef.

2 – Combine salt, pepper, onions, bay leaves, cloves, whole peppers, vinegar, and water and pour over beef.

3 – Cover and refrigerate 3 days, (turn occasionally).

4 – Remove beef from refrigerator. Save marinade.

5 – Place butter in a Dutch oven — brown all sides of the beef.

6 – Add marinade and water to cover the entire piece of meat.

7 – Then bring to a boil; simmer covered for about 4 hours.

8 – Serve over Tolsma's dumplings with a side of red cabbage.

Robert "Bob" Tolsma
Volunteer Division Chief
SCFD

Bob was born in Hackensack, New Jersey, in 1947. As a young adult he felt he had an obligation to serve the public. On his 21'st birthday he became eligible to be a volunteer firefighter and signed up that day with the Old Tappan Volunteer Fire Department.

He moved to Sarasota in 1977 with his young family to pursue a job opportunity and took a hiatus from volunteering. In 1989 he felt the urge to get back into the fire service and joined the Sarasota County Fire Department volunteers. Today he is Chief of the Volunteers.

Bob is vice president of Gee and Jenson, a civil engineering firm. He specializes in port engineering.

Bob and Nancy have been married 29 years and have two daughters, Kimberly and Debra.

Mike Regner whips up a batch of groceries that will stick to your ribs.

Kenny Coblentz
Lieutenant
Charlotte County
Fire Department

Kenny, a Lieutenant with the Charlotte County Fire Department, has been in the service for six years. He is married to wife, Andrea, and shares his home with their three dogs and one cat. His leisure time takes him to the water where he enjoys reeling in his next catch of the day, fish. Spending valuable time with his wife and family is what he treasures the most.

About the recipe...
This is a favorite of his mother's, which Kenny made while dating Andrea to win her heart over. It worked! He continues to make this recipe at home now.

Meatballs by Kenny

Kenny Coblentz — Lieutenant

Ingredients:

1 pound lean ground beef
3/4 cup oatmeal
2 slices bread
1/2 cup milk
1 egg
1 teaspoon parsley flakes

1 small onion
1 teaspoon salt
1/2 teaspoon pepper
1/2 teaspoon garlic powder
1 10.5 ounce can cream of mushroom
   soup

Directions:

1 – Combine all ingredients into bowl.

2 – Tear bread and chop onion. Add to bowl.

3 – Form balls and fry in pan until brown on sides.

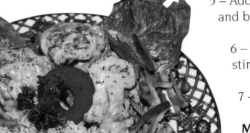

4 – Combine cream of mushroom and 1/2 can water

5 – Add this to pan after meatballs are cooked and brown.

6 – Let simmer on low heat 10-15 minutes stirring occasionally.

7 – Serve with rice or pasta and garlic bread.

Makes 3 – 4 Servings.

Jambalaya

Café on the Bay

Ingredients:

8 large shrimp
2 tablespoons olive oil
1 pound chicken breast cut in strips
1/2 pound Cajun sausage cut
1/4 cup chopped tomato

1/4 cup chopped pepper
1/8 cup chopped green onion
1/8 cup butter
Cajun spice mix

Directions:

1 – In sauté pan, heat oil.

2 – Add chicken and shrimp until 1/2 cooked.

3 – Season with Cajun spice mix.

4 – Add pepper and tomato and continue cooking.

5 – Just before serving, add green onions and finish with butter. Serve with rice.

Makes 4 Servings.

Chris Beaudoin
Chef
Café on the Bay

Keith Daum
Executive Chef
Café on the Bay

Keith Daum started in the restaurant business at age 28 to help out a friend during the holiday season. To his surprise, he loved the business so much he enrolled in the C.I.A. and it became his lifelong career. Keith went on to open two 4 star hotels and three other fine dining restaurants in the Rochester, New York area. He became a certified Executive Chef and won two silver medals at the A.C.F. food shows. In September of 1999 he vacationed to Sarasota to visit an old friend, Bill Herlihy. Keith was offered a job as an Executive Chef at Café on the Bay. Not sure about living in Florida, Keith went back home to New York. The rain and snow quickly made up his mind and he is presently with Café on the Bay.

941-383-0440

2630 Harbourside Dr.
Longboat Key, FL 34228

Breakfast Saturday
8:30 AM To 10:30 AM

Sunday Breakfast Brunch
9:00 AM To 1:00 PM

Sunday Lunch
1:00 PM To 3:30 PM

Lunch 6 Days
11:00 AM To 3:00 PM

Dinner 7 Days
4:30 PM To 10:00 PM

Extraordinary cuisine served in a truly exquisite waterfront setting. Come by land or sea. Casual attire is welcomed.

Les Keegan
Fire Lieutenant
SCFD

Les started his career in 1971 as a volunteer with the Fruitville Fire Department while still in high school. He was hired as a firefighter in 1973 for South Trail Fire Department and has survived four mergers in the 27 years that have quickly passed. He loves his current assignment at Station 7–A with the Sarasota County Fire Department. Les says, "My desire to cook came from my mother, who is an excellent cook. What I know about cooking I learned from her." While off duty, Les and his wife enjoy watching his 11 year old play Hockey for the J.P. Igloo Bruins.

Roasted Cornish Hens with Wild Rice Stuffing

Les Keegan — Fire Lieutenant

Ingredients:

4 cornish hens (20-24 ounces in size)
2 – 16 ounce cans of chicken broth
(the herbed broth works well)
2 – 16 ounce packages of Vigo brand
long grain and white wild rice

1 medium onion
1 package Jimmy Dean brand sausage
(mild or hot)
salt and pepper to taste
garlic to taste

Directions:

1 – Preheat oven to 375 degrees.

2 – Brown sausage in pan.

3 – Cook rice according to package instruction substituting 2 cans of chicken broth for 2 cups of water. (Remember you are making a double amount of the rice.)

4 – Add the sausage and the onion to the rice during cooking. (Optional – sauté the giblets and add to the rice.) Allow to cool some before stuffing.

5 – Stuff each hen full with rice mixture.

6 – Place on roasting pan rack or broiling pan rack and place in the oven.

7 – Cook for 1 hour and 30 minutes.

8 – Serve with your favorite vegetable, a warm loaf of Italian or French bread and remaining rice.

Makes 4 Servings.

Crab Cakes

Beach House Restaurant

Ingredients:

1 pound jumbo lump crab meat
1/4 or 1/2 ounce small diced red peppers
1/4 or 1/2 ounce small diced onions
1 bunch small finely diced scallion
  (green only)
1 small bunch parsley chopped
1 egg
1 pinch salt

1 pinch black pepper
1 ounce Dijon mustard
1 rib celery finely chopped
1 ounce horseradish (squeezed)
1/4 teaspoon Worcestershire sauce
1/4 teaspoon Tabasco sauce
3 1/2 ounces saltine crackers fine ground

Directions:

1 – Pick through crabmeat making sure there is no shell.

2 – Reserve in large mixing bowl, adding all other ingredients but adding the cracker crumbs last.

3 – Gently fold all elements until they are bound.

4 – Form into four ounce cakes.

5 – Sauté on each side until golden brown and firm.

6 – Finish in oven at 350 degrees for 3-4 minutes (if necessary) turning once.

7 – Serve with your favorite sauce and garnish to your liking.

Becky Shannon
General Manager
Beach House Restaurant

Becky Shannon moved to Florida in 1993 from her native state of Colorado. This is where she honed her professional skills through her successful management of the Fort Collins Marriot's Restaurants and as General Manager of the Armadillo. Upon her arrival, she joined the Chiles Restaurant Group and held a number of positions, most notably as Corporate Trainer and currently as General Manager of the Beach House.

As a mother of four sons, her time away from work is almost as action packed as a Friday night in season.

A Collection of
Side Recipes
from the
Fire Departments
& Area Restaurants
of Manatee and
Sarasota Counties
in the State
of Florida.

Side Recipes

Steve La Plante

Firefighter/EMT

Cedar Hammock

Fire Department

Steve comes from a family of Rhode Island firefighters. Both his father and grandfather were firefighters in Providence, Rhode Island, where he grew up.

Steve moved to Bradenton, Florida, in 1985. With firefighting in his blood, he later joined the Cedar Hammock Fire Control District as a volunteer. In 1991 he was hired by Cedar Hammock as a firefighter/EMT. He enjoys utilizing his certification as a fire officer one instructor to teach FO1 courses whenever possible.

Steve and Kim have been married 12 years and have two children, Derek and Alicia. He enjoys fishing, hunting, and camping with his family, especially in the Carolina's.

This recipe comes from our favorite restaurant in Pigeon Forge, TN.

Old Mill Restaurant's Corn Fritters

Steve LaPlante

This recipe comes from our favorite restaurant in Pigeon Forge, TN.

Ingredients:

1/2 cup bread flour
1/2 cup self rising flour
2 tablespoons milk
1 tablespoon melted butter

1/2 cup frozen cream style corn
2 tablespoons sugar
1 fig
1/2 teaspoon baking powder

Directions:

1 – Mix milk, egg, butter and corn.

2 – Stir in dry ingredients, mix well.

3 – Drop by spoonful into hot oil- 350 degrees.

4 – Fry until golden brown.

"Bill's Flavorful Potatoes"

Hall-Mark Fire Apparatus, Inc.

Ingredients:

1 large baking potato (peeled or unpeeled) per person, cut into 1" pieces

1 large onion for each 4 potatoes, cut into 1" pieces

1 large bell pepper for each 4 potatoes, cut into 1" pieces

6 tbsp (3/4" stick) of butter for each 4 potatoes, cut into 1/2" pieces

Directions:

1 – Preheat oven to 350 degrees.

2 – Combine potatoes, onion, and bell pepper in baking dish. Sprinkle with butter, salt, and pepper. Cover.

3 – Bake for 45-60 minutes or until potatoes are "fork tender." Stir mixture half way through cooking.

Hall-Mark Fire Apparatus, Inc.

Hall-Mark Fire Apparatus, Inc. was established in 1993 by owner James Hall. Our mission is to provide Florida fire departments with the best fire fighting apparatus and equipment to better protect our communities. We are the authorized sales and service center for Emergency One, Inc. We have a full time sales and service staff to better serve your needs.

45

Sweet Potato Crunch

Hans R. Rode — Firefighter / Paramedic

Ingredients:

2 1/2 pound can yams
2 eggs
1/2 cup evaporated milk
1 1/4 cup granulated sugar
3/4 stick butter or margarine
1/2 teaspoon cinnamon

TOPPING:
1 cup Rice Krispies cereal
3/4 cup butter or margarine
3/4 cup pecans

Directions:

1 – Beat together first 6 ingredients.

2 – Pour into greased 9 x 9 casserole dish.

3 – Mix the last three ingredients sprinkle evenly ever sweet potato mixture.

4 – Place in a preheated 350 degree oven and bake 30 minutes.

5 – Makes a great side dish with ham and your favorite vegetable.

Hans Rode
Firefighter/Paramedic, SCFD

Hans became a firefighter and EMT in 1987 with Sarasota Fire Department. In 1990 he became a paramedic and is presently working at Station #4-A as a paramedic/firefighter. Hans is a modest fellow that when asked if he had any accomplishments he was proud of, he replied... "I'm just and average guy." Hardly average, Hans received recognition from Sarasota County for the firefighter emblem and unit numbers) art work he did on the front of station #4. He was also recognized with a Team Heroism Award for his part in a team effort to project an exposed house from a structure fire while under cover of a SWAT team with a gunman on scene.

Hans and Leslie have been married 20 years and have three children, Johann, Jeremy, and Jennifer.

About the recipe...
"The Sweet Potato Crunch is a recipe from my wife's family that we all enjoy."

Take note of the art work/emblems on the building painted by Han's.

0

Dutch Dressing

Der Dutchman Restaurant

Ingredients:

2 quarts bread crumbled (broken up)
1/2 cup carrots, cooked and diced
1 cup celery, cooked and diced
4 eggs beaten
1 cup potatoes, cooked and diced

2 cups chicken, boneless and chopped
1/4 cup parsley
2 cups milk
1 teaspoon salt (to taste)
1/2 teaspoon pepper (to taste)

Directions:

1 – Toast bread on oven or skillet.

2 – Beat eggs and add milk, salt, and pepper.

3 – Mix all ingredients together.

4 – Bake @ 350 degrees for approximately 1 hour.

*Stir 2 times during baking time.

Makes 8-10 Servings.

Fanny Yoder
Head Cook
Der Dutchman Restauran

Fanny and her husband
Emanuel brought over 30
years of Amish style cooking
and baking experience to Der
Dutchman of Sarasota when
they arrived. When she's not
cooking or overseeing kitchen
operations, Fanny enjoys
quilting, singing, and watching her family grow.
Many of Der Dutchman's
cooks grew up learning the
Amish style cooking and baking that patrons gladly line
up for. We are pleased to
present our Dutch Dressing
recipe for you to enjoy.
Swing by for a taste of the
real thing and top it off with
one of our many delicious
homemade desserts.

of SARASOTA, FLORIDA

941-955-8007

**3713 Bahia Vista St.
Sarasota
Monday – Thursday
6 AM To 8 PM
Friday – Saturday
6 AM To 9 PM**

"An Old Tradition In A New Setting"

- **Breakfast Menu & Buffet**
- **Lunch & Dinner**
- **Banquet Facilities (Up to 300)**
- **Carlisle Gift Shop**
- **Bakery**

Steve Armstrong
Firefighter/EMT
Venice Fire Department

Steve was born and raised in Sarasota. He graduated from Riverview High School in 1980 and continued his employment with the family business, Armstrong Contracting. He spent three years working for SCFD as a mechanic before being hired by Venice Fire Department in 1993. He is a Firefighter/EMT assigned to an Aerial. In his off duty time he does mechanic work for both Nokomis and Myakka City Fire Departments.

Steve and Jill are newlyweds, married just six months. They are raising three sons, Jeremy, Trevor and Chad. He has a menagerie of animals including an occasional 4-H steer or pig that he lets local kids raise on his property. Steve loves building and racing swampbuggy's and modestly says of racing, "I've even won a few."

About the recipe...
"I got this southern recipe from my dad, and we just love it."

Most recent addition to the Venice apparatus fleet.

Black Eye Peas
Steve Armstrong — Firefighter/EMT

Ingredients:

1 pound bacon
2 medium onions
Lowry's seasoning to taste
salt and pepper to taste

5-6 cans of black eye peas
garlic salt to taste
any other seasonings you may like
large crock pot

Directions:

1 – Cut bacon into 1" strips.

2 – Chop onion.

3 – Sauté bacon and onion in frying pan.

4 – Add black eye peas, onion, bacon and salt, pepper, garlic salt and seasonings to crock-pot.

5 – Cook on low 5-6 hours stirring occasionally.

Makes 8-10 side dishes.

2

Bodacious Beans & Cornbread

Mary "Boot" Boutieller — Firefighter/Paramedic

Ingredients:

2 tablespoons olive oil
1 large chopped onion
1 large chopped green pepper
1-2 cloves chopped garlic
2 – 15 ounce cans black beans drained
15 ounce can kidney beans rinsed
    and drained

2 – 14.5 ounce cans Del Monte Mexican
    style stewed tomatoes
1 cup corn divided
2 Jiffy boxes cornbread mix
2 eggs
2/3 cup milk
1-1 1/2 cups shredded cheddar cheese

Directions:

1 – Sauté onion, green pepper, and garlic in olive oil.

2 – Add beans, tomatoes, and 1/2 cup corn. Heat through.

3 – Mix corn bread per package directions.

4 – Add cheddar cheese and 1/2 cup corn to cornbread mix.

5 – Pour bean mix into 9 x 13 baking pan.

6 – Spread cornbread mix on top.

7 – Bake at 350 degrees until cornbread is golden brown and done in the middle. About 30 minutes.

Makes 6-8 Servings.

Mary "Boot' Boutieller
Firefighter/Paramedic
SCFD

Mary was born and raised in New Jersey. Upon graduating from notorious East Side High School, she moved to Sarasota where she spent the next 10 years working as an administrative secretary in several law firms

She was hired by Sarasota Fire Department in 1989 as an EMT and received their fire academy training for state certification as a fire fighter. In 1993, she and her firefighter husband, John took a six month leave of absence to hike the entire 2100 mile Appalachian Trail They completed the trek from Georgia to Maine in just five and a half months

Since merger, Mary is assigned to Station #2-C of SCFD as a Firefighter Paramedic. She scored #1 on the current promotional list, and is awaiting promotion to the position of Fire Lieutenant

Matt Flynn
Battalion Chief
SCFD

Matt was born in Cleveland, Ohio, into a family of 11 children. One could say that he has fighting fire in his blood, as he is a third generation firefighter. His grandfather was a firefighter for the Cleveland Fire Department and rode some of the first motorized fire engines. His father was a Lieutenant in Cleveland as well. Matt and two of his brothers followed in their father's footsteps and pursued careers in the fire service. Matt has been in the fire service for 19 years and is currently a Battalion Chief. His wife Leigh is also in the fire service, and his daughter, Heather, is 10-years old. Matt and his family enjoy outdoor activities and they are diehard Cleveland Indians fans.

Flynn Family Potatoes

Matt Flynn — Battalion Chief

Ingredients:

6 - 8 medium potatoes
1/4 cup butter or margarine (melted)

1 pkg. zesty Italian dressing - dry mix
12 oz pkg. shredded parmesan cheese

Directions:

1 – Preheat Oven to 350 degrees.

2 – Wash, peel and slice potatoes into 1" chunks.

3 – Layer a 9" x 12" x 2" baking pan with potato chunks.

4 – Mix butter and Italian dressing mix, and spread pour over potatoes.

5 – Bake in oven @ 350 deg. for 40 - 45 minutes, stirring potatoes twice while baking.

6 – Remove from oven and sprinkle with cheese and bake an additional 10 minutes, or until cheese starts to brown.

7 – Serve hot with your favorite meats and vegetables.

Makes 6 Servings.

4

Mom's Corn Bread Casserole

Wayne Grubbs — Firemedic

Ingredients:

1 can cream corn
1 cup sour cream
1 can whole corn

1 stick butter
1 small box Jiffy cornbread mix

Directions:

1 – Melt butter

2 – Mix all ingredients. (Do not drain corn)

3 – Pre-heat oven to 400 deg.

4 – Pour into an 8" x 10" pan, and place in center of oven.

5 – Bake at 400 deg for 45 minutes. Check to see if it is done and if top is getting too brown.

6 – If it still is not done inside, cover with foil and bake @ 375 another 10 - 15 minutes. Do not over cook.

7 – When finished, let cool for 5 minutes before serving.

Makes 6 – 8 Servings.

Wayne Grubbs
Firemedic, SCFD

Wayne grew up in Miami, and after an early graduation from high school, he moved to Sarasota. His grandparents moved here in the 1920's to work in the nearly forgotten "turpentine business." His grandfather worked on the Longino Ranch, which was the last in the area to harvest turpentine from the trees.

Wayne joined the City of Sarasota Fire Department in 1978 after operating his own landscape business for two years. He continued the land-scaping on his days off for eight more years before he and his wife, Debbie, started "Country Pick'ns," a country craft-oriented store which operated in Sarasota for 14 years.

Wayne and Debbie have a five-year old daughter named Emily and a one-year old cockerspaniel named "Taffy."

*About the recipe...
"Mom made this for years and we loved it. Don't know if it's original but I do know it's good."*

25-foot Boston Whaler with twin 200 Yamaha's and 250gpm fire pump.

Jordana Thomas
Volunteer Firefighter, SCFD

Larry McGee, Firemedic

A former state competition gymnast, Jordana was born and raised in Minneapolis, Minnesota.

Her adult education includes a degree in emergency medical services technology, and a 1994 certification as a paramedic. She moved to Sarasota to accept a position as "statistician" with Sarasota Memorial Hospital in 1995.

As a single working mother of four, one wonders how she found time to volunteer with SCFD. She joined the volunteers in 1998 and remained active until her recent departure for a job opportunity with "The Discovery Channel" in Rockville, Maryland.

Her hobbies include volunteering, cooking, and maintaining a long distance relationship with her Sarasota firefighter boyfriend.

The 6900 acre wildfire at T. Mabry Carlton Reserve took 14 days to extinguish.

Yellow Squash Casserole
Jordana Thomas – Volunteer Firefighter

Ingredients:

6-8 medium summer or
   winter yellow squash
2-3 medium Vidalia or sweet onions
1 1/2 sticks butter

1 pound diced Velveeta cheese
6-8 large eggs hand beaten
sprinkle of bread crumbs
salt & pepper to taste

Directions:

1 – Slice yellow squash and onions thinly and steam until very tender.

2 – Drain thoroughly. Mix in butter and drain again.

3 – Place squash mixture in large casserole dish.

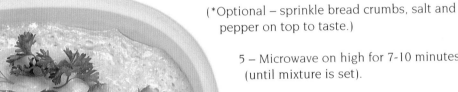

4 – Stir in eggs and Velveeta cheese.

(*Optional – sprinkle bread crumbs, salt and pepper on top to taste.)

5 – Microwave on high for 7-10 minutes (until mixture is set).

6 – Serve piping hot.

Makes 6-8 Servings.

Fried Rice Combination

Ovea Thai Kitchen

Ingredients:

2 cups cooked rice
1/4 cup sliced chicken
1/4 cup sliced pork
6-8 pieces large shrimp
1 teaspoon finely chopped garlic
1/4 cup vegetable cooking oil

2 tablespoons shredded carrot
2 tablespoons sliced onion
1 tablespoon chopped green onion
1 1/2 tablespoons soy sauce
2 eggs

Directions:

1 – Heat cooking oil in a wok. Add garlic and stir until cooked.

2 – Add shrimp, chicken, and pork.

3 – Break two eggs into the wok and scramble.

4 – Add cooked rice, carrots, sliced onion, and 1/ 2 tablespoon of chopped green onion.

5 – Add soy sauce and black soy sauce, mix together thoroughly, then sprinkle with 1/ 2 tablespoon of chopped green onion.

Ovea Thai Kitchen

Ovea Thai Kitchen is family owned and operated Tha. restaurant which is fast making a name for itself in hometown Sarasota. Born in Bangkok, owners "Cookie and Woody" have made the business a family affair, by employing their son, Ekawee and daughter, Awika, when they are not in school. The restaurant opened a year ago seating up to 45 patrons and is quaintly adorned with authentic Thai decor

The family prides themselves in serving their best Thai family recipes. By using the best quality ingredients to make their food dishes moderate prices, and warm and friendly service, they seem to have found the right combination to keep customers coming back

If you're interested in tanta lizing your Thai tastebuds drop in and sample their mouth watering Thai soups salads, entreés, and desserts

Ovea Thai Kitchen

941-365-7799

**501 N. Beneva Rd., #250
Sarasota
Tuesday – Sunday
Lunch 11:30 AM To 2:30 PM
Dinner 5:00 AM To 9:30 PM**

Real Thai Cooking

Family Operated With Friendly Atmosphere

Dennis Aber
Firefighter/EMT
Sarasota County
Fire Department

Dennis started his career with SCFD 11 years ago in south Sarasota County, the district now known as Battalion 4. Once surrounded by rural land, the palmettos and native vegetation near the fire station have steadily retreated with the onslaught of development. Conversely, the call loads have increased dramatically to reflect the population explosion. Dennis calls Station #32-A his home away from home and is always happy to take his turn behind the frying pan. The crew loves his cooking, and they say "his Baked Beans are to die for." Dennis enjoys cooking and woodworking in his spare time. He and his wife, Kathy, have been married 21 years and have a 17 year old daughter, Lisa, and 13 year old son, Ryan.

Mom's Baked Beans

Dennis Aber — Firefighter/EMT

Ingredients:

2 – 8 ounce cans B&M beans
4 to 6 ounces dark brown sugar
8 to 10 strips thick cut bacon

1 large onion (Vidalia or yellow) finely chopped

Directions:

1 – Drain bean juice from both cans (very, very well) and place beans in large bowl.

2 – Mix all dark brown sugar, well.

3 – Add all of the onions, mix well.

4 – Place all of the bean mixture into a glass baking dish, 9" x 9", so that the bean mixture depth is approximately 1-1/2 to 2 inches deep.

5 – Place bacon strips on top to cover entire bean surface.

6 – Place into a preheated 375 degree oven for 1 hour or until it is good and bubbly. Remove from oven and let cool for approximately 15 minutes.

NOTE: This recipe is great. But if placed in the fridge over night and reheated the next day, MAN IS THIS HEAVEN OR WHAT!!!! Thanks Mom.

Makes 4 To 6 Servings.

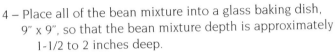

Sun Dried Tomato Soda Bread

Munroe's Restaurant

Ingredients:

4 cups all purpose flour
3 tsp baking soda
1 tsp salt
1 tsp ground black pepper
1 tsp dried thyme

1 dried rosemary
1/4 cup margarine
1/3 sun-dried tomatoes, chopped
1/3 cup pitted kalamata olives, chopped
1 1/4 cup buttermilk

Directions:

1 – Sift flour and baking soda into large mixing bowl

2 – Add salt, pepper and herbs – mix well

3 – Knead in margarine until mixture crumbs

4 – Add tomatoes and olives – mix well. Add the buttermilk and knead to a soft dough. Roll dough into an 8" round, score into 8 wedges and place on a greased cookie sheet.

5 – Bake at 350 for 30 minutes until risen and golden brown.

Top Photo:
Chef, Rick Munroe, just "loafing" around.

Bottom Photo:
The Munroe family Susan, Max, Rick, Ashley.

Grandma Maynard's Cornbread

Jim Frazier — Division Chief, SCFD

Ingredients:

2 cups self rising corn meal
5 tbs. flour
3 tbs. sugar
2 tsp. salt

5 tbs. cooking oil
1 1/2 cups skim milk (cold)
3 eggs eggs
1 tsp.vinegar

Directions:

1 – Pre-heat oven to 425 degrees.

2 – Pour 2 Tbs. of cooking oil in cast iron skillet and sprinkle a little corn meal in bottom.

3 – Place skillet in oven while mixing ingredients.

4 – Mix all ingredients except milk.

5 – Add vinegar to milk before adding milk to remaining ingredients. Then stir together thoroughly.

6 – Pour mixture into hot skillet, and bake 20-25 minutes or until brown.

Jim Frazier
Division Chief, SCFD

Jim was 21 years old when he left his home in Dearborn, Michigan, to move to Florida. His grandfather and three cousins are all firefighters and had steered him towards firefighting as a career. He applied with Sarasota Fire Department and was hired in 1975. He became a firefighter/paramedic and Lieutenant while on the line. During his 25 years of service, he served as president of the EMS Providers Association, and as Southwest Region director of the Florida Fire Chiefs Association. He recently retired as Division Chief of EMS/Legislative Liaison.

Jim and Lisa have had three children during their 25 years of marriage. At 20, Joshua is the oldest, followed by Nathaniel (18), and Rachel (9). They enjoy vacationing in Disney.

About the recipe...
"It's called Grandma Maynard's Cornbread because it was passed down to me by my grandmother, whom I lived with while I went to fire school. She was a great country cook from Kentucky, who never served a meal without some type of homemade bread or biscuits."

1999 E-One just delivered. Ringling art museum in background.

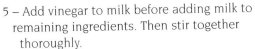

Roasted Garlic

Ophelia's

Stan Ferro
Ophelia's

Ingredients:

6 bulbs of whole garlic
2 cups extra virgin olive oil

Directions:

1 – Roast at 350 degrees for 50 minutes.

2 – Save oil.

Stan Ferro, a native of Massachusetts, exposure to the culinary world began in the kitchens of the restaurants his Great Aunt Ophelia owned, when he was a child. She was always the chef and he loved to help her. After moving to Cape Cod, Stan began cooking during the summer after his first year in college. Traveling in Europe on his honeymoon with Jane gave Stan exposure to European Cuisine. Upon their return, Stan worked for Marriott in Boston and was the chef at the Hasty Pudding Club at Harvard. When he moved back to the Cape, Stan mastered the art of carpentry and in 1976 renovated the Playhouse Restaurant. He was chef there for 14 years. In 1988 he renovated Ophelia's and was the chef there for five years. He now runs the business end of it. Stan is also an avid golfer and on the committee of the Siesta Key Chamber golf tournament.

Ophelia's
on the bay

941-349-2212

**9105 Midnight Pass Road
Siesta Key
Open 7 Days A Week
5 AM To 10 PM**

**Romantic Twilight
Bay Front Dining
Either Inside
or Outside**

26

DONZI AND SARASOTA COUNTY FIREFIGHTERS:
ONE HOT RECIPE!

35 ZF DAYTONA

DONZI
BEYOND PERFORMANCE

A Collection of
Dessert Recipes
from the
Fire Departments
& Area Restaurants
of Manatee and
Sarasota Counties
in the State
of Florida.

Dessert Recipes

Keith Haluska
Firefighter/Paramedic
SCFD

Keith started his career in the Fire Service as a volunteer in 1995. Always seeking a challenge, he went on to become a paramedic firefighter and is presently with the Sarasota County Fire Department. "Keith is a natural," his wife, Linda says, "being a firefighter/ paramedic is his 'calling,' and it fulfills Keith's desire to help, nurture, and care for others in their time of need." Keith and his wife of 12 years are blessed with two miracle daughters, 2 1/2 year old Marianna, and 8 month old Nicole. "Linda and the girls are the greatest gifts from God I have ever received," Keith says. His love for cooking comes from his mother and grandmother (who was a full-blooded Italian from Naples, Italy).

About the recipe...
This is one of my favorite holiday desserts that my grandmother made.

Cannolis

Keith Haluska — Firefighter/Paramedic

Ingredients:

CANNOLI SHELLS:
3 cups sifted all-purpose flour
1 tablespoon sugar
1/4 teaspoon cinnamon
3/4 cup port
salad oil or shortening for deep-frying
1 egg yolk
slightly beaten

CANNOLI FILLING:
5 heaping tablespoons cornstarch
1 cup sugar
1 quart milk
1 teaspoon vanilla or other flavor
2-3 pounds ricotta cheese
(optional - 1/2 cup semi-sweet chocolate
pieces)

Directions:

SHELLS:
1 – Sift flour with sugar and cinnamon onto a board. Make a well in center, and fill with port. With a fork, gradually blend flour into port. When dough is stiff enough to handle, knead about 15 minutes, or until dough is smooth and stiff (if too moist and sticky, knead in a little more sifted flour). 2 – Refrigerate dough, covered, 2 hours. 3 – In deep-fat fryer, electric skillet, or heavy saucepan, slowly heat salad oil (3 – 4 inches deep), to 400 degrees F on deep frying thermometer. 4 – Meanwhile, on lightly floured surface, roll one third of dough to paper thinness, making a 16-inch round. Cut into eight 5-inch circles. Wrap a circle loosely around a 6-inch-long cannoli form or dowel, 1 inch in diameter; seal with egg yolk. 5 – Gently drop dough-covered forms, two at a time, into hot oil, and fry 1 minute or until browned on all sides (turn, if necessary). With tongs or slotted utensil, lift out of oil, and drain on paper towels. Carefully remove forms. Continue until all dough is used.

*Note: Completed Cannolis shells may be dipped into bakers chocolate for extra flavoring (see photo). Shells can be made a day or two ahead of time and stored covered at room temperature.

FILLING:
1 – Mix cornstarch, sugar, milk and vanilla well. Cook until thick like pudding. Let cool. 2 – In a large bowl, whip ricotta cheese with an electric mixer about 1 -2 minutes. 3 – Add pudding mixture (and chocolate pieces if desired) blending well. Refrigerate, covered, until well chilled – at least 2 hours. 4 – Just before serving, with a teaspoon or small spatula, fill shells with ricotta mixture.

Makes 24 Servings.

PRODUCED BY FELD ENTERTAINMENT

64

Coca-Cola® Chocolate Cake

Cracker Barrel

Ingredients:

CAKE:

4 cups plain flour
8 tablespoons cocoa
3 teaspoon cinnamon
1 teaspoon salt
2 teaspoons soda
4 cups sugar

1 pound butter
4 eggs
1 cup buttermilk
4 teaspoons vanilla
2 cups Coca-Cola®

ICING:

1/2 cup butter
1/2 cup Coca-Cola®
6 tablespoons Cocoa
1 cup chopped pecans
2 teaspoons vanilla
2 – 1 pound boxes
    powdered sugar

Directions:

CAKE:

1 – Grease and flour an 11x17 inch pan.
2 – Sift together the dry ingredients and set aside.
3 – In a saucepan, heat the butter and Coca-Cola® until the butter melts.
4 – Add the eggs, vanilla, and buttermilk and mix well.
5 – Add the liquid ingredients to the dry ingredients and heat until smooth. The batter will be very thin.
6 – Pour into the prepared pan.
7 - Bake at 350 degrees for 30 minutes or until a toothpick comes out of cake clean. (Will fill 2 tube pans or 2 paper lined cupcake tins. Bake tube cakes for 60 minutes. Bake cupcakes for 15 minutes.)

ICING:

The cake must be iced while warm.
1 - In a saucepan, heat the butter and Coca-Cola®. Do NOT boil.
2 – Add all of the remaining ingredients and mix well. (Add powdered sugar a little at a time.) Icing should be at a consistency in which you can pour it over the cake.

Robert Ball
General Manager
Bradenton Cracker Barrel

I'm really excited to be involved with the Fire Fighters cookbook. It has some special meaning for me, because for nine years I was a police officer and cooperative firefighter. As a police officer we were assigned to a fire truck and worked along side the firefighters fighting fires. I have great admiration for their hard work and dedication to the community. I got involved in the food business 22 years ago, and have been with Cracker Barrel the last 12 years. I have been a General Manager in Kennesaw, Ga., Asheville, N.C., and Bradenton, Fl. At Cracker Barrel we are proud to serve quality food for a fair price. I hope you enjoy the Coca-Cola® Cake. Stop in and let me know how much you enjoyed it.

Richard Munroe

Chef/Proprietor
Munroe's Restaurant

Locals and seasonal visitors alike enjoy the bistro setting of Munroe's Restaurant. Proven to be Sarasota's favorite restaurant with casual elegance, friendly service, and creative, American foods.

Whether you start off your meal with one of our famous appetizers or finish with one of our colorful desserts, you won't go away disappointed.

For the late night guest, we offer live entertainment upstairs, with a late night menu and premium bar.

Warm Peach Compote With Basil

Munroe's Restaurant

Ingredients:

4 ounces sugar
1 cup water
2 pounds peaches, peeled-pitted & sliced
1 vanilla bean, split in 1/2 lengthwise
4 tablespoons butter cut into small pieces

1 handful, small fresh basil leaves
1 cup – assorted seasonal berries
   (raspberries, blueberries, & blackberries)
4 scoops vanilla ice cream

Directions:

1 – Heat sugar and water in a medium saucepan until the sugar dissolves. Add peaches & vanilla bean and simmer for 2 minutes.

2 – Remove the vanilla bean. Whisk in the butter a few pieces at a time then add basil leaves and cook until they wilt.

3 – Remove from heat – add berries and slowly fold the compote to mix the ingredients.

4 – Ladle compote out evenly into 4 bowls and garnish with a scoop of vanilla ice cream.

Fruit Pizza

Lynne C. Hall — *Volunteer Firefighter/EMT*

Ingredients:

CRUST:
1 cup butter or margarine
1/2 cup powdered sugar
1 1/2 cup flour

TOPPING:
12 ounce package vanilla chips
1/4 cup milk
8 ounce package cream cheese

GLAZE:
1/4 cup sugar
1 tablespoon corn starch
1/2 cup pineapple juice
1/2 teaspoon lemon juice.

FRUIT:
Grapes, strawberries, canned pineapple
or mandarin oranges, kiwi, blueberries,
star fruit.

Directions:

CRUST:
Mix butter or margarine, powdered sugar and flour.
Flatten out on a pizza pan and bake at 350 degrees for 15 minutes.

TOPPING:
Melt vanilla chips, milk, and cream cheese in the microwave, one minute at a time. Wisk until smooth. Ice the cookie with this mix when the cookie is cooled.

GLAZE:
Combine sugar, corn starch, pineapple juice, and lemon juice. Cook over medium heat, stirring constantly until thick. Brush over pizza when cooled.

FRUIT:
Slice and place fruit on top of iced pizza in a single layer. Be as creative as you wish.

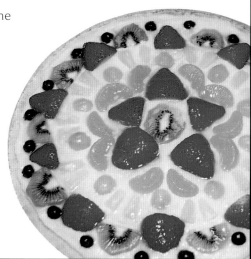

Lynne Hall
**Volunteer Firefighter/EMT
SCFD**

For over six years, Lynne Hall has been a volunteer with Sarasota County Fire Department. As a volunteer firefighter and EMT, she assists as additional man-power at stations, call-outs, and special events. She'll often work up to 50 hours a month. This is JUST a hobby for Lynne, though! In her "real life," Lynne is a third grade teacher at Ashton Elementary School. She has been teaching since 1985. Lynne takes most pride in her two daughters, ages ten and thirteen. Between their schedules and hers, Lynne is a busy lady. Her passion is helping people, whether it's her family, her students, or those she assists with the department. She is constantly giving of herself to others.

Mrs. Yoder
Yoder's

Yoder's began in 1975 in Sarasota by Levi and Amanda Yoder along with two of their daughters. Levi had been laid off construction due to the recession. Investing their life savings into a small 45 seat restaurant with no prior experience, Amanda started cooking just like she used to back home on the farm in Indiana. She especially loved to bake pies. Levi had a heart for people and loved making customers happy. The combination was a big success, and soon there were long lines of people waiting to eat, which totally surprised and delighted Levi and Amanda.

Peanut Butter Pie

Yoder's

Ingredients:

PUDDING:
1 cup cold milk
1/2 cup cornstarch
1 teaspoon salt
1 teaspoon vanilla
3 egg yolks
3 cups milk

3 tablespoons butter
2/3 cup sugar
CRUMB MIXTURE:
1 cup powdered sugar
1/2 cup crunchy peanut butter
1 9"-10" baked pie shell
2 cups whipped cream

Directions:

1 – Mix 1 cup milk, cornstarch, salt, egg yolks, and vanilla with wire whisk until smooth. Set aside.

2 – Pour sugar in saucepan, add milk and butter. Do not stir while heating (sugar keeps it from scorching on the bottom). Heat to just before boiling point.

3 – Whisk cornstarch mixture into scalding milk, bring to boil, remove from heat immediately (all the while whisking milk mixture until smooth), chill.

4 – Mix powdered sugar and peanut butter crumbs until crumbly.

5 – Place 1/2 of crumbs in pie shell top with chilled pudding.

6 – Place other 1/2 of crumbs (reserve a few for top) on top of pudding.

7 – Place whipped topping on top of crumbs and pudding and sprinkle remaining peanut butter crumbs on top.

Makes 6 – 8 Servings.

Frosted Pumpkin Bread Wheels

Merv Kennell — Fire Lieutenant/Paramedic

Ingredients:

BREAD:
1 tsp. nutmeg
1 tsp. cinnamon
1 1/2 tsp. salt
4 large eggs
3 cups sugar
1 cup oil
1 cup pumpkin (canned)

3 cups flour (regular)
2 tsp. baking soda
2/3 cup water
FILLING:
8 oz. cream cheese
1 stick margarine
2 tsp. vanilla
5 cups powdered sugar

Directions:

1 – Mix nutmeg, cinnamon, salt, sugar, oil together.

2 – Next add pumpkin, flour, baking soda and water.

3 – Pour mixture into 3 reg. size coffee cans and bake @ 350 degrees for approx. 1 hour (check at 50 minutes).

4 – When finished baking, remove from oven and allow to cool before slicing into 1/3" slices.

5 – Mix icing and spread between to pieces of bread.

6 – Then slice in half and arrange on plate in a pinwheel fashion.

Serves: Approx. 40 pieces /
2 pieces per serving.

Merv Kennell
Fire Lieutenant/Paramedic
SCFD

Violet Kennell

Merv Kennell is vice president of Firehouse Favorites. During the 24 years he has served with Sarasota County Fire Department he has worked in nearly every station and in every capacity at some point in time. Merv is currently a Fire Lieutenant/ Paramedic assigned to Station #7 on B-shift, and still loves the job.

Merv and his wife, Jennie, enjoy being active with their kids and family through home, school, and church. With a heart for mission work and kids, Merv has recently completed his third mission trip to Haiti to build a church supported orphanage.

Merv is excited by the opportunity to be a part of Firehouse Favorites, which through it's creation of the Sarasota Manatee Children's Burn Foundation, will help unfortunate children and their families when burn trauma disaster strikes.

About the recipe... People drive from miles around to buy these tasty morsels at my sister's bake sales in Watertown, New York. My crew wishes Mom would come by and visit more often since she introduced them to Frosted Pumpkin Bread.

Diana Galan
Firefighter/Paramedic
SCFD

Diana (DeDe) Galan joined South County Ambulance District as an EMT in April of '86. She became a paramedic in 1988 and received her certification as a firefighter in 1992. Diana is an excellent paramedic with 10 years of experience working off duty in Tampa General E.R.

Diana has no problem keeping herself busy on her off duty days. She just celebrated her first Mother's Day since the birth of her 10-month-old son "Christian." He shares his mother's affection with two pot bellied pigs Pueka and Pokita.

She likes watersports, fishing, camping, snow skiing and reading. Diana says her goal in life is "to be the best mother I can be and to raise a happy and well adjusted child."

Cherry Delight
Diana Galan — Firefighter/Paramedic

Ingredients:

9 ounce box of yellow cake mix
1-1/2 cups or 6 ounces of walnuts
1 stick or 1/2 cup butter

1 can (approximately 16 ounces) cherry pie filling
1 small tub whipped cream

Directions:

1 – Lightly grease glass baking dish 8" square. (Using cooking spray or butter).

2 – Preheat oven to 325 degrees.

3 – Pour can of cherry pie filling into pan and spread evenly.

4 – Pour cake mix over filling and spread evenly.

5 – Pour chopped walnuts over cake mix evenly.

6 – Melt butter in microwave and pour over walnuts.

7 – Place in oven for 20 – 30 minutes, checking periodically.

8 – Check with toothpick to see if it is done.

9 – When finished baking, remove from oven and let cool.

TIPS:
Cold…refrigerate for 1 hour if you have time.
Cut into serving sizes and top with a scoop of whip cream.
Warm….Serve with a scoop of vanilla ice cream.

Makes Approx. 9 Servings.

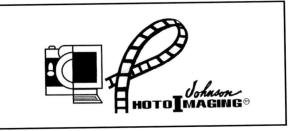

Bread Pudding

Pastry Art

Ingredients:

4 eggs
4 1/2 cups half & half
1 cup brown sugar
2 teaspoons vanilla

1 teaspoon cinnamon
pinch of salt
5 cups firm bread
   (crust removed and cut into chunks).

Directions:

1 – Combine first 6 ingredients in a large bowl, and whisk until blended.

2 – Grease or spray a 13"x 9" baking pan, add bread and pour egg mixture over. Press bread into liquid.

3 – Let bread soak 15 minutes or up to an hour. Bake at 350 degrees for 35-40 minutes or until pudding starts to puff up and a knife inserted in the center comes out clean.

OPTIONAL WHITE CHOCOLATE SAUCE:
1 – Bring 1 1/2 cups heavy cream to a boil.

2 – Pour over 5 ounces chopped white chocolate.

3 – Let sit 1 minute then stir until smooth.

4 – Pour over hot pudding and cut into portions.

John Andersen
Owner
Pastry Art

John was born in upstate New York in 1963. He moved to Florida in 1982 and became a retail district manager. Hungry for a change of pace, John spent four years as a restaurant food and beverage manager, prior to taking a position in Europe as a wine educator. In 1992, he expanded his food service background even further, starting his own wholesale distribution company for bakery and dessert items.

He shifted from wholesale to retail in 1992, when he bought into "Pastry Art" in Bradenton. He opened the Sarasota location in 1997 and today is owner of both locations. Certainly a factor in his success is his belief that "you get one opportunity to make a first impression."

Pastry Art

941-955-7545

Two Convenient Locations:
1508 Main Street
Sarasota
• • •
6753 Manatee Avenue West
Bradenton

Bakery

Café

Fine Coffees

Porter Shellhammer
Battalion Chief
SCFD

Porter is a 25 year veteran of the fire service whose name has become well known in the fire service instructional community. His resume bears witness to his desire for education and the pursuit of expertise. He has been teaching most of his career with specialty in tactics and strategy, incident command, and hazardous materials/incident mitigation. He was chosen to be a guest instructor at the National Fire Academy which is comparable to winning a "Grammy" for actors.

Porter's wife Joan tells us that the Strawberry Trifle recipe is her version of a recipe she originally found in a magazine, enjoyed, and later lost. It has become a family favorite referred to as "that strawberry thing."

About the recipe...
"We hope you enjoy this refreshing dessert as much as we do...it's a great party dessert, too."

"Strawberry Trifle"
Porter Shellhammer — Battalion Chief

Ingredients:

2 qts. strawberries, sliced (set aside 6 large, whole berries for garnish)
2 tbs. sugar
8 oz. pkg. cream cheese

1 cup sour cream
1/4 teas. almond extract
1 (prepared) angel food cake
whipped cream (for garnish)

Directions:

1 – Combine sliced strawberries and 1 tbs of sugar, and set aside.

2 – Tear angel food cake into 1inch pieces, and place in a large bowl.

3 – Mix together cream cheese, sour cream, almond extract, and 1 tbs of sugar until smooth.

4 – Gently fold the cream cheese mixture into the angel food cake.

5 – In a large glass serving bowl or trifle dish, place a layer of strawberries, then a layer of cake mixture.

6 – Continue the layers, with the top layer being cake mixture.

7 – Garnish the top with whipped cream and whole strawberries.

8 – Chill 2-3 hours before serving.

Makes 8-10 Servings.

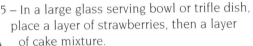

Free Form Apple Tart

Munroe's Restaurant

Ingredients:

1 granny smith apple, peeled, seeded and sliced

2 oz unsweetened pie dough, rolled into a 12" square

3 tbl sugar

1 tbl flour

1 tsp cinnamon

1 tbl walnuts, chopped

1 oz margarine

Directions:

1 – Sauté the apples with 2 tbl sugar and margarine – cook until sugar is dissolved.

2 – Add flour and cook until smooth. Add walnuts and cinnamon then cool.

3 – Place cooled filling in center of pie dough – pull the corners in to envelope the filling.

4 – Place on a greased sheet pan - sprinkle 1 tbl sugar over the top and bake at 350 for 20 minutes.

Rick Munroe and his girls.

Larry G. McGee Jr.
Firemedic, SCFD

Jordana Thomas
Volunteer Firefighter

Larry was born and raised in Sarasota. Upon graduation at Sarasota High, he joined the Marine Corp and learned "ground radio repair." After three years of active duty, he spent the next four years in the Marine Reserves while employed as a firefighter with Fruitville Fire Department (now SCFD). Hired in 1982, he has long been a member of the Special Op's team and is currently assigned to Station #8-A. Larry taught "Learn Not To Burn" in the schools for five years in his off duty time.

Larry's hobbies include tinkering with computers and coaching wrestling. He coached his son, Larry III, to a state "first place" in Greco Roman and Freestyle wrestling in 1999. He has two daughters as well, Carla (17) and Courtney (12).

Pizzafreet (Elephant Ears)
Larry G. McGee Jr. — Firemedic

Ingredients:

1 cup warm water
1 package yeast
1 tablespoon shortening

1 teaspoon salt
1/4 cup sugar
4-5 cups flour

Directions:

1 – Dissolve yeast in small amount of warm water.

2 – In medium bowl, dissolve sugar and salt and shortening.

3 – In the cup of warm water add 2 cups flour and blend with a spoon.

4 – Add yeast until smooth.

5 – Add remainder of flour.

6 – Kneed until smooth and let sit 30 minutes.

7 – In a skillet, melt shortening 2" deep. Heat to 350 degrees, very hot.

8 – Roll out small amounts of dough into 10" round and very thin. Fry to golden brown.

9 – Top with your favorite topping and cinnamon sugar.

Makes 8-10 Servings.

4

Mom's French Silk Chocolate Cream Cheese Pie

Chik-fil-A®, Tricia Mangrum

Ingredients:

1 stick butter
8 ounce cream cheese
1 1/2 cup granulated sugar
1 teaspoon vanilla

2 – 8 ounce Cool Whip
6 tablespoons dry cocoa
9 ounce graham cracker pie crust

Directions:

1 – Cream butter, cream cheese, and sugar with mixer.

2 – Add vanilla; add dry cocoa a little at a time.

3 – Stop mixer and fold-in one 8 ounce Cool Whip.

4 – Pour in graham cracker pie crust.

5 – Top with Cool Whip.

6 – Garnish with chocolate sprinkles or grated chocolate bar.

Makes 10 Servings.

Chik-fil-A®
Tricia Mangrum

Tricia started working for Sarasota Square's Chik-fil-A® when she was 15 years old. All throughout high school and college, she continued to work at Chik-fil-A®. Tricia earned an RN degree at Nursing School and her education was complete. However, her heart desired to make Chik-fil-A® a career since she loved it so much. Tricia became an owner of Chik-fil-A®, and it has been an extremely rewarding decision. " I love to work with young people," she says, adding "and teaching them life's most important principals; honesty, hard work, dedication and responsibility!" She is married to husband, Jeffrey, and they have one son, Hunter.

About the recipe... It was one of Tricia's Mom's favorites passed down to the family.

Robert Albritton

Albritton Fruit Company, Inc.

My family has been growing citrus in Florida for well over 100 years. My great-grandfather came to Sarasota in 1885 and planted his first groves. In 1946 my grandparents opened our first retail store, which is still operating on Proctor Road in Sarasota County. Over the years wonderful citrus recipes have evolved and been passed on from generation to generation. My sister Gail makes this delicious Trifle for our family every year for Christmas. It has long since become a tradition just as our family has become a tradition in the citrus industry in Florida. I hope you enjoy this special dessert and it becomes a tradition for your family too.

Aunt Gail's Trifle

Albritton Fruit Co., Inc.

Ingredients:

8 large navel oranges
1/4 cup plus 3 tablespoons Cointreau
Zesty — Orange Pastry Cream
   (recipe follows)
2 1/2 cups heavy cream, chilled

3 ounces bittersweet chocolate
2 10 3/4 ounces each — store bought all
    butter pound cakes (defrosted if frozen)
1/2 cup apricot jam, melted
1 1/2 cups broken pieces of crisp nut cookies

Directions:

1 – Using a sharp knife, peel the oranges, removing all of the bitter white pith. Working over a bowl, cut between the membranes to release the sections. Squeeze the juice from the membranes over the orange sections and add 1/4 cup of the Cointreau. Set a side to macerate for 30 minutes. Strain and reserve the juice and orange sections separately. Set aside 12 orange sections to decorate the top of the assembled trifle.

2 – Meanwhile with an electric mixer beat the Zesty-Orange Pastry Cream until smooth. In a large mixer bowl, beat 2 cups of the heavy cream until stiff. Fold one fourth of the whipped cream into the pastry cream, then fold in the remaining cream.

3 – Put the chocolate in a small heavy saucepan set over a pan of hot water. Let stand, stirring occasionally, until melted and smooth. Remove from heat.

4 – Using a sharp knife, cut each pound cake horizontally into thirds. Brush each of the 6 layers with 2 tablespoons of the reserved orange juice. Spread 2 tablespoons of apricot jam over the 2 bottom layers of each cake. Reassemble the cakes and cut them crosswise into 1/4 inch-thick slices.

5 – Line the bottom of a 4 1/2 - to 5 quart punch bowl or other large glass bowl with one-third of the cake slices. Moisten with one tablespoon of the Cointreau. Layer 1/2 cup of the cookie pieces and then one-third of the orange sections over the cake. Drizzle with one tablespoon of the melted chocolate and smooth one-third of the pastry cream over the top. Repeat layer the ingredients in this fashion two more times. Drizzle the remaining chocolate over the top. Cover the trifle with plastic wrap and refrigerate for at least 3 hours or for up to 3 days.

6 – To serve, beat the remaining 1/2 cup cream until stiff peaks form. Spoon dollops of the cream around the top of the trifle and garnish with the reserved orange sections.

Makes 20 - 25 Servings.

Zesty-Orange Pastry Cream

Albritton Fruit Co., Inc.

Ingredients:

4 egg yolks
1/3 cup plus 2 tablespoons sugar
1/2 cup all-purpose flour

3 tablespoons grated orange zest
3 cups hot milk
1/4 cup Cointreau

Directions:

1 – In a medium saucepan, whisk together the egg yolks and sugar until pale and thick, about 3 minutes. Beat in the flour and the orange zest. Gradually whisk in the hot milk and cook over moderate heat, stirring constantly, until the custard begins to boil. Cook for 2 minutes longer.

2 – Scrape the pastry cream into a large bowl and sprinkle with the Cointreau to prevent a skin from forming. Let cool, then cover with plastic wrap and refrigerate for at least 2 hours. (The pastry cream can be prepared up to 3 days in advance.) Beat the Cointreau into the pastry cream just before using.

Makes 4 Cups.

Amber Albritton
Albritton Fruit Co., Inc.

When I began my career at Albritton's in 1987, our stores carried fresh fruit, fresh squeezed juice, jellies and a few Florida souvenirs. With increased demand, our product mix has grown to provide shippers with not only the freshest citrus and juice available but with a large selection of gourmet items and specialty goods that have become a part of our growing list of products.

In November of 2000, we will be opening our largest store to date making this our 7th location. This time, with a new twist; a deli and a bakery. We will be preparing sandwiches and salads to order and will be baking fresh muffins and breads daily. Albritton's will continue in our tradition of providing excellent customer service and will do our best to make this new store a hometown favorite just like all the others.

Fruit Crisp

Tom Bonner — Firefighter/Paramedic

Ingredients:

5 cups blueberry, cherry, apple or any fruit
3 cups flour
1 tablespoon baking soda
1 teaspoon salt

2 cups brown sugar
2 cups quick oats
1 1/2 cups margarine
1 tablespoon cinnamon

Tom Bonner
Firefighter/Paramedic
SCFD

Tom said in his bio interview,
"As far back as I can remember, I was fascinated with
firetrucks and hoped some
day I'd drive one." Strangely
enough, he ended up pursuing a degree and career in
law enforcement. He moved
to Florida from his hometown
of Traverse City, Michigan,
in 1988 to work for the
Sarasota Sheriffs Office.
After six years as a deputy,
he decided his heart was in
emergency medicine, so he
moved to Washington D.C. to
obtain a degree in emergency
medical management and
intern as a paramedic. After
his training, he longed to be
back in the Sunshine State,
so he returned. He was hired
by SCFD in 1999. He and
his wife, Kim, have a seven
month old daughter, Kate.
Tom loves hunting, fishing
and cooking.

Directions:

1 – Preheat oven to 350 degrees.

2 – Mix: flour, baking soda, salt, brown sugar, quick oats, cinnamon,
and margarine until crumbly.

3 – Press 1/2 of this mixture on bottom of a 9x13 pan.

4 – Pour fruit over the top of this.

5 – Pour the remaining mixture over the top of the fruit.

6 – Bake for 35-40 minutes at 350 degrees.

7 – Serve with ice cream.

8

Baklava

William Leighton — Firefighter/Paramedic

Ingredients:

1/2 reg. size lemon
2 cups sugar
1/2 lb. walnuts
1 pkg. sugar cookies

1/2 lb. butter
1 pkg. fillo dough
1 cup water

Directions:

1 – Make your syrup first by mixing water, lemon juice, and sugar in a pan and bring to boil for about 10 min. (Set aside).
2 – Take the walnuts and a 1/2 pkg. (6-8 oz.) of sugar cookies and crush into small crumbs.
3 – Grease a 9" x 13" pan and place a couple of sheets of fillo at the bottom for a base.
4 – Lightly sprinkle the butter, nuts, and cookie crumbs on base
5 – Place another sheet of dough down and repeat the steps, saving a couple of sheets for the top.
6 – Roll the edges down and lightly butter the top.
7 – With a sharp knife, diagonally cut into diamonds before baking.
8 – Preheat to 375 degrees.
9 – Bake until golden brown (approx. 20 - 25 min.)
10 – Remove and let cool for a few minutes.
11 – Pour syrup mixture over the top, to taste.
12 – Allow to totally cool, then remove from pan and enjoy !

Makes 20 Pieces.

William "Bill" Leighton
Firefighter/Paramedic
SCFD

Bill was born in Sarasota Memorial Hospital in 1962. He and his brother grew up on Albanian cuisine that his Albanian born mother prepared for them. His father was a heavy construction engineer with Raymond International and built many of the oil wells that were later destroyed in the war in Kuwait. Bill became a mechanic after graduating from Riverview High School and worked for Sunset Dodge. A friend of his worked for Sarasota Fire Department and wet his appetite for a career in the fire service. In 1986 he was hired by Sarasota as a firefighter and has subsequently become a paramedic and S.W.A.T. Medic.

Bill is an eligible bachelor that enjoys weightlifting, fishing, and motorcycles. He also makes a mean "Baklava!"

*About the recipe…
This an old family recipe favorite from Albania.*

Lynne Hall

Volunteer Firefighter/EMT

SCFD

For over six years, Lynne Hall has been a volunteer with Sarasota County Fire Department. As a volunteer firefighter and EMT, she assists as additional manpower at stations, call-outs, and special events. She'll often work up to 50 hours a month. This is JUST a hobby for Lynne, though! In her "real life," Lynne is a third grade teacher at Ashton Elementary School. She has been teaching since 1985. Lynne takes most pride in her two daughters, ages ten and thirteen. Between their schedules and hers, Lynne is a busy lady. Her passion is helping people, whether it's her family, her students, or those she assists with the department. She is constantly giving of herself to others.

Mandarin-Orange Pineapple Cake

Lynne C. Hall — Volunteer Firefighter/EMT

Ingredients:

1 package yellow cake mix, without pudding
3 eggs
3/4 cup oil
1 can mandarin oranges

12 ounce cool whip
1 teaspoon vanilla
3 ounce package instant vanilla pudding
20 ounces crushed pineapple

Directions:

CAKE:

1 – Preheat oven to 350 degrees.

2 – Beat together cake mix, eggs oil, and the juice from one can of mandarin oranges.

3 – Add the mandarin oranges and mix until the oranges are in small pieces.

4 – Bake in a 9"x13" pan in the oven @ 350 for 35-55 minutes.

FROSTING:

1 – Whip together cool whip, vanilla, instant vanilla pudding, and crushed pineapple (with some juice drained).

2 – Frost cake when cool.

3 – Enjoy this simple yummy treat!

Bing Cherry & Pecan Pie

Munroe's Restaurant

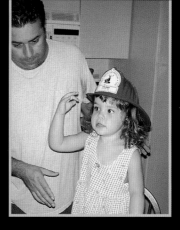

Ingredients:

10" par baked unsweetened piecrust
8 oz dried bing cherries
1/2 cup sugar
3 oz pecans, chopped
2 oz whole butter

1 tsp mace
1 tsp nutmeg
1 tsp cinnamon
4 oz water
2 tbl flour

Directions:

1 – Sauté cherries with butter.

2 – 2 oz of water and 1/4 cup of sugar.

3 – Cook until cherries are reconstituted.

4 – Add 2-tbl flour and toss until smooth.

5 – Add spices and cool.

6– Sauté pecans with sugar and water.

7 – Reduce until caramelized.

8 – Place cherry filling in the pie crust and cover with pecan topping.

9 – Bake at 350 for approximately 20 minutes.

NFPA Factoids And "Kitchen Fire Prevention Tips"

Question:
How many structure fires were deliberately set or suspected of having been deliberately set in 1999?

Answer:
72,000.

"Kitchen Fire Prevention Tips"
Keep your cooking surfaces clear of pot holders, dish towels, and food packaging. They can easily catch fire when placed close to a heat source.

Information Courtesy of NFPA

Susan Munroe helps Max with his cookies.

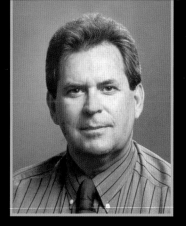

John William Shearer

EMS Quality Assurance Officer
SCFD
(Deceased)

Bill and I were fortunate to live on Siesta Key, and our apartment looked out over the Gulf. One of our special treats on the weekend was breakfast on the lanai while watching people walk the beach. Bill was the cook in the family and in addition to the usual "breakfast fare," he would prepare this coffee cake that was extraordinary. It was delicious and it became very symbolic of our "special moments alone together." I hope you enjoy it as much as we did and that you'll share it during your special moments as well.

"Bill's Banana Streusel Cake"

Bill Shearer (Deceased)

Ingredients:

1/2 cup butter or margarine
3/4 cup sugar
1 3/4 cups regular flour (unsifted)
1 tsp.vanilla extract
2 eggs (large)
1/2 tsp.baking powder
1/2 tsp.baking soda

1/2 tsp.salt
1/2 tsp.cinnamon
2/3 cup banana (mashed)
1/3 cup buttermilk or sour milk
   (sour milk equals1 tsp. vinegar per
   1/3 cup sweet milk)

Directions:

1 – Cream butter and 1/2 cup sugar.

2 – Add 3/4 cup of the flour and work into the creamed mixture with hands to form a crumb mixture.

3 – Remove 1/2 cup of crumb mixture, and set aside.

4 – To the remaining crumb mixture, add remaining 1/4 cup sugar, vanilla, and eggs. Beat until smooth.

5 – Combine remaining 1 cup flour with baking powder, baking soda, salt and cinnamon. Stir to blend. Set aside.

6 – In another bowl, combine bananas with buttermilk and sour milk.

7 – Add these two mixtures to the egg mixture, alternately, beginning and ending with dry ingredients.

8 – Blend well and turn into a buttered 10" pie pan.

9 – Take crumb mixture that has been set aside and rub between hands to make large lumps. Sprinkle over batter and bake at 375 for 35 - 40 minutes, or until cake tests done.

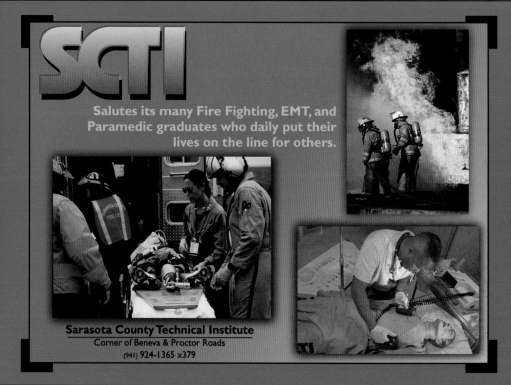

Easy Pudding Dessert

Big Olaf Creamery – Kim Mullet

Ingredients:

1/2 gallon vanilla ice cream
3 cups milk
2 packages instant pistachio pudding
60 Ritz crackers

4 tablespoons butter
whip cream
Heath Bars crushed

Directions:

1 – Melt ice cream in large mixing bowl for 1/2 hour.

2 – Slowly beat in milk, and then add 2 packages pistachio pudding until all is mixed.

3 – Crush Ritz crackers and add butter and mix into crumbs.

4 – Butter a 13x9 pan and press crumbs around, saving some for on top.

5 – Pour pudding over crumbs and chill overnight, then top with whipped cream, crushed heath bars, and the remaining crumbs.

Ken Mullet
Big Olaf Creamery

Ken is operations manager for the Siesta Key Big Olaf Creamery, and a partner in the Main Street Plaza location. In his free time he likes to golf, and referee H.S. basketball. When asked what he enjoys most in life Ken replied, "God, family, and friends!" He and his wife Kim are active in the Bayshore Mennonite Church and have a keen interest in the work of Christian Fellowship Missions in Haiti.

The easy pudding dessert is a delicious dessert that tastes best when made with Big Olaf's vanilla ice cream.

28

Charlie Russell
Firefighter/EMT
Englewood Fire Department

Charlie Russell, a Firefighter/ EMT, is presently with the Englewood Fire Department. Serving 17 years in the fire service to date, Charlie has been honored as the 1999 Firefighter of the Year. He is an outdoorsman enjoying hunting, fishing and sports. Back home in Mississippi is where this delicious recipe came from, straight from his Mom's kitchen. When asked what he loves most in life he replies, "What I love most in life is meeting new people and helping people. Living life to the fullest each day is important because you never know what tomorrow will bring."

Ms. Mud Pie

Charlie Russell — Firefighter/EMT

Ingredients:

2 cups plain flour
1 cup chopped pecans
2 sticks oleo
4 tablespoons sugar
2 cups cool whip
2 – 8 ounce cream cheese

2 cups powdered sugar
2 teaspoon vanilla
1 large package instant chocolate
   pudding mix
2 1/2 cups milk

Directions:

1 – Mix flour, pecans, melted oleo, and sugar in the bottom of 9x13 pan.
Bake at 350 degrees until lightly brown. Let cool – (do not overcook).

2 – Mix together cool whip, cream cheese, powdered sugar, and vanilla.
Spread over cool crust.

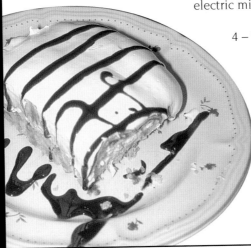

3 – Mix chocolate pudding mix and milk, beat well with
electric mixer and spread over cream cheese mixture.

4 – Top with cool whip and refrigerate overnight.

Makes 10 – 12 Servings.

Apple Streusel Cake
Munroe's Restaurant

Ingredients:

stick butter
1 cup, light brown sugar
2 eggs
6 tbl milk
3/4 cup chopped hazlenuts
2 cups self rising cake flour
1 tsp baking powder

1 granny smith apple, shredded
1 granny smith apple, sliced and tossed in brown sugar (for the streusel)
1 stick butter softened
1/2 cup flour
1/2 cup light brown sugar

Richard Munroe
Chef/Proprietor
Munroe's Restaurant

Locals and seasonal visitors alike enjoy the bistro setting of Munroe's Restaurant. Proven to be Sarasota's favorite restaurant with casual elegance, friendly service, and creative, American foods.

Whether you start off your meal with one of our famous appetizers or finish with one of our colorful desserts, you won't go away disappointed.

For the late night guest, we offer live entertainment upstairs, with a late night menu and premium bar.

Directions:

1 – Grease and eight inch cake pan and place sugared apples evenly on the bottom of the pan.

2 – Place all ingredients in a mixing bowl and beat with a spoon until smooth.

3 – Pour the batter into the cake pan and bake at 300 for 30 - 40 minutes, unmold and cool at room temp for 30 minutes.

4 – To make the streusel, place all ingredients in a bowl and knead with your fingers until the mixture beads.

5 – Place on a sheet pan and dry in a 250 degree for one half hour, remove and cool.

6 – Pack the streusel on top of the cake liberally.

Munroe's
Urban Bistro - Vintage Tavern

941-316-0609

1296 First Street
Sarasota
Lunch Monday – Friday
Dinner Monday – Saturday
5:30 PM To 10:00 PM
Closed Sundays

Sarasota's Favorite Restaurant

- American cuisine
- Bistro setting
- Live entertainment upstairs
- Desserts • Appetizers
- Late Night Menu
- Premium Bar
- Catering Available

Butch & Sandi
Mullet's Aluminum

Butch was born into an Amish family in Ohio. His dad owned and operated a country store and taught his children a very strong work ethic. In 1969 the family moved to Sarasota, Florida, and his dad opened Mullet's Appliances, which is now owned by Butch's brother and brother-in-law.

In 1978, Butch and his wife, Sandi, started Mullet's Aluminum. His brother, Bob, came to work for the company a few years later and is now vice-president and general manager. The company has now grown to over 80 employees and has become a leader in the aluminum industry. This has allowed Mullet's Aluminum to expand into many new aluminum, vinyl and glass products.

Butch, Sandi and their three children, Travis, Stasha, and Tiler, live on a ranch near Sarasota. Butch enjoys hunting, boating and raising cattle.

Butterscotch Date Pudding

Mullet's Aluminum
An Amish favorite dessert, which is an old family recipe.

Ingredients:

SYRUP:
2 cups brown sugar
2 cups boiling water
butter size of an egg –1/4 cup
1 teaspoon vanilla

BATTER:
1/2 cup sugar
butter size of walnut – 2 tablespoons
1/2 cup milk
1 teaspoon vanilla
1/8 teaspoon salt
1 heaping cup of flour
2 teaspoons baking powder
1/2 cup nut meats
1 cup dates

Directions:

1 – To make syrup bring all the ingredients to a boil.

2 – Pour syrup into 9 x 12 loaf pan.

3 – Drop batter by the spoon fulls into hot syrup.

4 – Bake at 350 degrees in the oven for 25-30 minutes.

5 – Serve with whip cream.

Flourless Chocolate Cake

Pastry Art

Ingredients:

8 large eggs
1 pound bittersweet or semisweet chocolate
chopped coarsely
8 ounces (2 sticks) butter, cut up
1/4 cup strong coffee or liqueur (optional)

Cocoa powder or powdered sugar
for decoration

This recipe highlights the type of chocolate used.
Bittersweet has less sugar and more chocolate flavor.
Use a good quality chocolate for the best results.

Directions:

1 – Preheat oven to 325 degrees. Line bottom of 8" spring form pan with parchment paper or wax paper, and grease sides. Cover pan underneath and up sides with foil. Set inside roasting pan and bring water to a boil. 2 – Beat eggs in a machine or a hand held mixer at high speed until doubled in volume, about 5 minutes. 3 – While beating eggs, melt chocolate and butter and liqueur in microwave or in a bowl set over hot water. Mixture should be warm – about 115 degrees. 4 – Fold egg foam into chocolate in 3 stages until completely blended. 5 – Pour batter into prepared pan. Set into roasting pan on oven rack and pour boiling water to come halfway up the sides. 6 – Bake at 325 degrees for 30 minutes or an instant – read thermometer is 140. Cake should rise slightly, edges just starting to set, and look a little undercooked. This is ok! It will firm up as it cools. 7 – Remove cake from water and set on a cooling rack until room temperature. Cover and refrigerate overnight. 8 – Remove sides of pan, invert onto wax paper or plate and remove parchment paper. Turn cake right side up onto serving platter. Dust with cocoa or powdered sugar or both. A lace doilly placed over the cake before dusting with sugar is very decorative. Softly whipped cream makes a nice contrast with the rich chocolate flavor. 9 – Chocolate dipped strawberries make a more elegant presentation.

Makes 12–14 Servings.

HELPFUL HINTS: When microwaving chocolate melt at 50% power for 2 minutes, stir then add butter and heat again at 50% power until smooth. Using a knife dipped in hot water and wiped dry will give nice clean slices. This cake is very rich, so a little goes a long way.

John Andersen

Owner
Pastry Art

John was born in upstate New York in 1963. He moved to Florida in 1982 and became a retail district manager. Hungry for a change of pace John spent four years as a restaurant food and beverage manager, prior to taking a position in Europe as a wine educator. In 1992, he expanded his food service background even further starting his own wholesale distribution company for bakery and dessert items.

He shifted from wholesale to retail in 1992, when he bought into "Pastry Art" in Bradenton. He opened the Sarasota location in 1997 and today is owner of both locations. Certainly a factor in his success is his belief that "you get one opportunity to make a first impression."

Pastry

Art

941-955-7545

Two Convenient Locations:
1508 Main Street
Sarasota

• • •

6753 Manatee Avenue West
Bradenton

Bakery

Café

Fine Coffees

Randall Stulce

District Chief
Sarasota Fire Department
Station #11, Battalion #3-B

District Chief "Randy" Stulce is a 25 year veteran that has seen his share of action. If cutting his at Station #1 wasn't enough, he filled in the voids teaching the basics to recruits on his days off. From the old days of burning hay or tires for "smoke day," to the new non-toxic smoke generators in the state-of-the-art Burn Building, Randy has been coaching students through the art of fireground survival. Randy's hobbies include snowskiing the powder in Colorado, plenty of physical B'ball with the crews, and occasionally sampling his mom's peanut butter fudge.

Chief Stulce's version of... "Follow the leader."

Peanut Butter Fudge

Randall Stulce — District Chief

Ingredients:

3 cups sugar
12 ounce can evaporated milk
1 stick butter
12 ounce jar of marshmallow cream

1 teaspoon salt
1 teaspoon vanilla
12 ounce jar of creamy peanut butter

Directions:

1 – Combine sugar, milk and butter in large heavy saucepan.

2 – Heat to boiling point.

3 – Stir over medium heat approximately 5 minutes. (Mix to soft ball stage, check by dipping spoonful in glass of cold water.)

4 – Remove and add marshmallow cream blending well, then add peanut butter again stirring until well blended.

5 – Pour into 12" x 9" x 2" pan and let cool.

6 – Cut and serve fudge. (DO NOT REFRIGERATE)

Makes about 3 pounds of fudge.

Turtle Royale

Scoop Daddy's

Ingredients:

2 ounces hot fudge
2 ounces hot caramel
1/2 cup pecans
2 scoops vanilla ice cream

1 banana
1 cherry
whipped cream

Directions:

1 – In a large dish, drizzle hot fudge and hot caramel decorating the bottom and sides of the dish.

2 – Lay a bed of fresh pecans.

3 – Position 2 scoops of vanilla ice cream on the pecan bed.

4 – Drizzle hot fudge and hot caramel over the ice cream.

5 – Cover with another layer of pecans.

6 – Cut a banana into quarters and stand them upright like 4 points of a crown.

7 – Cover with whipped cream and a cherry.

Scoop Daddy's

From the moment you ente SCOOP DADDY'S you'll fee like you've stepped into the fabulous fifties. Rock N' Rol to Buddy Holly, Chuck Berr and Fats Domino while enjoy ing our hamburgers, ho dogs, chicken sandwiches bratwurst, grilled cheese sandwiches, and Krispy Kreme donuts. You'll find yourself surrounded by fiftie memorabilia and thousands o refrigerator magnets as yot sit at our counter sipping at old fashioned ice cream soda a New York egg cream, a brown cow, or a thick, creamy milk shake. Please stop by and see for yourself why out super premium ice cream was voted "Best In America in a national taste contest." W look forward to serving you

941-388-1650

**373 St. Armand's Circle
Sarasota
Open 7 Days A Week
10 AM To 10 PM**

Serving Up Memories

- **Hamburgers** ● **Hot Dogs**
- **Ice Cream** ● **Milk Shakes**
- **Krispy Kreme Donuts**
- **Ice Cream Sodas**

*Voted Best In America
In National Taste Contest*

Sharon Schlabach

Sharon's Grandparents moved to Florida from Georgia and raised their families here. Sharon's Grandmother was a wonderful cook, always feeding people who stopped in to visit.

Sharon's parents, Buddy and Mattie Alday, raised their three sons and two daughters in Sarasota, Florida. In the early years Buddy would hunt wild hogs, turkey, alligator, and quail to feed his growing family.

Sharon went to beauty school 30 years ago while in high school, and was a hairdresser upon graduation.

Sharon loves to cook and can usually be found in the kitchen whipping up something, or canning vegetables or jellies with her mom and sister. Sharon hopes her 17-year old daughter, Ashley, will remember their family cooking and pass it down to future grandchildren.

About the recipe...
"Entertaining is what Southern Hospitality is all about. Good food and good company are a great combination. Here's a great recipe, you'll have to look up your own company."

Sharon's Chocoholic Cake

Sharon Schlabach

Ingredients:

CAKE:
3 grams Unsweetened Chocolate Squares
1/2 cup Butter
2 1/4 cup Light Brown Sugar
3 Eggs
2 cups Flour
2 tsp. Baking Soda
1/2 tsp. Salt
1 cup Sour Cream

1 cup Boiling Water
1 1/2 tsp. Vanilla

FILLING:
4 Egg yolks
1 cup Powdered sugar
1/4 tsp. Salt
6 oz. Semi-sweet chocolate
3 sticks Unsalted Butter (chilled)
1 jar Raspberry Jelly (seedless)

ICING:
14 oz. Semi Sweet Chocolate (CalleBut)
1 cup Heavy Whipping Cream
1 Tsp. Vanilla

Directions:

CAKE:
1 – Beat butter and sugar for 4 minutes. 2 – Add eggs one at a time, then vanilla. 3 – Mix flour, salt, and baking soda separately. 4 – Then alternate pouring dry ingredient mix and sour cream into batter. 5 – Slowly add hot water. 6 – Grease and flour baking pan, before pouring in batter. 7 – Bake @ 350 deg. for 30 - 35 minutes. 8 – Remove from oven and cool. 9 – Use dental floss to split layers.

FILLING:
1 – Mix egg yolks, salt, and powdered sugar. Beat 5 minutes.
2 – Melt chocolate and let cool. Then add to egg mixture.
3 – Add 2 Tbs. of butter at a time until completely mixed.
4 – Spread 2 T. of slightly warm jelly on top of cake.
5 – Chill... and then spread chocolate filling next.
6 – Repeat layer steps until the very top.
7 – Chill cake before icing.

ICING:
1 – Melt chocolate on low heat and mix ingredients, then cool.
2 – Pour over chocolate cake until Icing is sufficient for your tastes.

Makes 10 – 12 Servings.

Mandarin Bananas Flambé with Fresh Ginger and Ice Cream

The Colony Restaurants

Ingredients:

2 medium ripe bananas
1 orange cut in half
1/2 lemon
1/2 cup brown sugar
1/2 cup butter
1 teaspoon cinnamon
1 teaspoon fresh chopped ginger

1 tablespoon diced crystallized ginger
3 ounces rum
3 ounces banana liquor
1 ounce brandy
Vanilla ice cream
Mint for garnish

Directions:

1 – Melt butter and sugar in heavy nonstick skillet over medium heat, stirring constantly.

2 – Add liquor and flambé, squeeze juice from orange and lemon.

3 – Add cinnamon and stir until very thick and syrupy, about 2 minutes.

4 – Add bananas and stir just enough to heat through.

5 – Spoon bananas and sauce over ice cream and sprinkle with diced crystallized ginger and a sprig of mint.

Makes 4 Servings.

Tom Klauber
Food & Beverage Director
The Colony Restaurants

The Colony's Director of Food & Beverage Operations Tom Klauber is also Chef/Proprietor of Longboat Key's popular Pattigeorge's restaurant. Tom began his culinary career by working at his family's resort, later attending the University of Houston's Hotel & Management School and earning a degree from the Culinary Institute of America. He then traveled and studied abroad, receiving his diploma from La Varenne's Ecole de Cuisine in Paris, France. He gained experience in fine restaurants in Paris, Florence and Amsterdam before returning to The Colony, where he worked as executive chef and food and beverage director from 1982 to 1992. Prior to opening PGs in 1998, Tom was chef/owner at Gieussepp Wong in Aspen.

Tom Klauber has received numerous accolades, including being recognized in "Chefs in America" as one of the outstanding chefs in the United States, and receiving the James Beard Foundation "Rising Stars of American Cuisine" Award.

the Colony Restaurants

Monday – Saturday
Lunch: 11:30 AM To 2:30 PM
Dinner: 6:00 PM To 10:00 PM
Sunday Brunch:
10:00 AM To 2:00 PM

941-383-5558
1620 Gulf of Mexico Drive
Longboat Key

• • •

Enjoy an award-winning dining experience complemented by an unparalleled wine list with *spectacular* views of the Gulf of Mexico.

- **Prestigious DiRoNA Award**
- **The Wine Spectator's Award of Excellence**
- **Five Star Diamond Award for outstanding hospitality from the American Academy of Hospitality Sciences**
- **Member of Nation's Restaurant News Fine Dining Hall of Fame**

2

Chuck Chase

Firefighter/Paramedic

SCFD

Chuck's first involvement with the Fire Service began in 1968 in Millersburg, Ohio. The local funeral home hearse served as his first ambulance. The entire first aid kit was comprised of a bottle of oxygen and some bandages.

In 1981 he moved to Florida and began a new career in the field of Fire/Emergency Medical Services with the Fruitville Fire Dept. He especially enjoys being a paramedic and will tell you there is no shortage of equipment on his ambulance today.

Chuck is known for his sense of humor and the sheer enjoyment he gets from playing practical jokes. In his off duty time, he works as a Licensed Message Therapist. He and his wife Debbie enjoy boating, flying small aircraft, and travel.

Peanut Butter Brownie Pizza

Chuck Chase — Firefighter/Paramedic

Ingredients:

1 brownie mix (regular size box)
8 ounce cream cheese (softened)
1/2 cup brown sugar
1/4 cup peanut butter

4 Reese peanut butter cups
2 bananas
1/4 cup chopped peanuts
chocolate syrup

Directions:

1 – Preheat oven to 350 degrees.

2 – Prepare brownie mix according to box on round pizza pan, baking 20-25 minutes or until done.

3 – Let brownie cool completely.

4 – Mix together cream cheese, brown sugar, and peanut butter. Spread this mixture over cooled brownie.

5 – Chop 4 single Reese peanut butter cups and sprinkle over cream cheese mixture.

6 – Layer 2 sliced bananas over peanut butter cups.

7 – Sprinkle with 1/4 cup chopped peanuts.

8 – Drizzle with chocolate syrup.

Cherry Cobbler

Durango Oak Fire Steakhouse

Ingredients:

2 cups self-rising flour
1/2 cup butter (unsweetened)
2 cups whole milk

2 cups sugar
5 cups Comstock cherry pie filling

Directions:

1 – Melt butter and place in the bottom of a medium depth half hotel pan.

2 – Mix flour, milk, and sugar. Pour mixture over butter.

3 – Spoon pie filling over flour mixture, taking care not to mix layers.

4 – Place uncovered in 350 degree oven for 35-40 minutes until browned on top and thoroughly cooked through.

5 – Cobbler is done when cake separates from the sides of the pan.

6 – Serving suggestions: Serve a heaping #8 scoop of warm cobbler (equal amount of fruit and cake) with a #8 scoop of vanilla ice cream on one side.

Makes 12 Large Servings.

Darren J. Novosel
General Manager
Durango

Growing up in Pittsburgh, Pennsylvania no doubt predisposed Darren to become the diehard "Steelers" fan that he is. His collection of sports memorabilia is certainly biased in favor of his beloved team. To afford the collection, and pay his way through college, he found employment in the restaurant industry. With 16 years in the industry, Darren has been managing restaurants for 11 of them.

Darren and his fiancee` longed for a change of scenery to a more tropical setting so he accepted a transfer to Tampa which ultimately landed him in Sarasota and a G.M position with Durango USA. Darren says, "there's no better job for a guy who loves people and food."

*About the recipe...
Top off your meal with a tasty cobbler recipe from the kitchens of Durango USA.*

941-378-0595
**5451 Fruitville Road
Sarasota**

941-761-9516
**5502 Cortez Road West
Bradenton**

941-496-8383
**4369 South Tamiami Trail
Venice**

**Voted #1 Steak House
Across Florida By
Florida Today
Venice Gondolier
and *Naples* News Press**

Alex Horony
Firemedic
SCFD

Alex began his venture into the fire service as a 16-year old when he became a Fire Service — Explorer with the City of Brooksville. His early interest and subsequent training was rewarded with a position with the South Venice Fire Department in 1996. He has been serving as a Firefighter/EMT with Sarasota County for the past three years since the merger. Alex says, "my chosen field is gratifying and envigorating, and I enjoy the variety of crews I work with."

His wife Kristen and two-year old son Karl were well recieved in a recent Firehouse visit when accompanied by the 'Butterscotch Blast' recipe. Alex says, "the guys can't quit talking about the dessert; mean my family."

Firefighter, Steve Garris, lowers injured construction worker from roof in stokes basket.

Butterscotch Blast
Kristin & Alex Horony — Firemedic

Ingredients:

1 box chocolate cake mix
2 – 3.4 ounce boxes butterscotch instant pudding

12 ounce tub cool whip
8 ounces Heath candy crushed

Directions:

1 – Bake cake according to box directions. Let cool.

2 – Break cake into pieces.

3 – Mix pudding according to box directions.

4 – Pour pudding over cake pieces.

5 – Add cool whip and layer top with crushed Heath candy.

Serves 8 Firemen or 12-16 people.

Bread Pudding
Munroe's Restaurant

Ingredients:

1 baguette (day old preferred), sliced
   in 4 inch thick rounds
1 pint heavy whipping cream
1/2 cup sugar
1 zest of one lemon

6 whole eggs
1 tsp vanilla extract
1/2 cup milk
berries and mint to garnish

Directions:

1 – Place bread rounds in a casserole dish - squeeze in as many as possible.

2 – In an electric mixing bowl place milk, eggs, sugar, vanilla and lemon zest - whip at low speed for five minutes.

3 – Ladle custard mix over the bread slices in the casserole dish (you want the liquid to rise 2 inches from the surface).

4 – Sprinkle sugar over the entire dish, cover and bake at 300 for 30 minutes.

5 – Let stand for 30 minutes after cooking, cut into squares and place in large soup or pasta bowls for serving.

6 – Scald cream in a small sauce pan and ladle over pudding. Garnish with mint and berries as shown.

Susan Munroe with her daughter, Ashley.

Keith Haluska
Firefighter/Paramedic
SCFD

Keith is a firefighter/ paramedic presently working for the Sarasota County Fire Department. He has a great compassion for people and that is one of the reasons why working in the fire service is extremely rewarding for him. Keith and his wife, Linda, have been married for 12 years. God has blessed them with two beautiful miracle daughters, Marianna and Nicole. Keith enjoys water sports, computers, collecting fire memorabilia, and cooking. However, Keith's most treasured moments are those spent with his family, Linda and his girls.

About the recipe....
This is my mother-in-law's Polish family's traditional recipe that is served as one of their delicious desserts on Easter.

Donna Mae's Kolachy
Keith Haluska — Firefighter/Paramedic

Ingredients:

1 cup butter softened
8 ounce cream cheese
1 tablespoon milk
1 tablespoon sugar
1 egg yolk

1 1/2 cups flour
1/2 teaspoon baking powder
12 ounce Solo fruit filling
 (your favorite one)
sprinkle confectioners sugar

Directions:

1 – Cream softened butter, cream cheese, milk and sugar together.

2 – Add 1 beaten egg yolk and mix.

3 – Sift together, in a separate bowl, 1 1/2 cups flour with 1/2 teaspoon baking powder.

4 – Add flour mixture to creamed mixture.

5 – Cover and refrigerate at least 4 hours or overnight.

6 – Roll or pat out dough on a floured board to 1/4" thickness. Cut dough into 2" rounds. Depress center with finger. Fill the center with scant teaspoon of Solo fruit.

7 – Bake at 400 degrees in the oven for 10-15 minutes until slightly brown.

8 – Sprinkle with confectioners sugar before serving.

Makes about 36 cookies.

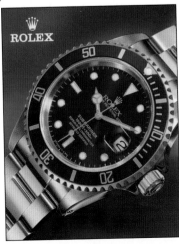

Pear Apple Tart

Café L' Europe

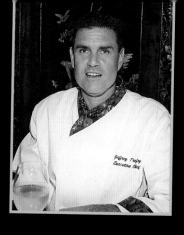

Ingredients:

8 ounces whipped cream
1 cup pastry cream
1/2 cup rosemary lemon reduction
(Combine 4 cups of water with 1 sprig of rosemary and the zest from one lemon. Reduce by boiling to 1/2 cup.)
6 six-inch puff pastry circles

1 tablespoon sugar
3 apples
3 pears
1/2 cup apricot glaze
1 pint strawberries
1 pinch powdered ginger
1/2 cup chopped pineapple

Directions:

1 – Combine whipped cream, pastry cream and chilled rosemary lemon reduction to form a light fluffy cream. Refrigerate.
2- Preheat oven to 425 degrees.
3 – Sprinkle sugar on puff pastry circles and bake to a light golden brown.
4 – Circles should puff up to at least 2 inches high. Let cool but do not refrigerate.
5 – With a piping bag starting from the bottom of the pastry fill them 1/2 full of the pastry cream mixture. Set aside.
6 – Slice apples and pears very thin.
7 – Alternate layers of apple and pear with the tips meeting at the top.
8 – Warm apricot glaze and brush on top carefully.
9 – Combine strawberries and pineapple in a food processor with ginger.
10 – Process quickly but not completely, so that the sauce is coarse.
11 – Place sauce on plate and then place tart on top of sauce.

Makes 6 Servings.

Jeff Trefry
Executive Chef
Café L' Europe

Upon graduation from the prestigious Culinary Institute of America, Jeff moved west to Santa Barbara, California and worked as a pastry chef for the El Encanto Hotel. To broaden his knowledge of the culinary arts and hone his skills, Jeff moved east and spent three years at Café L' Europe in the early 1980's. Jeff's career path led him to the Five-Star Five-Diamond Ritz Carlton Resort in Naples and he was promoted to Executive Sous Chef. In 1989, promotion placed Jeff as Executive Chef in charge of culinary operations at the Ritz Carlton in Kansas City, Mo. He then worked in Bermuda and Hilton Head Island, S.C. but is now back with Café L' Europe as Executive Chef. Jeff executes New European Cuisine with his own imagination and personal style. He is married to Janet and has three children – Megan, Jack and Mike.

Lisa Alday
Alday's Bar-B-Q

Jeff and Lisa have been in the BBQ/Catering business since 1980. "Alday's Cookouts," as it was known, was geared towards night and weekend catering. After marrying in 1981, their business continued to grow until they opened their first restaurant on Clark Road. The restaurant was a hit for barbecue lovers and quickly expanded to a new location serving over 1000 lbs. of pork weekly.

After 20 years in the business, Jeff, Lisa and their six children, still are providing catering and carryout of some of the finest oak fired barbecued chicken, pork, and ribs you can find.

Away from the BBQ cookers and telephones, Lisa enjoys rare quiet time and special moments with their kids. Jeff's hobbies include fishing, fishing, and fishing!

About the recipe...
Jeff's mother, Mattie Alday, loves to cook and bake almost as much as folks enjoy eating her creations. This cake is a favorite of the Alday family and friends.

Coconut Cake with Pineapple Filling
Alday's Bar-B-Q, Mattie Alday

Ingredients:

CAKE:
1 box yellow cake mix
   (I make it from scratch)
FILLING:
1 lg. can crushed pineapple (do not drain)
2 tbs. cornstarch
2 tbs. sugar
1 tbs. butter

ICING:
5 – egg whites (room temp)
2 cups sugar
1/2 teas. cream of tarter
1/2 cup water
14 oz. pkg. coconut

Directions:

CAKE:
1 – Mix as directed on box.
2 – Bake in two layers
3 – Split each layer with dental floss when cooled, to make 4 layers.

FILING:
1 – Mix above ingredients until thick over low heat and continue stirring to avoid burning.

ICING:
1 – Put sugar and water in pot...cook until it spins a thread, (therm reads 148 deg.)
2 – Beat egg whites (while cooking sugar water mixture) and add cream of tarter. Beat until stiff. Add syrup mixture slowly.

PUTTING CAKE TOGETHER
1 – Place bottom layer on plate using 1/3 of pineapple filling to top.*Repeat with 2nd and 3rd layer "Do Not Put Filling On Top Layer".
2 – Cover entire cake, top and sides with Icing.
3 – Then sprinkle entire cake with coconut.

8

Strawberry Pie

Yoder's

Ingredients:

2 cups water
1 cup sugar
3 tablespoons of clear jel mixed in
   1/4 cup cold water
3 ounce package of strawberry jel

1/2 teaspoon red food coloring
1-1/2 pints fresh strawberries
1 9"-10" pre-baked pie pastry shell
2 cups whipped topping

Directions:

1 – Cook water and sugar to boiling.

2 – Add clear jel mixture to water and bring to boil. While mixing with wire whisk remove from heat.

3 – Add strawberry jel and food coloring. Chill.

4 – Clean strawberries and slice. Mix with chilled jel.

5 – Place strawberry mixture into pie shell. Flatten mixture with back of large spoon into pie shell.

6 – Top with whipped topping.

Makes 6 – 8 Servings.

Mrs. Yoder and grandson, Brian Emrich
Yoder's

Yoder's offers over 20 varieties of homemade pies; best sellers include egg custard, Dutch apple, key lime, banana cream, chocolate peanut butter and fresh strawberry. Yoder's pies have become traditional for many at special events and holidays. Thanksgiving is the busiest time at Yoder's when they bake thousands of pies, with pumpkin pie being the favorite. Today six family members are involved in the business. Grandson, Brian Emrich, has his grandpa's heart for people and works as a manager and host. Brian always says, "save room for our dessert!" Shoo fly pie warmed up with ice cream is his favorite.

299

Steven Darling
Firefighter/Paramedic
SCFD

Steve has been with the Sarasota County Fire Department as a firefighter/ paramedic for over 16 years and moved to Florida via Colorado and Cape Cod, Massachusetts. Deanna works as an LPN nurse and is currently studying toward her RN license. She moved here 10 years ago from London, England. Steve and Deanna work together to make their key lime pie that has delighted friends, neighbors and relatives. Steve grows, picks, and squeezes the key limes at their home in Nokomis, Florida. The key limes must be constantly monitored and are quite a challenge to squeeze since they are very small. Deanna then takes over the finer part and actually makes the pies. Using fresh lime juice is the secret to having a pie that is not too tart.

The Firehouse Favorites gang at Marketing By Design. From left to right:
Alan McAnulty
Carolyn MacMillan
Bennie Barton
Jeni Dettman

Key Lime Pie
Steven Darling's wife, Deanna's recipe

Ingredients:

1/2 cup key lime juice
  (preferably fresh squeezed)
4 egg yolks
1 can sweetened condensed milk

1 graham cracker pie shell
  (or homemade pie crust)
almonds (optional)

Directions:

1 – Blend egg yolks and condensed milk.

2 – Slowly add lime juice.

3 – Pour into graham cracker pie shell.

4 – Bake at 375 degrees 20 minutes or until set.

5 – Cover and chill in refrigerator until served.

6 – Add whip cream and or tropical fruit to your taste. May decorate edges of pie with almonds.

Makes 6 – 8 Servings.

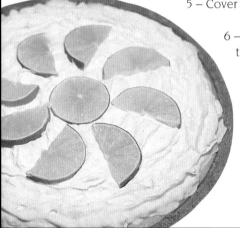

White Chocolate Mousse Cup

Ophelia's

Ingredients:

8 ounces white chocolate
3 1/2 ounces butter
8 eggs separated
4 ounces hazelnut liqueur
4 ounces powdered sugar
3 cups whipping cream

(This makes several dozen mousse cups; you could halve the recipe for a smaller number.)

Directions:

1 – Melt the chocolate and butter in a bowl over a double boiler.

2 – Beat egg yolks, hazelnut liqueur and powdered sugar until thick.

3 – Fold the chocolate and egg mixtures together.

4 – Whip egg whites until fairly stiff.

5 – Fold the egg whites into the chocolate and egg mixture.

6 – Refrigerate until chilled.

Joel Zaborowski
Ophelia's

Even before he could read, Pastry Chef Joel Zaborowski was making desserts in his family kitchen. He knew about sugar, flour and eggs from watching his stepmother, and apparently that was enough. Although he began following recipes for cookies and cakes when he was eight, his special kind of fearless improvisations continues to this day. When he was in his teens, he became serious about desserts and decided to pursue baking as a career. He attended Johnson and Wales University in Providence, Rhode Island majoring in Pastry Arts. Joel joined the staff at Ophelia's and in the fall they competed in the Taste of Sarasota. Joel took first place in the dessert division with his Triple Layer Chocolate Marscapone Flair.

941-349-2212

9105 Midnight Pass Road
Siesta Key
Open 7 Days A Week
5 AM To 10 PM

Ophelia's
on the bay

Ophelia's Famous Signature Dessert

Strawberry Fool

Café on the Bay

Ingredients:

2 pints Fresh strawberry
2 pints Heavy cream
1 cup Melba sauce (raspberry jam)

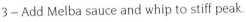

Café on the Bay

Nestled in the Longboat Key
Moorings, along beautiful
Sarasota Bay, sits Longboat
Key's Hidden Gem...Café on
the Bay. Elegant yet casual,
her charm beckons seafarers
and landlubbers alike for
breakfast, lunch or dinner.
You will delight in an offering
of extraordinary cuisine.
Enjoy the indoor dining room
or the covered outdoor ter-
race, both featuring spectacu-
ar marina and bay views.
Or you may simply wish to
enjoy your favorite cocktail or
one of our own exotic cre-
ations at our Marker 15
Lounge. This is one "Port of
Call" you will wish to visit
over and over again! Inquire
about our sunset special and
the pre-fixed dinner offering.
Breakfast Saturday
8:30 AM – 10:30 AM
Sunday Breakfast Brunch
9:00 AM – 1:00 PM
Sunday Lunch
1:00 PM – 3:30 PM
Lunch 11:00 AM – 3:00 PM
Dinner 4:30 PM – 10:00 PM
In the Longboat Key
Moorings Marina behind
Publix – right out of guard
gate, second left.

Directions:

1 – Clean and cup strawberries.

2 – Whip cream to soft peaks.

3 – Add Melba sauce and whip to stiff peak.

4 – Put strawberries in serving glass.

5 – Top with whipping cream mixture.

941-383-0440

2630 Harbourside Dr.
Longboat Key, FL 34228

Breakfast Saturday
8:30 AM To 10:30 AM

Sunday Breakfast Brunch
9:00 AM To 1:00 PM

Sunday Lunch
1:00 PM To 3:30 PM

Lunch 6 Days
11:00 AM To 3:00 PM

Dinner 7 Days
4:30 PM To 10:00 PM

Extraordinary cuisine served in a
truly exquisite waterfront setting.
Come by land or sea.
Casual attire is welcomed.

Blueberry Pie

Claiborne W. Moulton — Firefighter/Paramedic

Ingredients:

1 large egg
1/2 cup sugar
6 tablespoons butter (melted)

1/2 cup flour
1 pint or 2 cups blueberries
1/3 cup sugar

Directions:

1 – Grease a 9" pie plate (Pyrex pan).

2 – Add blueberries then sprinkle 1/3 cup sugar over berries.

3 – Beat egg.

4 – Add in sugar and mix.

5 – Add butter and mix.

6 – Gradually mix in flour.

7 – Pour batter evenly over blueberry.

8 – Bake at 350 degrees 30-50 minutes (depending on oven) until golden brown crust.

9 – Serve hot with vanilla ice cream or cold by itself.

10 – Enjoy my grandmother's recipe!

Makes 6-8 Servings.

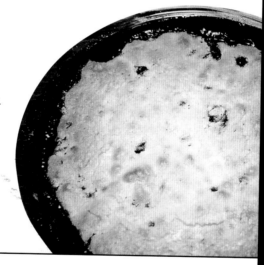

Claiborne Moulton
Firefighter/Paramedi
SCFD

Born and raised in Cajun Country (New Orleans) Claiborne moved to Sarasota in 1990 with his wife Evie He became a volunteer firefighter with SCFD in 1992 and served in that capacity for two years before being hired as firefighter, EMT. Claiborne has recently become a paramedic and is working at Station #12 on the B-shift. He sees physical fitness as a lifestyle and has no problem staying fit given his three sons ages 9, 6, and 4, who keep him running and lifting as their needs dictate He borrowed the Jambalaya recipe from his sister Anne and it has become a firehouse favorite wherever served

3

Wendy Shank
Volunteer Lieutenant Firemedic, SCFD

Wendy joined the SCFD Volunteers in 1996 and has remained active ever since. As a single mother of a seven-year old daughter (Kimberly), one wonders how she found the time to attend both Fire and EMT school (nights and weekends) while working full time for SCFD in an administrative position. She credits her firefighter boyfriend, Rick Haller, for helping to make it possible for her to attend school by caring for Kimberly and helping her study. Her dedication of time and energy has earned her the recent appointment to the position of Volunteer Lieutenant.

I asked her where the nickname "Bumpy" came from and she replied, "My friends call me Bumpy because I'm so graceful."

About the recipe...
"This recipe came from my grandmother Shank, the one who taught me to love baking."

Carrot Cake
Wendy Shank — Volunteer Lieutenant Firemedic

Ingredients:

CAKE:
2 cups flour
2 cups sugar
1 teaspoon cinnamon
1 teaspoon baking soda
1 teaspoon baking powder

1/2 teaspoon salt
1 1/2 cups oil
4 eggs
2 cups carrots (grated)
FROSTING:
1 pound box 10 X sugar

8 ounce package cream cheese softened
1/2 teaspoon vanilla
1/2 stick butter softened
1 cup chopped walnuts

Directions:

1 – Pre-heat oven to 350 degrees.

2 – Mix all ingredients for cake.

3 – Pour into 2, 9 inch greased cake pans.

4 – Bake 35-40 minutes until toothpick inserted comes out clean.

5 – Cool on racks.

6 – Mix all ingredients for frosting.

7 – Frost cake.

8 – ENJOY!

Seasonal Fruit Cobbler

Sarasota University Club

Ingredients:

2 cups all purpose flour
2 cups sugar
1 1/2 cups milk
4 whole eggs

1 1/4 tablespoon baking powder
1/2 tablespoon vanilla
2 teaspoons grated lemon zest
1 1/2 cups fresh fruit diced (your favorite)

Directions:

1 – Pre-heat oven to 350 degrees.

2 – Mix eggs, milk and sugar together until frothy.

3 – In separate bowl, mix all dry ingredients together.

4 - Combine all wet and dry ingredients together.
Don't over mix, mixture may be lumpy.

5 – Place your fruit in the bottom of casserole dishes or ramekins.

6 – Pour batter mixture over fruit and fill to top of dish.

7 – Bake in oven for approximately 15 minutes.
Check center with toothpick, until it comes out clean.

Suggestions: Serve with vanilla ice cream.
Drizzle top with Grand Marnier liquor as soon
as it comes out of the oven.

Makes 6 – 6-ounce Casserole Serving.

Paula B. Halling
Sous Chef
Sarasota University Club

A welcome addition to the
University Club kitchen in
Fall 1999, Paula is a Sous
Chef with many creative tal-
ents. In 1991, Paula gradu-
ated from Johnson and Wales
University with degrees in
Culinary Arts and Food
Service Management
Combined with over 14 years
of practical restaurant experi-
ence, Paula can meet any
number of culinary chal-
lenges. The seasonal Fruit
Cobbler recipe Paula has
shared is a special summer
treat. Once prepared and
tasted, it will remind you of
lazy summer days. This
recipe is a must share with
friends and family

Michael Tuttle
Baker
Pastry Art

Michael was born and raised in Syracuse, New York. At age 16, he started working in the restaurant industry in a small Italian restaurant as a dishwasher. In 1982, he made Florida his home. He found work as a cook and baker in various high end restaurants in the Sarasota - Manatee area including Longboat Key. Trained by some of the area's best Chef's, he found enjoyment in the creativity of preparing food.

Michael joined Pastry Art to pursue his strong suit in pastry baking. He enjoys meeting the customers of his creations and loves watching their reactions when they sample his tasty morsels.

Away from the ovens, Michael likes to write music, play his guitar, and surf the web.

Banana Split Cake

Pastry Art

Ingredients:

2 cups all purpose flour
1 teaspoon baking soda
8 ounces (2 sticks butter) softened
3/4 cup sugar
pinch of salt

2 eggs
1 teaspoon vanilla extract
1 cup or 2 medium size bananas mashed but not pureed
5 tablespoons of milk

1 cup walnuts chopped
1-8 ounce can crushed pineapple
cherry pie filling
chocolate fudge

Directions:

1 – Grease and flour two 8" cake pans and preheat oven to 350 degrees. 2 – Sift flour and baking soda and set aside. 3 – Using electric mixer beat butter, sugar and salt until well blended. 4 – Add eggs one at a time, then bananas. Scrape bowl and beat well. 5 – On low speed add dry ingredients, vanilla and milk. Mix for 30 seconds. 6 – Pour batter into prepared pans and bake at 350 degrees for 20-30 minutes or until knife inserted in center comes out clean. Cool on rack 15 minutes before unmolding. 7 – The cake can be made in advance, wrapped and chilled. Assembling the cake, slice each cake layer in half and level off the top. (Use these scraps to munch on while you're working!) There will be four cake layers and 3 layers of filling. 8 – Whip 2 cups heavy cream, 3 tablespoons powdered sugar and 1 teaspoon vanilla to stiff peaks and refrigerate until needed. 9 – Starting with bottom layer spread about 1 cup cherry pie filling up to edge of cake. 10 - Top with second layer and spread an 8 ounce can of drained crushed pineapple in same way. 11 – Top with third cake layer and spread with a thin layer of chocolate fudge, store bought or homemade. 12 – Top with last layer (use the flat layers for the bottom and top). Frost the cake with the reserved whipped cream. 13 – Holding walnuts in your open hand press onto side of cake. 14 – Decorate the top with rosettes of cream, maraschino cherries, fresh pineapple slices or sliced bananas dipped in chocolate.

*Tips and shortcuts: 1 - Use a banana cake mix or any yellow cake from the market. 2 – For added flavor, drizzle banana liqueur over each cake layer before filling. Substitute banana or cherry liqueur in whipped cream. 3 – The chocolate layer can be chocolate mousse, or a chocolate pudding mix. A ganache works very well: 1 cup of scalded heavy cream poured over 8 ounces of chopped chocolate. Stir and chill until cooled and thick. 4 – For maximum flavor toast walnuts ahead of time. 5 – Caramel can be used to swirl over top of cake if desired. 6 – If cake is to be eaten the same day it is made, thinly sliced bananas can be substituted or added to any layer.

Coconut Pecan Frosting

Suncoast Brace & Limb

Ingredients:

1 cup sugar
1 cup evaporated milk
1 teaspoon vanilla
3 eggs beaten
1/2 cup margarine

1 1/3 cups coconut
1 cup pecans
(1 box German Chocolate Cake Mix,
  if desired)

Directions:

1 - In saucepan, combine sugar, milk and eggs. Add butter.

2 – Cook over medium heat until mixture thickens and just begins to boil, stirring constantly.

3 – Remove from heat.

4 – Stir in remaining ingredients.

5 – Cool until spreading consistency.

6 – Frosts and fills 2 layer cake.

7 – Recommended frosting on a German Chocolate Cake. Yum!

Yields 3 1/2 cups.

3

Old Fashioned Southern Sweet Potato Pie

Lieutenant Vincent Thomas

Ingredients:

PIE FILLING:
3 large sweet potatoes
1 1/4 cup white sugar
1/4 pound softened butter
1/2 teaspoon vanilla flavor
1/2 cup milk
1/4 teaspoon nutmeg
dash cinnamon
3 drops (1/4 teaspoon) lemon flavor

PIE CRUST:
1 1/2 cup unbleached flour
1/2 cup Crisco
1/3 cup cold milk
1 teaspoon white sugar
1 pinch salt

Directions:

PIE FILLING:
1 – Boil potatoes until well done.
2 – Take out of water and let cool just enough to peel.
3 – Mix potatoes, softened butter, and 1/2 cup milk together until all strings are out of potatoes.
4 – Continue to mix slowly adding 2 eggs, vanilla flavor, nutmeg, cinnamon and lemon.
5 – Mix until all ingredients are well blended.

PIE CRUST:
1 – Blend flour, sugar, and salt. Add Crisco and blend together until absorbs the flour. Add milk slowly until it becomes dough.
2 – Maneuver all ingredients until it becomes flexible.
3 – Roll dough out on a flat surface so that it will fit the pan.
4 – Pour half the pie filling mix in each pan.
5 – Place in oven at 300 degrees and bake slowly for 1 hour.

Servings: Ingredients make 2 pies, 6 servings per pie.

Vincent Thomas

*Lieutenant,
Firefighter/Paramedic,
Special Op's,
Basic Fire Instructor,
Engineer, and Fire Officer 1
SCFD*

Vince "Troop" Thomas joined the Sarasota Fire Department in 1984. His nickname is self explanatory upon looking at his educational background which includes; firefighter, paramedic, special op's, basic fire instructor, engineer, and fire officer 1. Vince was assigned to the SCFD Station #3 as a member of the marine op's division until his promotions to Fire Lieutenant on 4/05/00. He's currently enjoying his first assignment as an officer at Station 5-C, and has only one regret. "I wish my father had lived to see this." Vince comes from a family of native Floridians... a rare find! He and his wife Yvette have two children, six-year old Vincent II and three-year old Brionna. Vince loves spending time with his family, and fishing in Sarasota Bay.

Chocolate Cake & Frosting

Sugar & Spice Restaurant

Ingredients:

CAKE:
1 cup Crisco
2 1/2 cups white sugar
2 cups boiling water
2 1/2 cups flour
1 cup cocoa-powdered
  Hershey's
1 tablespoon baking soda
1 teaspoon salt
3 eggs
2 tablespoons vanilla

FROSTING:
1/3 cup Crisco
3 tablespoons cocoa-
  powdered Hershey's
1/4 teaspoon salt
1/4 cup milk
1 teaspoon vanilla
2 1/2 cups powdered sugar

Directions:

CAKE:

1 – Pour boiling water over sugar & Crisco.

2 – Mix dry ingredients well.

3 – Add boiling water mixture, half at a time.

4 – Beat eggs and vanilla. Add to above mixture.

5 – Pour into a 9x13 pan.

6 – Bake at 300 degrees for 45 minutes (approximately).

7 – Serve at room temperature.

FROSTING:

1 – Mix all frosting ingredients (except powdered sugar) until smooth like a milkshake.
Add 2 1/2 cups powdered sugar.

2 – Mix until smooth.

3 – Spread over cake.

Makes 10 –12 Servings.

Rosemary and Reuben Beachy
Owners
Sugar & Spice Restaurant

Rosemary and husband Reuben were born into large families and raised in traditional Amish homes in Sugarcreek, Ohio. Rueben and Rosemary opened the doors of Sugar & Spice Restaurant in 1984. "Since our heritage was of the Amish faith growing up with big hearty meals served three times a day, why not cook the same way?" One thing that has become known about our people is good home cooking It takes a lot of time and hard work, and we are happy to do it for you. Our customers love the food and keep coming back for more. If you're ever in the area, please stop in and say hi. We're always happy to see new faces

Didier B. Goller
Pastry Chef
Sarasota University Club

Classically trained in France, Didier creates elegance and sophistication in all of his confections. Didier's background includes work experiences throughout Europe and the United States. Some of the notable pastry chef positions Didier has held include the Ritz Carlton Palm Beach, Hilton Hotel of Short Hills, Colony Beach & Tennis Resort, Michel Roux in England and at Sodigar in Toulouse, France. The Tart Tatin recipe that Didier is sharing for your enjoyment is a classic European dessert. This dessert is perfect for winter served warmed or in the summer with ice cream. Also, the apple chips made on their own make a great garnish for other desserts.

Tart Tartin

Sarasota University Club

Ingredients:

5 Apples
Granny Smith or Washington
8 ounces granulated sugar
1 drop lemon juice

5 ounces butter, cold
4 disc of puffy pastry
8 apple chips

Directions:

1 – Peel and core the apples and cut into quarters.
2 – In a dry saucepan, put sugar over a low heat and add lemon juice. Melt the sugar until golden brown in color. Remove from heat. Add the butter and mix until mixture looks like caramel sauce.
3 – Pour this mixture into a 5 ounce ramekin. Then arrange the apple quarters inside the ramekin.
4 – Cover with aluminum foil and poke a hole in top. Bake at 310 degrees until the apples become soft to touch but still retaining shape. (Approximately 20-25 minutes.)
5 – Uncover the tart and let it cool.
6 – Cut a disc of puff pastry 1-inch wider than the ramekin. Place disc on top and fold the excess pastry inside the ramekin.

7 – Bake at 310 degrees on a sheet pan until the puff pastry becomes golden brown. (Approximately 20-30 minutes.)
8 – When tart is finished baking, let stand for 2 minutes. Invert ramekin onto dessert plate. Remove the ramekin very delicately. The apple should stay perfectly all together without falling.
9 – Serve with fresh whipped cream or vanilla ice cream and garnish with apple chips.
APPLE CHIPS: Slice very thin slices of apple, leave skin on. Dip slices in sugar, place on parchment paper with a small amount of cooking spray, and then bake at 200 degrees until completely dry. (Approximately 4-5 hours.) The apples will become hard when removed from the heat. Store in an airtight container. If the apples become soft, place in oven again.
Makes 4 Servings.

Mango Cream

Irl Orr — Firemedic

Ingredients:

1 ripe mango
12 ounce Cool Whip
sprinkle of almonds (*optional)

Directions:

1 – Pare mango and cut into small pieces.

2 – Blend in a blender until smooth.

3 – Fold mango into Cool Whip. *Optional – Sprinkle with almonds.

4 – Chill.

5 – Serve with thin cookies.

Makes 6 Servings.

Irl H. Orr
Firemedi
SCFD

Irl grew up in Indianapolis Indiana, the son of ar Irishman. In his wilder days he traveled the U.S. as c drummer for a group knowr as "The Chessman" who hac several recordings witf Columbia Records. After the band, he decided to drum up a little business of his owr hanging wallpaper, which he did for 18 years. In 1980 he moved to Sarasota and was hired by SCFD in '82

He and his wife, Gini, have 10 children and 22 grandchildren. He enjoys his hobbies of deep sea fishing anc diving on his days off witf his own fishing charter business "Tarpon Tyme" ou of Englewood

Irl is affectionately callec "Grandpa" by his young firefighter peers and grand children. He will retire later this year

About the recipe..
"This is a very light desser with a fruity, moutf pleasing taste."

31

Frank Bielawski
Captain
North River Fire District

Frank was raised in Dennison, Ohio, with his four sisters and one brother. When his parent's retired, the family moved to Palmetto, Florida. He graduated from Palmetto High School in 1982.

Frank began volunteering at Braden River in 1984 and found his career. He put himself through fire school and was hired by Palmetto Fire District in 1985. He was promoted to Lieutenant three years later, and in 1992 he made Captain.

Frank married Marlene 16 years ago, and they have two sons, David (14) and Jarret (7). They are expecting another son in November. Frank loves baseball, and especially enjoys coaching his sons in Little League. Frank and his family are members of Bradenton Church of God.

About the recipe...
This Peanut Butter Pie recipe is my favorite as well as my own. The Firehouse crews love it when I make it.

Peanut Butter Pie
Frank Bielawski — Captain

Ingredients:

3 egg yolks
1 baked pie shell
1/3 cup all purpose flour
3/4 cup sugar
1/4 teaspoon salt

2 cups milk
2 tablespoons butter
1 teaspoon vanilla
1 cup powdered sugar
3 tablespoons peanut butter

Directions:

1 – In a heavy pot, combine flour, sugar, and salt.

2 – Slowly stir in milk.

3 – Bring to a boil and boil for 2 minutes stirring constantly.

4 – Add about half mixture to egg yolks. Stir well and add back to pot.

5 – Boil additional 2 minutes and let cool slightly.

6 – Add butter and vanilla and cool whip.

7 – Mix powdered sugar and peanut butter until crumbly and sprinkle on top.

Tiramisu

Cuoco Matto Restaurant

Ingredients:

1 pound of fresh mascarpone
1/4 cup granulated sugar
2 tablespoons rum
24 Italian ladyfingers
1 cup freshly brewed espresso
cooled

1/4 cup Kahlua
4 egg yolks
1/4 cup superfine sugar
1/4 cup + 2 tablespoons Marsala wine
2 tablespoons unsweetened cocoa powder

Directions:

1 – Whisk the egg yolks and the superfine sugar together in the top of a double boiler until pale yellow and fluffy.
2 – Place over hot not boiling water
3 – Beat, adding Marsala 1 tablespoon at a time, until the mixture is hot and thickened to be the consistency of a light, fluffy batter.
4 – Immediately remove the zabaglione from the heat and beat for another 3 minutes. Cool to room temperature.
5 – In a food processor, blend the mascarpone, granulated sugar and rum until smooth. Add the zabaglione and blend.
6 – In a mixing bowl, stir the Kahlua, and coffee together.
7 – Pour half of the coffee mixture into a flat dish or cake pan, arrange 12 biscuits, flat side up, side by side in the pan.
8 – Spread one half of the cheese mixture over the biscuits.
9 – Add another layer, moistening with the remaining espresso mixture.
10 – Pour the zabaglione over the top layer of the dessert.
11 – Sprinkle the cocoa over the top and enjoy.

Makes 6 Servings.

Frank Bologna
Executive Chef & Co-Owner
Cuoco Matto Restaurant

In Italian "cuoco" means cook or chef and "matto" means crazy. Frank Bologna is the Executive Chef and co-owner of this "Crazy Chef Italian Restaurant." Guests can dine or enjoy a drink at the bar, amongst the warm and entertaining ambiance of an open kitchen with an authentic wood-burning oven. The splendid tastes of Rosticceria Cucina Toscana (rustic Tuscan cuisine) are featured along with a distinct wine list at reasonable prices. Warm delicious Foccacia bread with a tangy balsamic vinegar and oil dipping sauce, is served promptly with every meal. Everyone will enjoy the personable, attentive service, superb food, and cozy atmosphere found at Cuoco Matto.

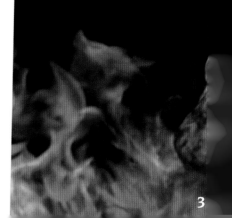

941-365-0000

1603 N. Tamiami Trail
Sarasota
Daily
11:30 AM To 11:00 PM

Serving
Lunch & Dinner
7 Days A Week

● ● ●

Catering available
on or off premise

3

Mary Lou Emrich
Yoder's

Yoder's offers over 25 varieties of homemade desserts, and even though they are known for their homemade pies, their chocolate cake recipe is an Amish classic found in many Amish cookbooks listed as crazy or wacky cake. Its uniqueness comes from having no eggs and you can mix the ingredients right in the pan before baking. Yoder's more than doubled up on the amount of Hershey's cocoa from the original recipe. "You can't make it too chocolaty for me!" says Mrs. Yoder. Everyone seems to agree.

Yoder's Easy Chocolate Cake
Yoder's

Ingredients:

CAKE:
2 cups sugar
3 cups flour
1 tbls baking soda
1 tsp baking powder
1 tsp salt
1 tbls vanilla

1-1/2 tbls vinegar
3/4 vegetable oil
2 cups cold water
1/2 cups Hershey's unsweetened cocoa
CHOCOLATE ICING:
3 cups powdered sugar

1 stick (1/2 cup or 1/4lb.) butter softened
3/4 cup Hershey's unsweetened cocoa
1 teaspoon vanilla
1/3 cup milk

Directions:

CAKE:

1 – Place sugar in the bottom of a 9 by 13 inch baking pan.

2 – Mix together flour, soda, baking powder, salt and cocoa, sift over top of sugar.

3 – Make three wells (with a large spoon) in the dry mixture.

4 – Put the vanilla in the first well, vinegar in the second and the oil in the third well.

5 – Pour water over all gradually, stirring with fork until smooth.

6 – Bake at 350 degrees approximately 25 to 30 minutes.

7 – Remove cake from oven, and cool completely before icing.

CHOCOLATE ICING:

1 – Mix all icing ingredients together.

2 – Spread icing on cooled cake.

*For a lighter taste, omit icing and top with whipped cream instead.

Spanish Custard – Flan

Columbia Restaurant

Ingredients:

6 tablespoons sugar
6 eggs
1 teaspoon vanilla extract
1 strip lemon peel
1 cinnamon stick
2 cups milk
Pinch salt

CARAMELIZED SUGAR:
1 cup sugar
1 tablespoon water

Directions:

1 – To make custard, boil milk with lemon peel and cinnamon stick.

2 – Lightly beat eggs with wire whisk.

3 – Blend in sugar, vanilla extract, and salt. Add milk gradually; strain.

4 – Pour into ovenproof custard cups with caramelized sugar in bottoms.

CARAMELIZED SUGAR:
Place sugar and water in small skillet. Cook over medium heat, stirring constantly, until sugar is golden.
Pour immediately into 6 ovenproof custard cups.

5 – Place cups in pan of hot water (2 inches deep) and bake in oven for 1 hour at 300 degrees. Never let water boil or custard will be filled with holes.

6 – Remove from pan and cool in refrigerator.

7 – To serve, unmold by pressing edges of custard with spoon to break away from cup, then turning upside down.

8 – Spoon caramelized sugar from bottoms of cups over top of each custard.

Makes 6 small Servings.

Richard, Adela and Casey Gonzmart
Owners
Columbia Restaurant

Our family has been creating some of Florida's favorite Spanish cuisine for nearly 100 years. We feature the freshest seafood and steaks as well as our won tradition family recipes. Through the years we have received some of the highest awards in the restaurant industry, but our highest praise comes from our loyal customers who dine with us again and again

Join us daily for lunch o dinner, and take in the beautiful sites of St. Armands Circle while enjoying the delicious dishes our che prepares especially for you

The Gonzmart family looks forward to welcoming you to the Columbia Restaurant

Frank Wankowski
Captain
Bradenton Fire Dept

Captain Frank Wankowski was born in Kearney, New Jersey, in 1962. Although he dreamed of being a policeman someday, he started working as a mechanic after high school. In 1982, his family moved to St. Pete Beach and made friends with some local firefighters. His interest in becoming a firefighter grew until he enrolled in fire and EMT school.

Frank was hired by Bradenton Fire Department in 1985. He has earned "Firefighter Of The Year" on two occasions, once for delivering a breech baby in the back seat of a car. He was promoted to Lieutenant in '95 and subsequently Captain in '98.

He and Terrie have been married 14 years and have two sons, Craig and Jarrett. He loves "grouper fishing," hunting and Nascar.

Carrot Cake

Frank Wankowski — Captain

Ingredients:

CAKE:
2 cups sugar
1 cup margarine
4 eggs
2 cups flour
2 teaspoons baking soda
2 teaspoons cinnamon
1 teaspoon salt

1 1/2 teaspoons vanilla
3 cups grated carrots
3/4 cup chopped walnuts
FROSTING:
6 ounces cream cheese (room temp)
1/2 cup butter (softened)
2 teaspoons vanilla
4 cups powdered sugar

Directions:

CAKE:

1 – Grease and lightly flour a 9x13 pan.

2 – Sift flour, cinnamon, baking soda, and salt together.

3 – Using a mixer, cream margarine and sugar until fluffy.

4 – Add eggs, one at a time.

5 – Add carrots, vanilla and nuts – mix well.

6 – Pour mixture into pan.

7 – Bake at 325 degrees for 55-60 minutes.

FROSTING:
1 – Using a mixer, mix butter and cream cheese until fluffy. Add vanilla and sugar. Beat until creamy.

2 – Frost cake.

Fresh Fruit Tart

Pastry Art

Ingredients:

CREAM FILLING:
3 tablespoons flour
4 tablespoons sugar
pinch of salt
1 cup milk
1 large egg

1 egg yolk
1 teaspoon vanilla extract
1 tablespoon butter

PASTRY CRUST:
(yields 1 – 8" crust)

4 ounces (1 stick) butter
softened
1/4 cup confectioner's sugar
1/2 teaspoon vanilla extract
1 cup all purpose flour
sifted

Charles Carson
Pastry Chef
Pastry Art

Directions:

CREAM FILLING: 1 – Whisk flour, sugar and salt in a 1 1/2 quart non reactive saucepan. 2 – Whisk in milk, egg and yolk. 3 – On low heat, stir constantly until cream thickens and starts to bubble. Continue to boil and whisk for about 30 seconds. 4 – Remove from heat and whisk in vanilla and butter. Pour into a glass or ceramic dish and chill until cold, stirring every 10 minutes. Cover with plastic. This can be made one day ahead.

PASTRY CRUST: 1 – In a bowl beat butter and sugar until well blended. 2 – Mix in vanilla and flour. Blend well and form into a round disc. 3 – Chill, wrapped in plastic at least an hour. Dough can be made a week in advance. 4 – Roll out dough to about 1/4" thick and place in a fluted tart pan, patching crust as needed. An alternate method is to make a free form shell on a baking pan or flat cookie sheet. Make sure to fold the outer edge onto itself, and pinch the dough to form a thick border 1/2" high. 5 – Chill formed shell 1 hour before baking. Prick dough several times with a fork and bake 20-25 minutes at 350 degrees. The crust should be golden brown. Cool completely before filling.

ASSEMBLING THE TART: 3 tablespoons apricot jam, 1 tablespoon hot water 1 – Spread pastry cream into baked crust before topping with fruit. 2 – Slice assorted fruits and arrange over custard. Try not to have any cream show through. In a small bowl, microwave jam and water to make a glaze to brush or spoon over fruit.

NOTE: Wrapped well this dessert will hold two days in refrigerator.

Born and raised in
Philadelphia, Charles is a
professionally trained Chef
from The Restaurant School
in Philadelphia, Pennsylvania.
He spent 16 years working in
restaurants and catering in
Philadelphia and Knoxville,
Tennessee before moving
to Sarasota.

Charles has been making
tasty lunches and desserts at
Pastry Art for the past year.
He truly enjoys sampling his
work including his favorite
Pastry Art dessert product,
the Apple - Raspberry
Coffee Cake.

In his free time Charles
enjoys fishing and walking
off those pastry samples on
Sarasota's beautiful beaches.

Michael Garey
General Manager
Café L' Europe

Michael Garey was born and raised in Buffalo, New York. He moved to Sarasota, Florida as a teenager and began in the restaurant business as a busboy in 1977. In 1979 he started as a busboy at the Café L' Europe. Moving up the ladder, he became a dining room captain in 1981 and assistant manager in 1982. In 1984, he left Café L' Europe to help open and manage Mr. Wong's Chinese restaurant. Michael came back to Café L' Europe in 1986 as General Manager, the title that he holds today. Mr. Garey is currently President of the St. Armands Merchants Assoc. and conceived and organized two events for the Florida Wine Festival, the Wine Marker's Dinner, and Sip and Shop. He is married to his wife, Catherine and has three daughters, Alexandra, Jenna and Amelia.

Warm Chocolate Cake
Café L' Europe

Ingredients:

2 ounces melted butter for coating
8 ounces butter for cake
1 cup of flour (reserve 1/2 cup)
4 eggs

14 ounces bittersweet chocolate
 (reserve 6 ounces)
1/2 cup sugar
1/8 cup water

Directions:

1 – Preheat oven to 325 degrees.
2 – Prepare 6 ounces ramekins by brushing with melted butter and dusting with flour. Cool in the refrigerator.
3 – In a double boiler combine 8 ounces chocolate with 8 ounce butter. Melt until smooth. Set aside in a warm spot.
4 – Separate eggs and whip the whites to soft peaks. Set aside.
5 – Warm together the sugar and water until dissolved.
6 – In a mixer, whip egg yolks and sugar mixer on high speed until the yolks have doubled in size.

7 – Reduce mixer speed to slow and incorporate 1/4 cup of flour, chocolate butter mixture and then fold in t he whipped egg whites.
8 – Fill each ramakin 1/2 full with the chocolate mixture.
9 – Add in 1 ounce of the reserved chocolate to each of the ramakins then fill all the way to the top.
10 – Bake for approximately 20-25 minutes. They should rise but the tops should not be too dry.
11 – Remove and serve immediately.

Makes 6 Servings.

Orange Crème Brulee

Café on the Bay

Ingredients:

3 cups heavy cream
6 egg yolks
6 tablespoons sugar

2 tablespoons orange liquor
1 tablespoon orange rind
4 tablespoons brown sugar

Directions:

1 – In double boiler heat cream.

2 – In mixer, whip egg yolks and sugar.

3 – Add hot cream to egg mixture.

4 – Add orange rind and liquor to mix.

5 – Return mixture to double boiler and stir with whip until it thickens.

6 – Pour in 4 cups and let set for 4 hours

7 – Top with 1 tablespoon of brown sugar each.

8 – Put under broiler to brown the sugar.

Makes 4 Servings.

Bill Herlihy
General Manager
Café on the Bay

Twenty-two years ago, Bill Herlihy began working in the restaurant business in the Finger Lake Region in Western New York. He moved to Rochester, New York in 1984, where he first met Café on the Bay's current Executive Chef, Keith Daum. In 1988, Bill decided to relocate to sunny Florida and 2 years later he met Michael Garey and Titus Letschert. Shortly thereafter, he started as a dining room captain at Café L' Europe. After 6 years of learning from "the best" Bill became General Manager of Café on the Bay. Keith Daum and Bill were reunited after 12 years. Bill has a nine-year old daughter, Delanie, and is very active in local charities. He has been the Co-Chairperson of the St. Jude's Gourmet Luncheon on Longboat Key for the last five years.

941-383-0440

**2630 Harbourside Dr.
Longboat Key, FL 34228**

Breakfast Saturday
8:30 AM To 10:30 AM

Sunday Breakfast Brunch
9:00 AM To 1:00 PM

Sunday Lunch
1:00 PM To 3:30 PM

Lunch 6 Days
11:00 AM To 3:00 PM

Dinner 7 Days
4:30 PM To 10:00 PM

**Extraordinary cuisine served in a truly exquisite waterfront setting.
Come by land or sea.
Casual attire is welcomed.**

Advice from Chef,
Rick Munroe

Munroes Restaurant

Ask the Expert...

Q. How often should I sharpen my kitchen knives?

A. The most important thing is to keep your knives sharp. Every time you use a knife, a portion of the edge becomes bent and dulls. If you run the knife over a sharpening steel before each use, you will unbend the bent edge. To do this, pull your knife at a 20-degree angle across the steel. You will need to cover the entire blade and alternate sides.

Almost any type of sharpening steel will work; however, do not use the sharpener on electric can openers. They tend to overheat and ruin the blade of your knife.

Once a year, your knives will need to be taken to a professional sharpener. Your local butcher will be able to recommend one.

A Collection of
Spa Cuisine
(Healthy Heart)
Recipes from the
Fire Departments
& Area Restaurants
of Manatee and
Sarasota Counties
in the State
of Florida.

Spa Cuisine Recipes

Foods for Health

Fruits and vegetables are particularly important for good health; they are known to provide protection from chronic illnesses such as coronary disease and certain cancers. Below we diagram which foods provide the best sources of antioxidants and vitamins and explain the main types of fat.

Antioxidants: selenium, zinc, manganese and copper. Compounds called flavenoids, which can be found in red wine, tea and onions may also have antioxidant properties.

Beta-carotene or Provitamin A: can be converted to vitamin A in the body. Beta-carotene is a powerful antioxidant, is fat-soluble and appears to help protect fatty parts of cells. Food sources include; bright yellow and orange fruits and green vegetables — carrots, apricots, peaches, tomatoes, red and yellow bell peppers, green leafy vegetables.

Vitamin C: is water-soluble and can regenerate vitamin E, It attacks "free radicals" in your system. Food sources include — citrus fruits and juices, kiwi fruit, blueberries, strawberries, green bell peppers, tomatoes, green leafy vegetables and new potatoes.

Vitamin E: is thought to be the first line of defense against damage to the fatty parts of cells. Food sources include — vegetable oils, almonds, hazelnuts, whole grain cereals and bread, avocados, eggs, cheese and other dairy products.

Antioxidant Minerals: selenium, zinc, manganese and copper are particularly prevalent in foods such as whole grain cereals, nuts, meat, milk and other dairy products.

Dietary Fats: a small amount of fat in the diet is important for good health. Consuming too much can lead to obesity, heart disease and the development of certain types of cancers. There are 3 main types of fat — saturated, monounsaturated and polyunsaturated.

Saturated Fates: these are not essential in the diet and a high intake is associated with a higher risk of developing heart disease. They are known to raise blood cholesterol levels and should be consumed in moderation. Food sources include — whole milk, cream, butter, cheese, fatty cuts of red meat and red meat products such as hamburger and sausage, cakes, cookies and ice cream.

Monounsaturated Fats: are known to reduce the blood cholesterol levels and can help protect against heart disease. Food sources include — olive oil, peanut oil, canola oil, nuts, seeds and meats.

Polyunsaturated Fats: All amounts of these fats are recommended for good health and can help reduce blood cholesterol levels. Food sources include — sunflower oil, corn oil, margarine's, pine nuts, walnuts, sesame seeds and soybeans.

Healthy Tips for Cooks

- Choose lean cuts of meat and remove any visible fat before cooking.

- Grate or shred cheese finely and use a sharper variety in order to use less and make it go farther.

- Use vegetable stocks and broths instead of meat stocks for sauces and gravies.

- When using oil in a recipe, measure it out with a spoon for accuracy rather than free pouring from the bottle.

- Use mashed potatoes to top savory dishes instead of pastry.

- Thicken sauces with cornstarch or arrowroot instead of roux.

- Grill, poach, broil, steam or boil food whenever possible — purchase good quality non-stick pans that enable less oil for sautéing.

- Avoid frying foods as much as possible. If you do fry foods, use oils such as canola or olive oil, which are high in unsaturtates.

- Roast meats and poultry on a rack so that some of the fat will drain away from the roast.

- Use fresh herbs and lemon to season vegetables instead of butter.

- Choose fruit canned in fruit juice rather than syrup.

- Prepare healthy snacks such as fresh fruits, fresh vegetables and corn tortillas with fresh salsa.

- Wash or scrub vegetables rather than peeling them.

- Cook vegetables "al dente" to retain nutrients.

- Serve cooked vegetables immediately as they loose vitamin "C" rapidly.

Richard Munroe
Chef/Proprietor
Munroe's Restaurant

Locals and seasonal visitors alike enjoy the bistro setting of Munroe's Restaurant. Proven to be Sarasota's favorite restaurant with casual elegance, friendly service, and creative, American foods.

Whether you start off your meal with one of our famous appetizers or finish with one of our colorful desserts, you won't go away disappointed.

For the late night guest, we offer live entertainment upstairs, with a late night menu and premium bar.

Whole Grain Herb Mustard

Munroe's Restaurant

Ingredients:

1-3/4 cups white wine vinegar
2 small onions, diced
8 sprigs, fresh tarragon, chopped
8 sprigs, fresh basil, chopped
1/2 cup water
1/2 cup, white mustard seeds

3 tbl dry mustard
1 tsp black pepper
2 tsp light soy sauce
1 tbl honey
1 tsp tumeric

Directions:

1 – Combine vinegar, onions and herbs in a mixing bowl. Boil 1/2 cup of water and pour over ingredients - cover and let stand for three hours.

2 – Pulverize mustard seeds with a motar & pestle (or food processor).

3 – Strain vinegar / herb marinade into a sauce pan – add mustard seeds, dry mustard, pepper, soy sauce, honey and tumeric – mix well and simmer for 5 minutes.

4 – Ladle into a sterilized mason jar.

4

Grandma's Vegetable Garden Ketchup

Munroe's Restaurant

Ingredients:

5# ripe tomatoes, chopped
1 medium yellow onion, chopped
1 stalk celery
1 clove garlic
1 red bell pepper, chopped
1 bay leaf

1/8 tsp celery seeds
3/4 tsp mustard seeds
1 cup white wine vinegar
4 tsp honey
2 tsp molasses

Directions:

1 – Puree tomatoes, celery, onion, garlic and pepper in a food processor until smooth.

2 – Place puree in a heavy sauce pan and simmer for 5 minutes.

3 – Add bay leaf, celery seeds, mustard seeds, vinegar, molasses and honey - simmer for 45 minutes, stirring occasionally.

4 – Strain ketchup and ladle into a sterilized mason jar.

Keith Haluska mixing a batch of soda bread for photos.

NFPA Factoids And Kitchen Fire Safety Tips

Question:

What percentage of fires in vehicles or structures were deliberately set or are suspected to have been deliberately set

Answer:

13.1%.

"Kitchen Fire Prevention Tip"

You can prevent burns and stove-top fires by turning pot handles toward the center of the stove.

Information Courtesy of NFPA

Marianna Haluska rolling out the "Kolachy" dough.

Merv Kennell helping with recipes in "Munroe's" kitchen.

NFPA Fire Safety Tips

"Electrical Safety"

Heat producing appliances such as toasters, coffee makers, waffle irons, and electric frying pans, use a lot of electric. Never plug more than one such appliance into an outlet.

"Smoke Detector"

Never paint smoke detectors, it can adversely affect their performance, or render them inoperable.

Information Courtesy of NFPA

Merv, Rick & Keith taking a break from cooking.

Minted Citrus Vinegar

Munroe's Restaurant

Ingredients:

3 oranges
2 lemons
2 limes
4 sprigs mint

1 teaspoon saffron
1 tablespoon sugar
1 apple cider vinegar
1 mason jar

Directions:

1 – Zest all citrus fruits, then peel. Stack the peeled citrus fruits in the Mason jar.

2 – Arrange all other ingredients around the fruit in the jar.

3 – Pour vinegar in to fill, seal tightly then shake the jar to help dissolve sugar.

4 – Store in the refrigerator for up to 4 weeks, shake periodically to blend the ingredients.

Hot Chili Vinegar

Munroe's Restaurant

Ingredients:

1 jalapeno pepper
1 habanera pepper
1 cerrano pepper
1 lemon zest of
1 lime zest of

1/2 teaspoon red chili flakes
1 teaspoon black peppercorns
2 ounces carrot julienne
1 quart white wine vinegar

Directions:

1 - Cut all the chili peppers in ? and de-seed them. Discard the seeds and be sure to wash your hands after doing so.

2 – Heat vinegar to 130 degrees, add all ingredients and simmer for two minutes.

3 – Cool and strain.

4 – Place strained ingredients into a bottle and funnel vinegar over to fill. Cork and store in a refrigerator for up to four weeks.

Rick & daughter Ashley sharing a moment in the kitchen.

NFPA Fire Safety Tips

"Electrical Safety"
Never leave a detachable appliance cord plugged into an outlet when it's not attached to the appliance.

"Smoke Detector"
Smoke detectors lose their sensitivity over time and should be replaced every 10 years, if not sooner.

Information Courtesy of NFPA

The girls decorating their first batch of cookies.

'Jiggy" at the grill.

Cranberry Ketchup

Munroe's Restaurant

Ingredients:

12 oz. Cranberries
1 lg onion, chopped
1 cinnamon stick
1/2 tsp whole allspice
1/2 tsp black peppercorns

1 cup water
1 cup sugar
1/2 cup cider vinegar
1 1/2 tsp salt

Directions:

1 – Simmer cranberries and onion in 1/2 cup of water for 20 minutes and place in food processor.

2 – Blend to make a smooth puree, strain into a medium sauce pan and simmer for 20 minutes.

3 – Add cinnamon, allspice, peppercorns, water, vinegar, sugar and salt to the sauce pan and simmer for 20 minutes, stirring occasionally.

4 – Strain and funnel into a sterilized mason jar.

Chief Kehoe whips up a batch of Chicago style pizza dip.

Provencal Oil

Munroe's Restaurant

Ingredients:

1 quart extra virgin olive oil
3 cloves garlic
3 sprigs fresh basil
6 Kalamata olives
6 sun dried tomatoes, reconstituted

1 tablespoon black peppercorns
1/2 teaspoon saffron threads
2 sprigs fresh parsley
1 lemon zest of

Directions:

1 – Heat oil in a sauce pan to 150 degrees, remove from heat and add garlic, olives, tomatoes, black pepper and lemon zest.

2 – Cool oil – add remaining ingredients and stir.

3 – Strain oil and reserve – place the strained ingredients in a bottle.

4 – Funnel enough oil to cover ingredients – cork and store at room temperature for up to two weeks or refrigerated up to four weeks.

Keith & Nicole Haluska.

NFPA Fire Safety Tips

"Kitchen Fire Prevention Tip"

Don't toss wet or frozen food into hot grease or oil. The violent reaction will splatter hot oil.

"Electrical Safety"

If an electrical appliance gets wet inside, have it serviced before using it again.

Information Courtesy of NFPA

The Haluskas dressed for cool Florida weather (70°) Ha!

Ashley samples the cookies.

Keith in the kitchen.

Bouquet of Lettuces with Southern Orange Salad

Munroe's Restaurant

Ingredients:

1 navel orange peeled & segmented
4 dried apricots
1 ounce red onion julienne
2 ounces pecans roughly chopped

1 scallion chopped
2 ounces green bell pepper julienned fine
3 ounces fresh assorted baby lettuces
3 ounces citrus vinegar

Directions:

1 – Rinse lettuce and dry in a paper towel.

2 – Place at twelve o' clock in a large salad or pasta bowl.

3 – Toss all remaining ingredients in a mixing bowl and place at six o' clock on the salad bowl.

4 – Drizzle remaining vinegar over the lettuces and garnish with dried figs and chopped pecans.

0

Lentil & Spinach Salad
Munroe's Restaurant

Ingredients:

3 ounces yellow lentils
1 plum tomato wedged
6 ounces baby spinach leaves, rinsed
6 ounces water (or chicken stock)
2 ounces Provencal oil (or olive oil)
1 lemon juice of

1 teaspoon salt & pepper
2 ounces julienned sweet peppers
1/2 ounce julienned red onion
1/2 ounce minced cucumber
1/2 ounce minced tomato

Directions:

1 – Cook lentils in water until tender – they should absorb all the water – cool and reserve.

2 – Toss cool lentil with lemon juice, salt & pepper, cucumber and minced tomato – refrigerate for 1/2 hour minimum (can be prepared a day ahead).

3 – Arrange spinach, peppers, onion and tomato wedges as shown.

4 – Scoop lentils onto center of spinach bed and drizzle Provencal oil over the salad.

Firehouse Favorites models Nicole, Linda, & Marianna.

NFPA Fire Safety Tips

"Electrical Safety"
Never replace an electrical fuse with a penny or other conductive material.

"Smoke Detector"
You should have a smoke detector placed on each level of your home, and near every sleeping area.

Information Courtesy of NFPA

Linda helps prepare salad ingredients for photo.

Easy Vegetarian "Cobb" Salad
Munroe's Restaurant

Ingredients:

1 plum tomato diced
1 ear white corn shucked
4 shitake mushrooms julienne
1 ounce red onion diced
1 ounce sweet peppers diced

1 stalk celery sliced
3 ounces spinach chiffonade
2 scallions sliced
2 ounces whole pecans roasted
1 lemon juice of

Directions:

1 – Cook corn and shuck the kernels.

2 – Arrange all ingredients as shown and
squeeze lemon juice over the salad.

Empire Club
Munroe's Restaurant

Ingredients:

1 piece of pita bread
4 ounces smoked turkey breast
1 plum tomato sliced
1/2 small red onion sliced

1 leaf romaine lettuce –
  cut into 2 inch squares
1 pickle wedge
10" bamboo skewer

Directions:

1 – 1/4 the pita bread.

2 – Layer the sandwich as follows: pita, turkey, tomato, lettuce and repeat to the last pita.

3 – Secure sandwich by stabbing the skewer thru the center. It should stand up on the plate.

4 – Garnish with pickle wedge and have whole grain mustard and Lingonberry jam for condiments.

Linda Kennell enjoys what was once a hotdog & bun

NFPA Fire Safety Tips

"Household Fire Prevention and Fire Safety Tip'
Never bring gasoline inside the home. Store gasoline in an outside shed or detached garage, in an approved container

"Escape Plan'
Every household should have an scape plan, and practice i at least twice a year

Information Courtesy of NFP

Travis Kennell & Granpa Jenkins playing fireman like dad

NFPA Fire Safety Tips

"Household Fire Prevention and Fire Safety Tip"

In most cases, automatic fire sprinkler systems control or extinguish fires in less time than it takes for the fire department to arrive.

"Fireplace/Chimney"

Never burn trash in your fireplace.

Information Courtesy of NFPA

Captain Patek handles first alarm assignment.

Garlic Pickles

Munroe's Restaurant

Ingredients:

4 large cucumbers
8 cloves garlic browned
4 sprigs basil
1/2 small white onion sliced
1 tablespoon capers

1 tablespoon black peppercorns
1 tablespoon sugar
1 pint white wine vinegar
1 teaspoon granulated garlic
1 mason jar

Directions:

1 – Heat vinegar to 130 degrees in a saucepan and add all ingredients except basil and cucumbers.

2 – Place cucumbers and basil in the Mason jar.

3 – Strain vinegar – place strained ingredients in the Mason jar with the pickles, cover with cooled vinegar and seal.

4 – Keep refrigerated and marinate for four weeks for 1/2 sours or 8 weeks for spicier pickles.

New Havana Sandwich

Munroe's Restaurant

Ingredients:

4 ounces roasted Pork Tenderloin
1/2 green apple peeled & sliced
3 ounces onion julienned
3 bread length pickle slices
1 tablespoon olive oil

1 piece Cuban bread cut sandwich length
  & grilled
1 tablespoon whole grain mustard
1/2 teaspoon cumin
1/2 teaspoon nutmeg

Little chefs in the making

Directions:

1 – Grill Cuban bread, place the pickle slices along the bottom.

2 – Sautee the onions to caramelize, add apples, cumin & nutmeg and remove from heat while stirring.

3 – Slice the roasted pork loin very thin and layer on top of pickles.

4 – Drizzle olive oil over the top piece of bread and the pork layer.

5 – Spoon onion/apple mix on liberally top of pork.

6 – Finish with dollop of whole grain mustard.

NFPA Fire Safety Tips

"Escape Plan'
Always try another exit if you encounter smoke when you're escaping a fire

"Smoking Fire'
Never dump ashtray contents into a wastebasket, without wetting the ashtray contents

Information Courtesy of NFPA

Marianna enjoys mixing dough.

3

Nally Sharpe, James Herrmann,
Gary Ewing in the kitchen.

**NFPA Fire
Safety Tips**

'Electrical Safety"
Never replace a circuit breaker
with one that exceeds the
circuits amperage rating.

'Smoke Detector"
Test your smoke alarms
every month by pushing
the "test" button.

Information Courtesy of NFPA

Grilled Chicken with Orange Salad

Munroe's Restaurant

Ingredients:

8 ounces boneless, skinless chicken
   breast
2 oranges segmented
2 ounces dried cherries
1 lemon segmented

1 tablespoon olive oil
1/2 teaspoon sugar
1/2 teaspoon salt
1 ounce citrus vinegar

Directions:

1 – Make the orange salad in a large mixing bowl
by tossing all ingredients.

2 – Grill the chicken breast and place in
the center of the plate.

3 – Spoon orange salad liberally
on the chicken.

4 – Serve with grilled vegetables
and couscous or rice.

Longboat Key Fire Chief
Julius Halas prepares a meal
for the crew.

Chicken en Papillote

Munroe's Restaurant

Ingredients:

4 6oz boneless, skinless chicken breasts
1 tbls olive oil
1 clove garlic crushed
1 tsp ground coriander
1 tsp ground cumin

1 tsp chili powder
1/2 tsp salt
1/2 tsp ground black pepper.
1 lemon, juice of

Directions:

1 – Blend together spices, lemon juice and oil.

2 – Place each chicken breast on a 12" square piece of parchment paper. Score each chicken breast diagonally and brush some of the seasoning mixture on each piece.

3 – Fold the paper loosely over each chicken breast and twist to make a seal, making a total of four packages. Place the packages on a baking sheet.

4 – Bake in a preheated 350 oven for 30 minutes.

5 – Undo the packages and place chicken breasts on service plated – serve immediately.

NFPA Factoids And Kitchen Fire Safety Tips

Question
How much property loss was reported in 1999 due to incendiary or suspicious vehicle fires?

Answer
195 million dollars

"Kitchen Fire Prevention Tip"
Install your fire extinguisher on a wall away from your stove, near a door, and out of reach of children.

Information Courtesy of NFPA

Decorating cookies is almost as much fun as eating them.

NFPA Fire Safety Tips

'Household Fire Prevention and Fire Safety Tip"
Make sure your doors, door locks, security bars, and storm windows can be quickly opened from the inside, by all members of the household.

'Fireplace/Chimney"
Each year have your chimney professionally inspected and cleaned.

Information Courtesy of NFPA

Beef Tenderloin Flautas with Grilled Pepper Salad and Chili Oil

Munroe's Restaurant

Ingredients:

2–3 ounce beef tenderloin steaks
10" flour tortilla 1/2 wrapped
1 small poblano chili
1 small red bell pepper
1 small Romano pepper
1 plum tomato

3 ounces corn oil
1 teaspoon chili powder
1/2 teaspoon cumin
1/2 teaspoon dry mustard powder
1/2 teaspoon salt

Directions:

1 – Grill the tenderloin steaks to desired temperature, grill the flour tortilla, and grill the peppers and tomatoes.

2 – Arrange on a large plate as pictured.

3 – Heat oil in a small sauté pan and add spices, stir and fuse.

4 – Drizzle oil over the food and serve immediately.

Joshua MacMillan

NFPA Fire Safety Tips

"Household Fire Prevention and Fire Safety Tip"
Keep matches and lighters out of sight and reach of children.

"Escape Plan"
If you have to escape through smoke, crawl on your hands and knees with your head 1 to 2 feet from the floor. Their is a higher oxygen level lower to the floor.

Information Courtesy of NFPA

BREAKFAST
9

LUNCHEON
25

HORS D'OEUVRES
45

APPETIZERS
57

SALADS
89

ENTREES
107

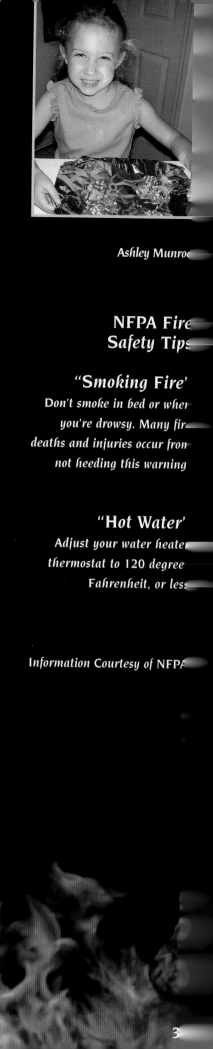

Ashley Munroe

NFPA Fire
Safety Tips

"Smoking Fire'

Don't smoke in bed or when
you're drowsy. Many fire
deaths and injuries occur from
not heeding this warning

"Hot Water'

Adjust your water heater
thermostat to 120 degree
Fahrenheit, or less

Information Courtesy of NFPA

Ashley & Marianna

NFPA Fire Safety Tips

"Smoking Fire"
Give smokers large, deep, non-tip ashtrays.

"Hot Water"
Outfit tubs and showers with anti-scald fixtures or turn on cold water first, then add hot until desired temperature is reached.

Information Courtesy of NFPA

SIDES
247

DESSERTS
263

SPA CUISINE
321

Marianna Haluska

NFPA Fire Safety Tips

"Space Heater Safety"

If you must use space heaters, turn them off before you go to bed or leave home

Keep space heaters at least three feet away from anything that can burn.. people included

Information Courtesy of NFPA

Marianna Haluska waves a friendly goodbye from her "favorite" fire truck and says "look forward to our next edition!"

Start to Finish...

a photographic essay on the two year process of creating Firehouse Favorites.